LAUGHING IN MY SLEEP

An Autobiography

Frank Topping

Hodder & Stoughton
LONDON SYDNEY AUCKLAND

Acknowledgements

The publishers are grateful to the following for permission to reprint photographs:

British Forces Broadcasting Service: Broadcasting to HM Forces everywhere
Kent Messenger Group: Preparing to move to North Wales
National Children's Homes: Richard Briers at NCH gala, The Queen at NCH gala
Snap People's Theatre Trust Ltd: As John Steinbeck
Yorkshire TV: Stoke Mandeville Junior Paraplegic Games, Backstage at *Cats*

British Library Cataloguing in Publication Data
A catalogue record for this book is available
from the British Library.

ISBN 0 340 58599 4

First published in Great Britain 1993
Second impression 1993

Published by Hodder and Stoughton,
a division of Hodder and Stoughton Ltd,
Mill Road, Dunton Green, Sevenoaks, Kent TN13 2YA
Editorial Office: 47 Bedford Square, London WC1B 3DP

Typeset by Hewer Text Composition Services, Edinburgh
Printed in Great Britain by Cox & Wyman Ltd, Reading, Berks.

To June –

With me in the laughter
Wife and lover,
With me at the table
Cook and mother,
With me on the road
When there is no other.

Contents

Foreword

Which Methodist minister, whom we hear regularly on the radio, has been an altar boy and an office boy, a factory worker and a hospital porter, a radar operator and a stage electrician, a television floor manager and an assistant film director, a radio producer and a television presenter, a repertory actor and a song-and-dance man, a university chaplain and the author of many books?

Answer: Frank Topping.

If you knew that before peeping in these pages, then you knew even more about Frank than I did. For years I have been accustomed to Topping popping up in many places, but until I read this book I had not realised that his life has been such a great entertainment, for him and for those with him. If not exactly a pilgrim's progress, it has certainly been more than a wayfarer's wanderings. Indeed, it is an allegory in itself. And the joy of this book is that you can hear his voice in every sentence.

He was born in Birkenhead, where his father was a shipyard worker (and trombonist) and his mother a barmaid. Since then he has been many things in many places. He is a man to whom things happen. He is always on the move, but never restless. Strengthened through his life by a growing belief that you do not embrace faith, but that it embraces you, he has never been afraid, in the comfort of that embrace, to try something different. But that is neither restlessness nor recklessness. It is the cheerful courage of someone intrigued to discover what would happen if he were to do that rather than this. And he has been happily supported throughout by a wife who has moved house many times more often than most people change cars.

He is a great performer, but when he performs he is not acting as a preacher, he is acting that which is being preached, which is a very good way of getting over a message. As Frank himself would say, there is no sin in chuckling in church. And certainly when it comes to laughter, there is no stopping Topping.

Brian Redhead

1 Brass Bands, Nuns and Vikings

There is a mist today, a lazy white haze drifting on the sea. A few miles away, shrouded in the fog, the Needles lighthouse sounds her horn and further away, somewhere in the English Channel, a coaster groans in reply.

The sea is sleeping, the deep sound of her breathing is in the shift of the shingle, soothing and soporific. It is a dreaming sea, and a sea to dream by.

By noon the mist will have lifted. On the grey horizon a yacht might be seen ghosting towards the Solent. But now the sea is blanketed, reluctant to reveal her stories, and yet, suddenly, a noise that has been distant roars into close proximity and a fishing boat emerges from the mist, thrusting a path through the fog. A man is in the wheelhouse, another is coiling rope at the stern. The wake of the boat breaks the rhythm of the sea on the shingle and, like a sleeper disturbed, the stones toss and turn on the beach. Then, as suddenly as she came, the boat is swallowed by the fog. Frowning, the sea slips and slides and settles back into the deep breathing of her sleep and we are alone once more to dream our secret dreams.

In a beach hut on the English coast in the misty morning, memories swirl around my brain and I have to ask myself, where does reality begin and dream end? Or is it all a dream with the awakening somewhere beyond our span of years? I know that the events happened, but, in my mind they are like photographs which capture a fragment of a moment, a tantalisingly incomplete split second, which raises as many questions as the picture answers.

What is this girl thinking as she gazes through the window? What

was said to make her smile so beguilingly? And those men in the
fishing boat emerging from the fog, who were they? Were they
content in their work or had they just exchanged sharp words?
Were they fresh or tired? Starting a day or ending a night?

Mist and memories are by their nature ephemeral, insubstantial,
not to be trusted. Memories, like dreams, avoid accurate recollec-
tion. They hide behind laughter, attempt to erase fears, prejudice
and guilt. They reveal only as much as we can bear, shielding us
from naked knowledge of details and motives that might transform
dream into nightmare.

A child is on the beach. The mist on the surface of the water
curls at the feet of the child. He is standing on the edge of a curtain
of vapour, the edge of a memory in which I can see another beach,
another sea, another child.

A lady, with a fur stole about her shoulders, sat at one end of
the carriage; the fur stole had a fox's head. The lady was very
'frilly'. She had lace around her neck and lace on her cuffs and
she smelled of scent. She was large and looked strong, but she
behaved as if she were fragile. Her hands, when not in use, dangled
from her wrists.

When she boarded the train a porter had lifted her suitcase to
the rack. She had given him sixpence from a tiny leather purse,
holding the coin delicately at arm's length as if anxious not to
touch the porter. At my end of the carriage was a man in a
bowler hat. He was reading the *Liverpool Echo*. The leather strap,
with holes in it, held my window open a few inches and I could
hear the hiss of steam, the trundle of luggage trollies and a voice
shouting, 'Platform Two! Chester train!'

The train shuddered, took the strain of the carriages and slowly
began to move, the great engine hissing and puffing, a weight-lifter
gathering strength. I was tense with expectation. I could not have
been more excited if I had been about to set sail for America in
the *Queen Mary*.

This was my first experience of travelling unaccompanied. It was
summer 1948. In September, I would be starting at a new school,
a school run by a religious order, the Irish Christian Brothers.

The pain of that experience lay ahead, unimagined. But this was my first holiday away from home and I was determined to drink in every second of it.

As the train weaved its way towards the outskirts of the town, I recognised landmarks that were familiar and yet seemed different seen from the train. I saw the hill in Mersey Park from which I had so often gazed down at the river and dreamed of sailors and explorers. As we passed the shipyard, I tried to imagine my father at work deep in the bowels of a submarine or a destroyer. I almost shouted when a clear view of the river suddenly opened up, wide and sparkling in the sun, with a tanker doggedly pushing out to sea, a white wave creaming her bows or, as sailors say, 'with a bone in her teeth'.

The train was speeding along now, swaying and rattling and making a kind of mechanised music. I noticed that the man in the bowler and the frilly lady were gently rocking, their movements synchronised to the rhythm of the train. I looked away quickly when I realised that the lady was watching me watching her. Everything outside the window was strange now; I might have been in a foreign country. I felt a sudden surge of excitement. That was what I was doing, I was going to a foreign country – Wales!

The man in the bowler hat had put down his newspaper and took a bag of sweets from his pocket. Staring out of the window, he unwrapped a boiled sweet and popped it into his mouth. It transformed him. Perhaps it was because he looked so sad and sucked with such concentration. Instead of being a bowler-hatted man with a newspaper, he became a gargoyle, a beetle-browed troll with a swollen cheek. He sucked so fiercely that I found myself licking my lips. When he turned his head and looked at me I drew back into my seat. Then he smiled, a ghastly broken-toothed smile.

''Ere you are, son, 'elp yerself. They're boilies.'

I was surprised that his speech sounded so Liverpudlian; somehow I didn't expect it from a man in a bowler hat.

I was hungry, but his proffered bag of 'boilies' presented me with a dilemma. My mother had told me never to accept sweets from strangers, in case they were poisoned. I looked at the frilly lady, but she was dabbing at her nose with a lace handkerchief, in a world of her own in which small boys and trolls sucking boiled sweets did not exist. I decided to take the risk. After all, he was eating from the same bag and I wouldn't take the top one! After scrabbling about a bit, I extracted a sweet and muttered, 'Thank you.' There was no bitter taste. It was all right, but I would make this sweet last as long as possible; after all, I might not be so lucky a second time.

I did have some food in my suitcase, sandwiches that my mother had made for the journey. Big sandwiches, which we used to call 'doorsteps'. But I couldn't face opening my case, not in front of the frilly lady. I was embarrassed at the thought of her seeing my ancient underwear. So I sucked my boily slowly, and turned my face to the window.

I knew that my adventure trip to Wales was being organised by the Society of St Vincent de Paul, but I had no idea that the holiday was intended for 'poor' children. I did not think of myself or my family as poor, neither were we in any kind of need that I knew of. In retrospect, seeing in my mind's eye the back-to-back houses standing in the shadow of the shipyards, remembering the rattle of the trains that shook the crockery in Grandma Topping's house, thinking of the forbidding 'back entries' and back-yard lavatories, the mangle outside the kitchen door and the tin bath for the weekly scrub, reminding myself of these things I suppose these days we might have been thought of as 'disadvantaged' children, but it never occurred to me. Poverty was something that happened to people starving in India or in the 'olden days' when, as my mother told me, poor children had no shoes. We had shoes and we did not starve, so we were not poor. Anyway, I did not think about it. It simply did not enter my head that this holiday was a form of charity. I did not know how much my mother had paid, but she had paid something. As far as I was concerned, it was a 'paid for' holiday. Nor did I have any concept of the struggle it must have been for my mother to 'kit me out' for the Grammar School. I was not poor or disadvantaged, I was simply there, living in a shipyard worker's family, part of the Irish Catholic community. I was surrounded by such an abundance of characters and experiences that my eyes and ears could hardly contain them. The language was rich, the river romantic, uncles, aunts and cousins numberless. I suspected that my being chosen for this holiday treat had more to do with gaining three certificates for Religious Knowledge from the Bishop's examiner than anything else.

My father was known as 'the quiet man' because he did not talk a great deal. He was a caulker at the shipyard, an ancient trade concerned with decking, planking and the watertightness of ships. His great passion was his 'G' trombone, a bass trombone. He was of average height, fair complexion, blue eyes and black hair. He was a dreamer and in his silences he lived in his dream world. He began to lose the sight of his left eye when he was quite young, a fact that was brought to light when he volunteered for the Royal Canadian Mounted Police Force. He got as far as Canada by the simple device of changing the hand that held the card in front of his eye during the eye test and reading the letters twice with his good eye. However, the police surgeons in Canada were not so easily deceived and he was sent home on the next boat. The quiet man who smiled a lot, a secret smile, eventually went blind in his left eye and from time to time wore a black patch, which I liked for its piratical effect.

His brother, Tom, was also a trombonist, but a tenor trombonist. He was fair and sandy-haired and a bit of a clown, more outgoing. If my father smiled, Tom laughed. Together he and my father used to play musical jokes in their brass band. There was a piece called 'The Acrobat', with the tenor trombone representing the acrobat. Full of loops and swirls, it is a wonderful solo for tenor trombone. At the end of the piece the acrobat descends from the high wire, and the trombone describes the descent in swoops of sound which get lower and lower. Uncle Tom would stand to perform his solo, and at the end, on the lowest possible note, he would take his trombone away from his mouth. The deep rasping note would continue and he would pretend to search for its source, a search which would ultimately reveal that the impossibly deep note was coming from my father's bass trombone.

My mother's maiden name was Kelly and one of her favourite brothers was John. John Kelly, 'Jack', was a publican. He never gave the children a coin without doing a trick with it. He would twist it from finger to finger across the back of his hand, then stick the coin in the middle of his forehead and declare, 'It's no good this, it's made of putty. 'Ere you are, sunshine, you might as well have it.'

Uncle Peter Kelly was famous for being always just about to leave. He would call at our house and say, 'I can't stop long, I've got to catch that bus.' Throughout the next hour or two, he would look at his pocket watch and say, 'Is that the time? Where's me bonnet? I've got to catch that bus!' Offered a cup of tea, which seemed to be permanently available, he would immediately accept despite his resolutions about getting 'that bus'. He gave us a temporary feeling: every visit was a fleeting visit, even if he stayed all day.

Grandma Kelly, an eccentric in her own right, used to fall out with George, the cat, and refuse to speak to him. She would make up a dish of food for him and then insist on one of her children giving it to him because she and he were not on speaking terms. She also employed go-betweens when she was not speaking to Grandad. Grandad had a drinking problem. He used to take the pledge regularly. One of Grandma's ploys to defeat his weakness was to send one of the children with his sandwiches and billy-can to meet him at the dock gate when the lunch-time hooter blew. The child was instructed to 'stay with your Dad till the back-to-work hooter blows'.

Grandad Kelly was a great singer of music hall songs. He and Grandma had a permanent weekly booking at the Argyll Theatre. There was also a streak of the adventurer in Grandad that appealed to me. As a boy he had run away to sea and sailed to Australia in a clipper ship.

Both of my parents came from large families and everybody lived in the next street, round the corner, or down the hill. So many uncles and aunts, it was hard for a small boy to keep count. There was my mother's sister, Molly, and her son, Tom, there was Uncle Peter and Uncle Gerrade, and a second cousin called Mary Brennan, and her son, Joe, who all lived with Grandma Kelly. And then there was Uncle John at the Stork Hotel and, living near the docks, Uncle David and his family, and Uncle

Jim and his, and there were more aunties, Maggie, and Winnie, and Winnie's husband, Uncle Arthur, who wasn't a Catholic, but by common consent was a 'nice feller', and, whispered – after a swift glance over the shoulder – 'a *Freemason*'. If you add to this list all the children of the uncles and aunts, it begins to approach a population crisis, and these were just the Kellys. The Toppings were as numerous. Christmas get-togethers meant pilgrimages to houses overflowing with people, songs, stories, booze, melodramatic argument and sleeve-rolling rows. In pubs, Grandfather Topping, a 'convert' to Catholicism, had, occasionally, to be restrained by his sons from 'punching a prod' (i.e., a Protestant), an act which, in his cups, he believed to be a mission required of him by his adopted faith.

I was born on March 30th, 1937 in a room over a corner shop in Rock Ferry, a shop in which my mother sold everything from fire-lighters to sausages. My mother, who started her working life in a flour mill, saved up £60, bought the lease of the shop and ran it very successfully. Her sales line was, 'Ask – and if it's not in stock today, it will be tomorrow.' By the time I was three years old we had left the shop. The principal reason for giving up the business was an accident in which I was badly scalded and nearly died. Not surprisingly, the incident was so traumatic and distressing that my mother felt she ought to concentrate on nursing the baby. Despite giving up the shop, mother never lost the feeling that she was an entrepreneur, nor did she cease to remind us that being your own boss was the only secure way of life.

It is true that we lived in a rough area in a tough seaport, but we were not poor, despite the fact that I was rattling along the Welsh coast to a holiday arranged specially for 'the Children of the Poor'.

A tribe of Red Indians had set up their tepees in a field near St Asaph. The priest who had met us off the train pointed it out and I caught sight of the encampment as the bus laboured up the steep hillside. Without a hint of a smile the priest said, 'Heap big Redskin pow-wow. Me – Chief Holy Joe, you – Braves.' Recognising a true brother, we stared down at the rows of bell tents. They did look like wigwams, complete with blue smoke drifting in the sunlight.

From then on, at the camp, we greeted each other by raising our right hands and solemnly intoning, 'How!'

In the days that followed, our imaginations were released to run riot in the Welsh countryside. We were Explorers of the Wilderness, Soldiers in far-flung foreign fields and once, we were the Knights of the Round Table in a real castle led by a bald King Arthur who wore a white handkerchief crown, knotted at the corners. But the day that has lingered longest in my memory is the day that I learned to row.

I don't remember much about Rhyl apart from the boating lake, a lake made magical because it surrounded one of the most tantalising places in the world, an island. I had never met Danny before the holiday, nor have I seen him since. By the time we were clambering into the rowing boat we were old friends who had shared many campaigns. We had been taken to an amusement park but the moment we realised that there was a rowing lake, with an island, fairground attractions ceased to exist. Danny had been taught to row by his father, who was a seaman. So what better teacher could I possibly hope for? As we pushed off from the jetty, deeper memories stirred and ancient enemies hove into sight. We could see them plainly, waiting between us and the island – the French!

The children in the other boats may have been lost in innocent worlds of their own but, as far as we were concerned, they were firing grapeshot into our rigging and attempting to rake our decks with thunderous broadsides. Captain Danny Black was seriously wounded before feverishly calling on his young lieutenant to take over conning the ship.

His rowing instructions were very good and in no time at all I was experiencing the thrill of propelling a boat through water. It was exhilarating – perhaps too exhilarating. I made the mistake of trying to make the boat go faster, and catching an enormous crab fell backwards off the thwart, losing an oar in the process. The captain was suddenly transformed into a bosun who grabbed the remaining oar with one hand and with the other caught the wayward oar before it drifted beyond our reach. 'Damned Frenchies!' the bosun shouted. 'That's both our officers gone! It's up to you and me now, lad!' Holding an oar each and paddling the boat like a canoe, we drew away from the roar of the guns. And that is how the bosun and the ship's boy, sole survivors of a murderous engagement with the French fleet, reached the safety of Castaway Island.

On the island we did battle with a tribe of hostile natives and then fought pirates with our cutlasses, finishing them off in time to have our sandwiches and a swig of orange grog. We lay on our backs in the long grass and watched the clouds drifting over the undergrowth of our tropical island. We felt the breeze on our legs and listened to the hum and click of summer insects.

When we came to leave the island, I made the fatal mistake of standing with one foot in the boat and one on the island, with the inevitable result.

Heavy, wet, grey flannel shorts do make your legs rather sore, but I hardly noticed. After all, it had been one of the most exciting days of my life. As we walked back to the bus I noticed people staring at my dripping trousers, women shaking their heads sadly; but how were they to know that I had just been in battle with the French and fought hand to hand with pirates on the Spanish Main? How were they to know that if it hadn't been for the bosun and the ship's boy, the people of Rhyl might, even now, be a subject race?

There must be another boat out there in the fog. I can hear the metallic noise of a Seagull outboard engine. I must give mine a run soon, though I have gone off engines lately.

I can't hear the squeal of gulls and terns this morning. I wonder if fog grounds them, like aeroplanes?

Through the mist, I can see a mythical bird, the Liver bird. I can see the Liver building across the Mersey, with the huge bird perched on top of it, wings permanently outspread. I can see the cranes of Cammell Laird's shipyard, terraced houses and back alleys. I can see the altar of St Anne's Church and the gleaming, gold monstrance being held aloft at the service of Benediction. I can smell the incense. The Latin responses of

the Mass drift on to my lips. I can hear the plainchant tunes
of the Tantum Ergo, Kyrie and Agnus Dei. I can see my first
school and the nun who taught me to read, the nun I once
wrote about.

> I will never forget
> Sister Adrian,
> in her black, voluminous habit
> looking out at the world
> from a starched white wimple.
> At five foot two
> she stood like a giant
> above the infants of Class One –
> and so full of knowledge.
> I remember
> she unlocked a door for me
> with a single letter,
> the letter Aitch.
> I couldn't understand that letter,
> couldn't pronounce it
> when I saw it on the page.
> Aitch was a mystery to me.
> The eyes in the wimple
> crinkled with wisdom
> and secret humour
> and she said,
> like someone telling a joke,
> 'Ah, 'tis a stupid letter, that one.
> It shouldn't be called Aitch at all.
> It should be called the letter, "Huh".
> Huh – as in H-im,
> Huh – as in H-er,
> Huh – as in H-ome,
> Huh – as in H-eaven.'
> And suddenly the scales fell from my eyes
> and I had conquered the letter Aitch,
> or rather, she had.

I used to think
that there was so much to learn
after Sister Adrian
and the letter Aitch,
though I longed
for the end of learning,
for the end of tests and examinations,
for the end of schools,
as if the need to learn
would stop
the day I left school.

And then came work
and wife and children,
and learning became a hunger,
a need to know,
a need to explore, to discover,
to experience.

Then, at last, I saw the joke,
I realised the impossible nature,
the immensity of the task.

Oh, Sister Adrian, you knew
it would take eternity
to explore the letter Aitch,
to explore, 'Huh – as in H-im,
Huh – as in H-er,
Huh – as in H-ome,
Huh – as in H-eaven.'

Fog does strange things to noises.

The lighthouse fog-horn is close sometimes and sometimes distant, almost as if the lighthouse was sailing slowly back and forth. I know I'm not confusing it with other horns; this one is too familiar. I hear its call throughout the year. At night, lying in bed at the cottage, its clear tone conjures up the tower, the light and the great white 'needles' of rock standing in the sea. It is not a deep sound, not the basso profundo of the great Cunard *Queens*, nor is it a trumpet call. If anything, it is like the sustained note of a 'G' trombone, like the sound I used to hear when my father practised in the front room of our terraced house in Birkenhead.

I cannot remember why Father Mulvaney's band marched from Birkenhead to Liverpool. As the River Mersey is the only thing that separates the towns, the idea of marching from one to the other has more than a touch of Irish about it, but then, Father Mulvaney's band had more than a touch of Irish about it.

'All right den, lads! "Faith of Our Fathers" for a quick warm up, okay?'

The bandmaster's 'scouse' dialect cut through our private reveries and conversations. We had gathered under the lofty iron roof of the Birkenhead Transport bus depot, a gloomy place in which a malevolent wind searched between giant out-of-service double-decker buses. I was thirteen years old and the depot was eerie and mysterious. Lit by dismal bulbs swinging in the breeze, the buses loomed over us like mournful prehistoric beasts, sightless and abandoned. But I was not afraid, surrounded by sturdy euphonium players and the gleaming trombones of my father and my Uncle Tom. The presence of Father Mulvaney was also reassuring. He stood, large and bountiful, smiling through circular spectacles, one hand gripping his briar pipe and the other resting on a crucifix stuck, like a six-shooter, in his cassock cummerbund.

Having practised 'Faith of Our Fathers', the bandmaster called us to assemble in the street. It was a bright day but rather gusty and, emerging from the gloom of the bus depot, I found myself squinting with some surprise at the number of people who had gathered at the starting point.

Father Mulvaney beamed at us. We looked, I imagine, reasonably smart in our Norwegian Police uniforms – well, they could have been Swedish or Belgian, I don't know which, but a job lot from somewhere. Sparing no expense, Father Mulvaney had delighted the proprietor of the local army surplus store with his order for assorted uniforms: navy blue; brass bands, for the use of.

We were not the only band. A school ensemble consisting mainly of bugles and drums was to lead the procession. Behind them, the 'Knights of St Columba' would hold their banners aloft. The women's sodality of 'Our Lady of the Sea' was to be followed by Father Mulvaney, OMI, cassock, cape and biretta, at the head of his band. Taking up the rear was an equally motley collection of altar boys, a troupe of dancers in national costume and a band of Irish Bagpipers. The difficulty of playing in a brass band sandwiched between youthful bugles and the dirge-like drone of bagpipes is best left to the imagination. Haphazard and highly individual drum-rolls and bugle blasts were already clashing with the disturbing groans of the Irish bagpipes. It was like listening to an orchestra tuning up before a performance; there was a feeling of excitement and expectancy in the air.

As there did not appear to be a ready supply of Catholic hymn tunes arranged for brass band, our bandmaster had painstakingly worked out his own arrangements and written out the different parts for us in neat blue-black ink. The arrangements had proved satisfactory. At rehearsal in the Lourdes Hall, Father Mulvaney had rubbed his hands with glee and announced, 'It's great, boys! MacNammara's Band itself couldn't hold a candle to yer!'

In the street, a considerable number of Birkenhead housewives had gathered at their doorsteps, attracted, no doubt, by the possibility of hearing, 'Come to the Cookhouse Door, Boys', 'Faith of Our Fathers' and 'Phil the Fluter's Ball', played simultaneously. The housewives also appeared to be in uniform. It was a uniform that seemed to separate women from girls. I remember being surprised at seeing a girl who had been at school only a year earlier and who had now been transformed into a 'housewife'. There she stood, in the uniform: mule slippers, wrap-around apron and hair-curlers encased in a headscarf. Amongst the older women a Woodbine cigarette in the corner of the mouth seemed to be an optional extra.

Without warning, and before we had sorted ourselves into our correct processional order, the bugles struck up and the boys stepped off smartly. Taken by surprise, the 'Knights', the sodality, the band and everyone else began to hop and skip and shuffle around each other. The pipers, realising that things were starting, began to inflate their bagpipes, filling the air with what sounded like a chorus of Greek mourners working up to a climax. From somewhere in the middle of this chaos, Father Mulvaney rallied his men. 'To me, Band! St Anne's Band, to me!' The 'Knights' had started to run after the bugles, their long-poled banners transforming them into a troop of medieval jousters, hotly pursued by the maidens of 'Our Lady of the Sea'. Father Mulvaney, smiling as bravely as if he had heard the last trump, stood firm. 'Don't panic, boys. We'll catch them up at the traffic lights.' And we did.

I'm not in the habit of attributing what appear to be the more wilful twists and turns of the weather to the hand of an interfering deity but, in this instance, it is difficult not to suspect that the Almighty found the opportunity for humour irresistible.

During the fourth verse of 'Faith of Our Fathers', whilst marking time at the traffic lights by the Co-op, the heavens opened. Not misty wetness, not a shower or even a squall, but huge half-crown raindrops splattered down on the music clipped to our instruments. The blue-black ink ran instantly. Crotchets and quavers slid off the page and dribbled into the gutter. Some players struggled valiantly, desperately playing from memory, some succeeded for a while, some got it wrong, some played spirited renderings of ink blobs, others gave up and slowly, with a noise like a Spanish village corrida band in its death throes, Father Mulvaney's pride and joy squawked, whistled and tooted into an uncertain silence. The traffic lights changed. In embarrassed confusion and out of step we sploshed on towards the ferry.

'"Sladeburn", lads! "Sladeburn"!'

This was not a last-ditch celtic war cry, simply an instruction to select the only printed piece of music in the repertoire, the march 'Sladeburn'. The call for 'Sladeburn' was the beginning of an epic feat of endurance probably unrivalled in annals of brass-band history.

We played 'Sladeburn' through the streets to Woodside, the ferry landing-stage. We played it in torrential rain as we disembarked at Liverpool. We played it through the traffic. In shop

windows we saw our reflections playing 'Sladeburn'. We played it
at T-junctions and crossroads, around Belisha beacons and traffic
islands. We played it at the rally in a car park, again and again.
Back through Liverpool, on the Pierhead and on to the ferry, white
and wrinkled wet fingers depressed brass valves. The rain never
eased off for an instant. Our shoes like pulp, our socks squelching,
'Sladeburn' echoed through the deserted streets of Birkenhead. By
this time, we had not merely memorised 'Sladeburn', every last
note had been branded on our brains, etched into our souls. For
months to come, 'Sladeburn' haunted my dreams. To this day the
word 'Sladeburn' brings back not only the melody but the entire
harmonic arrangement and the smell of rain-soaked army surplus
uniforms steaming at the huge fireplace in my Uncle John's pub,
'The Stork'. I remember my mother proclaiming the whole event
a 'miracle', on account of the fact that she had not heard of a
single participant who had caught a cold. But try as I might, I
cannot recall the cause for which we had marched so gallantly.

I do remember why we played a trumpet fanfare at a Mass in St
Werburgh's Church. The Mass was a special celebration in honour
of the declaration of the Dogma of the Assumption of the Blessed
Virgin Mary, body and soul, into heaven. I remember toying with
the idea that if I had died the day before the declaration, not
believing in the physical assumption but simply thinking of it as
a picturesque way of honouring the memory of Our Lady, I would
have died a good Catholic. But if I died, holding this view, the day
after the declaration, I would die a heretic. The thought troubled
me, and was to trouble me, along with other questions, for several
years to come.

I think I'll make a cup of tea on the Gaz stove. It's good being
here at the beach hut. I wonder why huts hold such a fascination
for me? Potting sheds, garden houses, beach huts – perhaps it's
the intimacy, or the smell of wood.

This particular hut is pleasantly haunted by the ghosts of many
summers, towels hanging on the doors to dry in the sun, the smell
of seaweed and Ambre Solaire, and the laughter of my wife, June,
urging her mother and father or her twin brother, John, or her

sister, Joan, to brave the breakers on the beach; our own children shouting with pleasure and clutching ice-creams; wonderful picnic lunches and tea, brewed up on this old stove. I'm glad the children enjoyed this hut, and still do.

My father was always building huts, altering them or extending them. Our back-yard shed, my father's workshop, grew by stages until it covered the entire back-yard area. The garden shed on the allotment was my favourite, perhaps because of its musty, earthy smell. It is a smell that I associate with him. One whiff of anybody's garden shed brings back a vivid picture of my father's neat and orderly allotment and the shed with its tools, seedling trays, pots, tarred string and watering cans.

I learned to ride a bike during the war, on the paths around the allotments, standing on one pedal and pushing it along like a scooter. There were crashes, falls and scraped knees before I eventually managed to swing a leg over the saddle and stay upright. When the moment of triumph came, the realisation that I could balance the thing, I remember shouting for sheer joy and seeing my father look up and smile his slow smile before returning to his spade and the great task, laid upon him by the Government, to 'Dig for Victory'.

The war was in full swing when my father was badly injured in an explosion in the shipyard. The incident left him with several fingers that no longer functioned properly and the marks of that explosion remained on his face for the rest of his life. When he recovered he returned to the shipyard and also took up duties as an ARP street warden.

Curiously, the war did not seem to impinge on my life all that much; perhaps I was able to take it in my stride because being such a small child when it broke out, war seemed to be the natural order of things. Apparently, I once asked my mother if there was ever a time when there wasn't a war, because my memory did not reach back to a time of peace. Air-raid warnings, gas masks, going to the shelters, collecting bits of shrapnel and playing conkers were everyday events, the apparent norm.

As a child, my mother seemed to me to be a tall and powerful woman who was forever rolling up her sleeves with determination in her fight against Hitler and life in general. She was taller than average, about five foot, seven inches, with thick, dark auburn hair and brown eyes. She sang a lot as she went about her work, romantic ballads of the day, traditional Irish songs and music hall tunes learned from her parents. She was also a great story-teller, with a natural ability for mimicry. When she quoted conversations with neighbours, she became the person she was quoting, voice, gestures and facial expressions. She also had a gift for improving the story she was telling, adding a little colour, or perhaps giving the tale a neater conclusion. If any of the family had witnessed the original event, she would call on them to verify her version by saying, 'Didn't she, Frank?' or 'Isn't that right, Joe?' We were always loyal, even if we had difficulty in reconciling her account with our memory of what had actually happened. After one such evening of stories, in the intimate privacy of washing-up in the kitchen (a time usually reserved for singing in harmony), somebody was bold enough to question her about a detail in one of her stories. She smiled what we called 'an old-fashioned smile' and said, 'Ah, would you spoil a good story for a ha'porth of truth?'

During the war, my mother worked as a barmaid at the Fairfield Hotel, a local pub whose customers were mainly shipyard workers. When a ship had been sunk, the pub would be almost empty and silent. Bombs could drop, destroying houses and shops and the men could remain chirpy, even make jokes about it, but a ship was personal. Not only did these men know every rivet, bulkhead and companionway but, inevitably, there would be a father, brother, cousin or school-friend serving aboard the ship. In a shipyard town, ships are family.

Noises, bangs, whistles, sounds of all kinds, seem to live in the accessible parts of my brain. I don't know why, but they do. The shipyard hooter, the air-raid 'warning' and the 'all clear', the drone of German aircraft and the bomb that rumbled noisily and then suddenly became silent, the clip-clop of the coalman's shire horses on the cobbles of the back entry and the clinking of harnesses, fog-horns on the river and seagulls, all these sounds seem to live in the forefront of my memory.

I remember excitement, but not fear; I remember the excitement of waking up, having slept the night under the stairs, to find that the windows had blown in. That day, on the way to school, I was amazed to find that a whole street, or at least most of it, had disappeared overnight. One night, with searchlights ranging across the sky, I heard people running down our back entry and somebody shouting, 'Granny, where's Granny?'

One image that remains with me vividly and which caused me great concern at the time, was seeing my father and mother struggling at the front door of our house, my mother pleading with my father not to go out into the street to deal with an incendiary bomb that had landed in the middle of the road. Even then my distress had nothing to do with the incendiary or the air raid that had begun, it was the physical struggle between my father and mother that upset me.

Once, in the country, I watched a dog-fight between a Spitfire and a Messerschmitt. I watched it as I might watch a football match, with no awareness of the horror of what was happening. When the Messerschmitt was hit, its engine screaming, a trail of black smoke smearing the summer sky, a group of farmworkers cheered, and I cheered with them.

We lived at 21, Mossley Road, Birkenhead, a street that was situated between two parks, Victoria Park and Mersey Park. I suppose they were a kind of compensation for the meanness of the shipyard workers' terraces. Because of the parks, in my mind I grew up surrounded by greenery and open skies. The summers were long and balmy and with my friends, Roy and June Smith, we lived not in a world at war, but in the magic world that children always inhabit, a world full of hide-outs and secret places with secret names.

A few days ago, on the river at Keyhaven, I saw Roy for the first time in more than thirty-five years. Like the fishing boat emerging from the fog, Roy had suddenly appeared out of a far deeper mist. Both of us were sailing. My scow being lighter and faster than his boat, I was overtaking him. Then I heard the greeting that bridged the thirty-five-year gap. 'Frank, you old bugger! What are you doing here?' The gap had been wider on my side than his. He had kept occasional track of me because of my work on television, radio and in the theatre and as a result recognised me first.

At 'The Gun' in Keyhaven, we found a table and Roy reminded me of forgotten adventures. Funny things, time and circumstance; we seem to be at their mercy, to be picked up or put down by some capricious controller of both. Although I don't really believe this, it often appears as if this is what is happening.

In Birkenhead our family would undoubtedly have been described as 'a good Catholic family'. My brother, Joe, went from St Anne's School to St Anselm's College and then to St Mary's College, Grange-over-Sands, which was a seminary school that trained young men for the Holy Ghost Fathers, a missionary order. As a result of his being away at the seminary I never really got to know him until much later. My other brother, Tom, was eight years younger than me and as I left home when I was sixteen, this age gap and the separation meant that we did not really begin to know each other until we were adults. Even now the gulf of our separate childhoods divides us. I regret that. I think we missed out on the special bond-forming that happens when brothers grow up together as children.

Nevertheless, I enjoyed a great sense of family. There were uncles, aunts and cousins galore and I also enjoyed a sense of belonging to the family of the Church. It was as if the priests and nuns were uncles and aunts as well. For me those days, above all others, are redolent of things Catholic: the rich aroma of incense, brass thuribles clinking, sanctus bells, acolytes with candle torches, the glittering monstrance held aloft at Benediction, processions in the garden of St Anne's Convent, next to the parish church, and perhaps most of all the singing of medieval Latin plainsong which seemed to unite us with centuries of worshippers. It used to fill me with a mysterious sense of floating out of time, and stepping into the ageless Communion of Saints.

I can see myself, almost as if I were watching some other boy, serving at Mass, struggling to transfer the small but heavy brass altar lectern from the epistle to the gospel side of the altar. I dropped it once. Red-faced with embarrassment, I recovered the book and placed it, closed, in the correct place on the altar, looking anxiously at the priest. To my amazement and relief he gave me a secret wink (in those days the celebrant stood with his back to the congregation) and thus absolved, I returned to my place with a lighter heart.

The priest was Father Mulvaney, to me, a larger-than-life figure who guided me through learning the Latin responses of the Mass and praised what I now realise must have been my pathetic attempts at playing the cornet. I sometimes wonder what direction my life might have taken if he had been the priest who had listened to my rebellious teenage questions. By the time I was asking those questions, he had moved on.

My brothers and I went in turn from St Anne's School to St Anselm's College, a school run by the Christian Brothers, a religious teaching order. I cannot say that I enjoyed my time at St Anselm's. I don't know why I'm being so reticent, I hated the place. I don't know what it is like now, I hope to God it has changed. In my day, the Order believed in corporal punishment which they administered with a strap. The strap was an instrument designed to inflict pain and yet, presumably, keep within the law regarding corporal punishment in schools. It was a flat piece of leather, perhaps a quarter of an inch thick, a few inches wide and about eighteen or twenty inches in length, handle-shaped at one end. Boys would dispute as to which was the most painful, a stiff new strap, or one made flexible by time and use.

After the comforting sense of family that I had enjoyed until then, the shock of my first days at St Anselm's was traumatic. It was as if I had fallen into a different century, a Dickensian era perhaps, where the shibboleth 'Spare the rod and spoil the child' was fervently believed and acted upon. Even now, I can see a black cassocked figure who, having put a question, towers over me, tapping the edge of my desk with the dreaded strap.

Inflicting pain on a child in order to induce it to learn strikes me as a medieval, if not a primitive and barbaric approach to education. I suppose the idea was that fear of 'the strap' would concentrate our learning efforts. It had the opposite effect on me. As an actor I enjoy the benefit of an extremely good memory. I am what people call a 'quick learner', but I also know how easy it is to lose the thread of thought when one is distracted. Gimlet eyes and a tapping strap frequently brought thought to a frustrated standstill when I was at school. Overshadowed by those black-gowned, strap-tapping figures, even if I knew the answers to the questions, I was rarely able to stutter out the required words. I have no doubt that most of the Brothers meant well, but I am equally convinced that for some there was an interior struggle with the spectre of sadism.

Perhaps my memory is distorted. Undoubtedly some of the Brothers were kind and gentle and there must have been laughter and happy days. If such days existed they have been squeezed out, overpowered by memories of fear and frustration. I do not suppose that I was punished any more than other boys, perhaps less than most; possibly other boys did not feel or react in the same way, but for me, every day was dominated by the fear of being beaten. For a child, for anybody, that is a living nightmare. I suppose, as an accidental by-product, it taught me something about survival.

For local Catholic families, getting a place at St Anselm's was considered an enviable achievement. I shared that belief and started at the school with eager anticipation and high hopes. At the end of the first year's examinations, I was placed seventeenth out of a class of about thirty. I had also begun to play truant. I spent a number of unhappy years at St Anselm's and longed for the day when I would leave school. I had no idea of what I wanted to do, other than to get away from St Anselm's and the Christian Brothers. When I see the Irish comedian Dave Allen on television making wry jokes about being what he calls 'a practising atheist' after being educated by Catholic priests, I can but sympathise and remember the text about those who cause little ones to stumble. I no longer feel bitter, but I still get a sinking feeling whenever I think of the place.

For the most part the lay members of the teaching staff live in my memory as humane and kindly, but the one bright light on my horizon was the man who taught English Language and Literature, John Farrell.

John Farrell did not believe in corporal punishment. He maintained discipline by his quiet but infectious enthusiasm. He introduced us to authors, poets and playwrights as if they were personal friends. He arranged for us to see plays and films. He opened up the world of English literature in such a way that we did not feel that we were working, or being educated. It was just great fun, which is, I think, the best tribute I can offer to his skill as a teacher. He was an encourager and even duffers were made to feel that they had achieved something when he returned their essays. We were to meet again, years later, when by chance I employed him as a broadcaster. We became friends and colleagues and remained so until the day he died. We even acted together in sketches that he had written for the radio. Once, he told me that he had left St Anselm's because he could not live with the school's approach to education. I was not surprised.

It was only a few years before he died that I learned just how deeply committed he was to his faith. I discovered that he was a Franciscan Tertiary, a member of the Third Order, which I believe is the most difficult of the orders to follow. To live the life of a religious in a community is one thing, but to live such a life as a married layman, with the worldly responsibilities of husband, father and wage-earner, is a very different proposition altogether.

Like many another child, I escaped into the secret world of make-believe, the dream-world that is untouched by grown-ups who see life as a 'vale of tears'. A favourite place of escape was Thurstaston Common. We used to cycle to Thurstaston, on the west side of the Wirral Peninsula, where the common was wild with shrubs and purple flowers and red sandstone rocks. We were Knights, come to the jousting fields, our armour, flannel and tweed with leather-patched elbows; our helmets, peaked caps emblazoned with a grammar-school badge. Chase and skirmish filled the long afternoon until, weary of battle, we made the ascent to the top of Thurstaston Hill to stand like breathless conquerors and stare across the estuary of the Dee to the blue mists of Wales and its northern mountains. Up on this hill, where clean wind flipped our ties over our shoulders, we were free; free from the trammels of theorems and French verbs, free from the tyranny of the strap. There is something spiritual about a breeze. Somehow, the wind on the hill filled us with an exultation that could not be contained and almost invariably we released it by throwing back our heads and laughing. Even now, in the open air, on a hill, in a boat, with the wind in my face I am filled with a sense of freedom and a sense of the ridiculous that reduces current anxieties to their proper size.

I did have two good friends at St Anselm's, Alan Trowers and Michael Golashewski. Together we joined the 'Cads', the Co-op Amateur Dramatic Society, as junior players, and took part in a number of youthful productions. Plays were an extension of our games, another form of escape, and I grabbed every opportunity. Eventually, acting in plays proved to be the key that opened up a whole new world to me, but that came after I left school.

The fog is beginning to lift. The tide is ebbing and the breathing of the sea is shallower, faster. There is still nothing to be seen but there is a new sound, the deep throbbing of diesel engines. It must be a ship, a tanker, a container vessel or perhaps a Townsend Thoresen. Townsend Thoresen, Voght and Maguire. There must be many Anglo-Scandinavian shipping concerns, not surprising I suppose, this particular brotherhood of the sea, same sea, same families really. In my first job after leaving school, as a kind of messenger boy for a firm of ship's agents, charterers and brokers, in Liverpool, I boarded hundreds of ships, English, Swedish, Norwegian, Danish, and officers and crews were completely interchangeable. The only thing which identified the nationality of the ship was the flag – not the men who sailed her.

I was sent on errands to the Mersey Docks and Harbour Board, took messages and papers to ships in crowded docks and was welcomed aboard by captains who nearly always seemed both tough and kindly.

Everything about the port excited me. The river, its tugs, ferries, customs and harbour authority boats, liners, Isle of Man cruise ships, cargo vessels unloading, ships in for refit and whalers back from frozen seas, this was the river that had beckoned my grandfather when he was a boy to run away to sea, the river from which he had sailed in a tall ship to Australia. It was also the river from which my father had sailed to Canada to join the Royal

Canadian Mounted Police Force. From this river my uncles had sailed to war whilst my father had helped to build the warships and submarines of the wartime navy, and now I bustled around its docks and sailed every day on a ferry service whose origins lay with medieval monks who used to row across the river.

The ferry boats crossing the Mersey are chubby vessels. I once heard them described as 'floating Bessie Braddocks', in honour of the local, large and redoubtable lady MP of that name. Some of the ferry boats had been at Dunkirk and now sported brass plaques which proclaimed their part in the great retreat. I always travelled on the upper deck, in the open air, and if I closed my eyes I could hear loud-hailer commands, explosions, the shouts of men in the water and low-flying Stukas betraying their arrival with the plaintive screech of black-backed gulls.

Voght and Maguire sent out hundreds of telegrams to ships and ports all over the maritime world. One of my jobs was to calculate the cost of the telegrams. I became so familiar with the different rates that if asked, 'How much is seventy-two words to Copenhagen, quickest rate?' or 'Hong Kong, cheapest?' I could give the exact cost almost immediately, out of my head. It became an office joke. People would ask me for the cost of telegrams to some of the remotest places on earth, to see if they could catch me out. Providing I knew which part of the world they were talking about I could nearly always give the right answer in a matter of seconds.

The arrival in Liverpool of whaling ships delighted some and horrified others. Whalers endured tough conditions and very long voyages, months at a time, perhaps even half a year. The first port they put into was always an occasion for celebration and 'a night on the town' which was good news for the pubs in which they spent their money but not so good for the pubs they smashed up. After one such 'whalers' night on the town' I was sent to Water Street police station to pay the bail for two whalers who had spent the night in the lock-up. The instructions were simple: pay their bail, put them in a taxi and take them back to their ship. Carrying out these instructions was not so simple. I arrived at the police station to be shown through a couple of iron-barred gates and into the inner sanctum of the lock-up. I paid the bail and the prisoners were released into my custody. When the prisoners emerged, I could hardly believe my eyes. They were Viking giants, Nordic seagods, the biggest men I had ever seen.

They had thick blond beards. Their faces were so deeply tanned that their eyes appeared startlingly blue and their teeth an amazing white. Their clothes were splattered with blood and various bits of them were bandaged, principally heads and hands, and what was not bandaged had sticking plaster on it. Each had a swollen black eye. Neither of them seemed in the least concerned either with their situation or their wounds. They smiled and laughed as if this stage in the proceedings was a natural part of any whaler's celebratory night out. They spoke very little English but enough to learn that I was responsible for their release. They both gave me a friendly pat on the back, which nearly flattened me, and shook hands with such strength and vigour that I did not know what to concentrate on, the pain in my crushed fingers or the fear of having my arm dislocated at the shoulders.

When we got outside, despite my protests, they dismissed the taxi and announced that they wanted to buy me 'a liddle trink'. I protested loudly and firmly and just as firmly they each took hold of an arm and propelled me towards the nearest pub. I think my feet were actually off the ground as we proceeded pubwards. They bought me 'a liddle trink' in every pub from Water Street police station to their ship, which was quite some distance along the dock road, but long before we reached the dock road, I was shouting 'Skol!' in a pretty fair imitation of their Viking accents and knocking back 'liddle trinks' like a champion tea-taster. Unfortunately, their 'liddle trinks' were somewhat more alcoholic than tea and I have little memory of the last part of the journey except for seeing what seemed like hundreds of bearded Vikings standing around me roaring with laughter. In fact they were still roaring with laughter when I woke up in my own bed the next morning.

When I turned up at the office, Mr Voght, without the trace of a smile, said, 'You took your time over that bail job didn't you?' I could just hear his voice through the sound of the roaring Vikings in my head. 'Well,' said Mr Voght, 'how much is twenty-eight words to Buenos Aires, cheap rate?' For once, I hesitated whilst trying to work out the answer. In the pause, there was a roar of Viking laughter. I looked up at Mr Johannes Voght, but he wasn't laughing, just smiling and I noticed, perhaps for the first time, that he had amazingly white teeth.

2   Stage Falls, Stumbling Faith and a Death in Cyprus

It is a beautiful morning. The sea is dazzle-bright, almost too sparkling for my eyes. Hurst Spit shingle bank is a pale serpent, basking in the sun. The white lighthouse on the beach and the red tower light on the castle look as if they have been freshly painted.

I've been for a paddle along the water's edge and have just finished trying to remove the inevitable beach-grit and sand from in between my toes. My face has caught the sun, but my feet look as if they belong to someone else, pallid, bloodless from their cold dip in the sea. In England no matter how hot the sun may be, the sea is always cold.

I once spent an afternoon looking at people's feet, or rather their shoes. It was an exercise we were given when I was a drama student at the North West School of Speech and Drama in Southport. We sat in a coffee shop, by the window, and watched the feet of people in the street. At first, it seemed rather a daft idea, watching people's feet. Initially we noted the obvious, male feet, female feet, but gradually our observations became more subtle. We began to see tired feet, old feet, neurotic feet, worried feet, neat or misshapen; scuffed boys' shoes, glossy, patent girls' high heels, careful bows or broken laces; pigeon-toed sandals and down-at-heel boots.

Eventually we began to imagine and describe the faces that might belong to particular feet and were amazed to discover how much the feet had informed us about the person.

Years later I was to play the novelist John Steinbeck, in a play based on his experiences as a war correspondent. To my surprise, the first speech in the play was about feet. Steinbeck said that one of the lasting impressions he had of a troopship was of feet; his observations were so similar to ours that he might have been sitting at the next table in that Southport coffee shop.

Whilst working for Voght and Maguire, much of my spare time was taken up with the Birkenhead Co-op Amateur Dramatic Society. The junior players took part in a festival of one-act plays to be adjudicated by Christabel Burniston, founder of the English Speaking Board and Co-Principal of the North West School of Speech and Drama. Our play, a Regency comedy in which I played a gentleman called Schilling, was awarded high marks in the festival. My character was described by Mrs Burniston as having 'ingenuous charm'.

I was not quite sure what 'ingenuous' meant but it sounded complimentary. Mrs Burniston talked about drama and the theatre as a territory that offered possibilities of limitless exploration. As she spoke, I realised that even though she might be unaware of my presence, she was dangling before my eyes the keys to another world. I was entranced, spellbound. I could see a path opening up before me. I had no clear idea about where it would lead, but I knew that somehow I had to follow it. There and then I determined to discover how I could become a student at the North West School of Speech and Drama.

I learned that 'O' levels were required, so, in spite of all I felt about my old school, I asked if I could return in order to achieve 'O' levels. Surprisingly, perhaps, the school agreed.

In the short time that I had been away, less than a year, my attitude to school and teachers had altered dramatically. Somehow both had diminished in an extraordinary way. The black-cassocked hovering giants of yesterday had shrunk to my size, even smaller in some cases. And something had happened to me. The teacher might tweak the ear of the boy in front of me, but I no longer waited to be humiliated. When the strap-toting brother approached me, I found that I was able to meet him eye to eye and without speaking he would pass me by, aware, perhaps, that the fragile confidence trick of authority was at risk. Whatever the reason, I was left alone, which suited me admirably. Somehow, I achieved my aim. Not only did I get into drama school but I also won a scholarship.

The North West School of Speech and Drama altered my life considerably. It was 1953 and the school had not long been established. There were many part-time students, but there were only five full-time, four girls, Ann, Robina, Maureen and Joyce, and me. Joyce was a widow with two small children. She was also a pianist and composer and I think her fees were paid partly in kind, in that she provided most of the musical accompaniment required by the school. The full-time students studied for a London Guildhall School of Music and Drama Teaching Diploma. The subjects included Theatre History, Phonetics and Phonology, i.e., speech sounds as you hear them and sounds as you make them; English Literature, plays and poetry, History of Costume, Anatomy, Speech Therapy, Mime and Movement and some basic psychology.

Being such a small group, we full-time students were privileged in the personal attention we received, and I loved every minute of it. We had teaching practice in the evenings with small children whose parents wanted them to learn to speak the so-called 'standard' English. We also performed in the local community. On one occasion we were presenting an extract from Sheridan's *The School for Scandal* before an audience of pensioners. I was playing Sir Peter Teazle. At one point in the scene I was required to stamp angrily across the stage and fling myself into a chair. I did not know that in the preceding action the chair had accidentally been moved so that only three of its legs were on the stage. The fourth leg was suspended in space. When my moment came, I threw myself at the chair. To my horror, the chair tilted off the stage and crashed to the floor, whilst I continued my journey through the air, landing very heavily at the feet of the front row of pensioners. There was a chorus of 'Ooohs!' from the audience, but such was my embarrassment that the 'Ooohs!' had hardly died away before I had leaped back on to the stage and was delivering my next line for all the world as if nothing had happened. All of this was too much for Maureen, my Lady Teazle, and most of my following speech was addressed to the quaking shoulders of a Lady Teazle who could no longer face either me or the audience.

Since then I have been far more cautious about stage furniture and props, but you cannot be perpetually prepared for accidents. When the gremlins are out to get you, they get you, as I was to discover in later years both in the theatre and on television. At Leatherhead Rep, on the first night of the farce, *Dry Rot*, in which Peter Bowles played Alfred Tubbe, my wife June, well padded, played the Peggy Mount policewoman's role and I played a French jockey, I was precipitated into a forward roll from a sofa whilst clutching a glass of whisky. By some miracle I did not spill a drop of drink. This unintentional piece of tumbling raised such a roar of laughter from the audience that the director, after rebuking me for introducing new 'business' without consulting him, said, 'Nevertheless, it's very funny. Keep it in.' I had to practise for hours to achieve the same 'accident'.

Again, in a television production I was required to make a running entrance across the set and on to a circular rostrum. The rostrum was on wheels which should have been locked. They weren't. The rostrum with me on it, arms outstretched like a tightrope walker who has just lost his balancing pole, careered across the studio, crashing to a stop against the scaffolding of the tiered seating for the studio audience. Once again I had landed in the front row. However, all this excitement lay in the future.

At drama school I was still learning. I must say that there is a limit to how much acting you can teach someone. You can be taught an approach to acting, how to set about researching a character. You can be taught to dance, sing, move and open your mouth. Opening your mouth is essential for any actor but particularly for Merseysiders who have a tendency to speak, like ventriloquists, through clenched teeth. I believe that a gift can be coached, stretched, improved, but the gift has to be present in the first place. You can, perhaps, be taught to perform adequately, and there are many 'adequate' actors in the theatre, but a good actor – I don't like the expression 'a great actor' – a good actor has not only done all the basic technical spadework, but he or she has something else, something indefinable. I remember the piano accompanist,

William Blezzard, who had accompanied many performers, actors and singers, telling me that throughout his life he had only ever worked with three people in whom he recognised that indefinable 'something', but he had recognised it within the first few minutes of their performance.

This indefinable 'something' takes different forms. There are actors who are electric on stage, but privately you might not notice them in a room full of people. There are others who seem to light up any room they enter, whether it is on a stage or at a private gathering, but that is not the gift I mean when I think of a good actor. Personal charisma is exciting, but it is not always synonymous with good acting. Good acting may be indefinable but, as William Blezzard says, you know it when you see it. Sir Ralph Richardson used to say that it was just a trick, and perhaps it is, but I believe that it is the one trick that cannot be taught. Theologians sometimes say that faith 'is not taught, but caught'. I think an element of that idea may well apply to the indefinable something which makes a performance outstanding; like faith there is something spiritual about it, a mystery captured, accidentally perhaps. Well, all this is rather 'high-falutin''. At drama school I was learning how to stand up straight, open my mouth, breathe and interpret a Leichner make-up chart.

A school in Bootle, near Liverpool, had asked the North West School of Speech and Drama to provide a make-up artist for one of their productions. They sent me. I can't remember if the production was *Aladdin* or *Choo Chin Chow,* but I do remember the task of transforming about thirty or forty miniature Liverpudlians into thirty or forty miniature Chinamen. I was horrified at the prospect. I bought a Leichner make-up chart labelled 'Oriental', from Boots, I think, and then a goodly number of the appropriate sticks of greasepaint and set off for Bootle.

Bootle may have enjoyed a miracle of replanning, or maybe it hasn't, since I visited it, but at that time it was back-to-back at its most depressing. The real miracle was the inside of the school, a startling contrast of bright colours and noise and laughter. It may have been miserable outside but inside the staff had created another world.

The first four children were experiments as far as I was concerned, until I realised that for the large 'chorus' of 'townspeople' I needed to work like a cartoonist. I had to create an oriental impression which could be achieved by drawing a few very particular lines on a suitably unmarked canvas. I got the staff to prepare the 'unmarked canvasses' with an appropriate base colour and then they passed them on to me for the few and particular oriental lines to be drawn in. As time progressed, I became increasingly deft, and finished in time to offer more subtle touches to the children playing principal roles. Later, the headmistress said it was wonderful 'to have someone with such specialist skill'. I didn't have the nerve to tell her that apart from myself, these were the first faces I had ever 'made-up' in my life.

As a drama school the North West School was very uninstitutional. The building was a large family house in Roe Lane, Southport. It had been adapted slightly but still retained the atmosphere of a family home.

Christabel Burniston's co-principal was the versatile Miss Joclyn Bell. The two names put together have a marvellously theatrical ring to them. Joclyn Bell presided over most of our studies. Small, trim and neat, she attempted to teach us to breathe to our best advantage. In class she once demonstrated an exercise for me, a sequence of muscle control in breathing, and I was astonished to discover that her stomach muscles were as hard as rock. In my romantic dreams about acting I had never considered the importance of physical fitness for an actor.

Gradually our muscles must have improved, as each day began with breathing exercises followed by physical exercise, 'limbering up' as we called it, and then relaxation. Relaxation usually involved lying on the floor and relaxing muscles from head to toe whilst Miss Bell 'talked us through', painting word pictures of idyllic places. Lying on the sand of one of Miss Bell's sun-drenched beaches, beneath a gently swaying palm tree, with the sound of a rhythmical sea lapping a white coral shore on one occasion I actually went to sleep.

Of course I had a silent and utterly innocent passion for Miss

Bell, as once I had for Miss Merryman at my junior school. It was not the same as the teenage crush I had on a girl called Pat, who lived in a nearby street at home. With Miss Merryman and Miss Bell it was more like worship than love; after all they existed on a different plane. Nor was it in any way similar to the rough and tumble of the flirtatious games played with Robbie, Mo and Ann. Those games were sometimes boisterous but as we were always in a group, it was rather like puppies playing. Well, almost. There was a very definite sense of family, which in a curious way protected us from ourselves.

It is hard for me to describe the metamorphosis I was experiencing, not only as a student, but as a young man growing up. For the first time in my life I had left the terraced house community of a shipyard town to live in a different society, another world. Joyce Goldsworth, our resident pianist/student, lived with her parents, Doctor and Mrs Barbour. They provided me with a home from home, but in so doing, unconsciously introduced me to things that so far had been outside my experience. Very often, it was little things that surprised me, such as napkin rings. I doubt if I had been in what was, to me, such a large private house before. A Scottish family, they took me with them to Southport's annual Caledonian Ball. They even provided me with a dinner suit, and a dress-shirt with, wonder of wonders, dress-studs instead of buttons! By the end of the evening I found myself dancing Eightsome Reels and Dashing White Sergeants as if I had been born to them.

From time to time, Miss Bell's mother would take 'the young-sters', Robbie, Mo, Ann and me, to a Southport restaurant for tea and crumpets, or toasted teacakes. Joyce's brother, Bill, who was a GP in partnership with his father, was a keen amateur painter and I remember going with the family to a local gallery for a preview of an exhibition in which some of his work was being shown. I don't know if he was joking, but he assured us that one of his paintings, in a place of honour, was upside down.

Joyce seemed to know a great number of people in Southport and I was frequently being introduced to friends and acquaintances who revealed aspects of a small town society that were revelations to me. Everything seemed to be different: speech, manners and mode of living. Although I was welcomed, I felt somewhat detached, out of my depth, I suppose. I enjoyed staying with Joyce and playing in the garden with her children, Mardi and David, or listening to Joyce playing the piano, or going for a spin in Joyce's Hillman Minx Coupé. The Hillman was the first car I ever drove, on the beach at Southport. I will always be grateful to Joyce. She taught me a great deal, perhaps without knowing it.

We enjoyed a good relationship. I suspect that thrown together by chance we were accidentally good for each other, a gauche and naive teenager who needed a guiding hand, and a young and recently bereaved wife and mother. Perhaps I was a shoulder of a kind, I don't know. I do know that I remember those days with warmth and affection.

The last production I was involved in at drama school was Christopher Fry's *The Firstborn*, in which I played Shendi, the son of Miriam who was the sister of Moses.

It was the major production of the year and I was incredibly intense about the role. When I learned that the budget did not extend to wigs I dyed my hair black. I could not tolerate the thought of playing a Mosaic Jew with flaming red hair. I don't know how good or bad I was at Shendi; I was very immature in many ways, but then so was Shendi.

Most actors either relate their performances to their own experience, or enter into a vicarious understanding of someone else's experience, or perhaps a combination of both. I know that I felt great sympathy for Shendi. In what must have appeared to have been a hopeless situation, enslaved by the Egyptians, he had attempted to climb out of slavery by accepting a position of authority, as an overseer for the Egyptians. Like me, I felt, he had an uncertain position amongst people who were not his own, and also was regarded with some suspicion by his own people. He was, I think, suffering what nowadays we call 'a crisis of faith'. A similar, unresolved turmoil was causing me a great deal of private 'agonising'. I was stimulated, perhaps even disturbed by Fry's verse and found my mind leaping about down a variety of mental back alleys, looking for a catechism where none existed. It was all very enjoyable and we spent marvellous hours debating irrelevancies, but I suppose that is a natural and necessary part of coming to terms with what, where and who we are, and I was fortunate to be doing it in a pleasant environment with agreeable people.

The priest was Irish and old. He shook his head, sighed a great sigh and looked at me in silence. I could hear the presbytery clock ticking in the sparsely furnished room.

It was a comfortless room, brown linoleum, a square of old carpet, a table with two upright chairs; sepia photographs and Victorian pictures. Suspended across a corner of the room was a large wooden crucifix with a disturbingly realistic figure of the dying Christ. I could smell the odours of celibate priestly living, furniture polish, beeswax candles, stale tobacco, and BO from a cassock on the door.

Eventually he spoke. 'Sure, it isn't you who is asking these questions at all,' he said. 'It's the devil! It's the devil – in the form of intellectual pride.'

He leaned back with the air of one who has all but said, 'So put that in your pipe and smoke it!'

'Well, Father,' I said, 'supposing it is the devil asking these questions, how would you answer the devil?'

He turned his head and gave me a sly, sideways smile. 'Ah sure that's easy. Wouldn't I look him in the eye and say, "Get thee behind me, Satan!"'

And with that all my questions about transubstantiation, indulgences and the Assumption were to be satisfied. Couldn't he see that I was hanging by a thread?

1956. The bustle of Famagusta is behind us. We are in the country now. Ahead is the village of Paralimni. We can see the orange-groves and the vines and the occasional carob tree. Here and there isolated eucalpytus trees cast dappled patches of shade. It is hot, in the eighties. A woman, black dress, black headscarf, heavy shoes, is leading a donkey along the edge of an orange-grove. The trucks, RAF uniforms, everything, is covered in dust. It's in our hair, our mouths and eyes. Even the trees and the bushes blend with the pastel coloured earth and bleached rocks.

The buildings rise up out of the earth like rectangular stones. Black holes in white walls are windows into cool interiors. In the street a woman is working a cement mixer. Old men with grizzled moustaches sit in groups outside doorways and children are playing, shouting. There is a donkey crossing the street. We slow down. 'What the hell was that! A bomb? A machine gun? God, the noise! Did someone scream?' Stop truck. It's Alan! Oh God, there's blood on the windscreen. He's hit. He's slithered down into the cab through the observation hole in the cab roof. Why is everybody shouting? 'Don't be bloody stupid! Fire at what? You can't open fire on a street full of old men and children!' 'I don't know. I didn't see anything. It must have come from . . .' 'Shut up! We've got to get him into the back of the truck.' 'No, you don't have to be careful, he's dead. What? . . . Because I just bloody *know* he is, that's all.' A Greener police gun, lying on the ground behind a hole in a wall. Large shell full of lead shot. No need to aim, just point and . . .

'He was married, you know.'

'Yes.'

'Got kids. Did he say anything?'

'He just said "They've got me", sort of – surprised.'

They call us the Wild Men of Greco. Men are threatened, 'Watch it, or you'll get posted to Greco!' Cape Greco is about seven miles from Paralimni. There isn't a proper road, so the trucks make a lot of dust. No fresh water. My first meal here was six Rowntrees clear gums, two slices of Spam, a bar of chocolate and a tangerine.

They sent us dehydrated rations, but there is no fresh water. We bring the water in bowsers, tanker trucks, from Ayios Nikolaos, unless General Grivas's lads shoot holes in them. Fresh water is rationed for drinking and cooking purposes only. We wash our clothes in the sea, and swim a lot. We've been given bars of soap that are supposed to lather in salt water. They don't. A kind of scum forms, that's all. We shower and shave when we can get to Ayios Nikolaos; in between shaves we grow stubble and look like Humphrey Bogart in *The African Queen*. Clothes washed in salt water go sticky, then stiff, then disintegrate. Free order of dress, wear what you like. We look like bandits. When we drive into Ayios Nikolaos, the blancoed RAF police scowl, groan and make a show of shuddering.

The Army used to guard the camp, but there was too much friction between the Artillery and the dishevelled Brylcreem boys. It's first light. I've been on guard duty all night, just been relieved. I've clambered down to the water's edge, over the rocks beyond the lighthouse. There's a pale sky with a white line along the horizon. Nothing in sight, just sea and sky. I can see a bird, a big one. Wonder what it is? An eagle? It appears to be gliding along the horizon, except that it is only a few hundred yards away. The sky is getting brighter and the bird banks away towards the east, lifting, soaring, and suddenly, there they are, the mountains! The Syrian mountains! Absolutely as clear as crystal. Gradually the sky gets lighter and the mountains begin to fade, then the sun blips on to the horizon and the mountains have gone. A mirage of some sort, like a dream, like the dream I'm living now, waiting for the sun to blip on to the horizon when this whole island will disappear and I'll find myself awake and at home.

Escort duty. Stand on the passenger seat, like Alan, top half of my body through the circular hole in the cab roof, waiting for the bang. Waiting here, that's worse. Waiting for the gate to open and the trucks to rumble out. It's all right once you're on the road. If your number is on it, well that's that, nothing you can do about it, in fact it's exciting. It's the waiting in the camp that is almost unbearable. It's like diving off a high diving board; once you've gone it's all right, it's standing on the edge that's terrifying.

Two Turkish Cypriot boys, about fifteen or sixteen, are in the camp, being held in some kind of detention. By candlelight in our tent they are teaching us to sing 'Uskudari', in Turkish, and we are drinking Cypriot wine. Strange how it all has the same flavour, wine or spirits, I think it's the Retsina.

Williamson – his father is Henry Williamson who wrote *Tarka the Otter* – has organised a short-story writing competition. I'm producing a pantomime for Christmas; it's called *Like It or Lump It*. I wanted a stage and the discip. sergeant has built one out of concrete! Wonder where he got the cement from?

Another ambush, bloody Paralimni again. In my tent I was shivering, shaking. Fear or the effects of sunburn, or both. Blisters on my back, like inflated tennis balls. MO says people of my colouring and skin shouldn't live here! Who's arguing? Swim with my shirt on in future. The trouble is you can't hit back, not with ambushes in the street. You just have to take it and lick your wounds. The word is, if someone does something suspicious, shoot first. A boy shouted to me in Paralimni and then threw something. I suppose I should have shot him. I didn't. I caught what he had thrown; it was a pomegranate. If I had shot him it would have destroyed me. Somebody ran amok the other day in the camp, firing a sten gun all over the place. I think I know how he feels. I felt very bad the night after the pomegranate, couldn't sleep, and it wasn't the blisters. When I did sleep, it was worse. I was in a hole, like a well, hanging from the edge. The hole fell away beneath me for ever. I couldn't get a foothold and my fingers were losing their grasp and suddenly I was falling, down and down with that awful sensation in the stomach, and then I woke up on the floor. Hang on! Cling on! That's what I've got to do. But why? What for? What's so good about living like this? Sweating, shivering, shaking, being afraid. I do have the means of oblivion, just a squeeze on the trigger and no more anxiety, no more fear, oblivion. Or would it be like that? Oblivion or an eternity of shooting at laughing boys throwing pomegranates? Dear God, what is it all for?

The 'Big Blow' came last week. It was early and we weren't ready. Apparently the weather didn't obey the rule-book and, as everybody knows, the military live by the book. We were supposed to have dug trenches around the tents before the weather changed, but we hadn't even started when the storm hit us. I woke up suddenly. I didn't just stir, I was wide awake and alert. I could see the sky through the ventilation hole in the tent. The fly sheet had gone and the tent poles were swaying. A rope outside was lashing the side walls.

There were three of us to a tent, all Merseysiders in ours, Derek, Geoff and me. I shook Derek and shouted, 'Derek! The tent's going!' I called to Geoff and rushed out of the tent. Outside a weird and ghostly 'Dance Macabre' was in progress. Shadowy figures were leaping about, shouts and wails swallowed in the wind. There was an eerie light that disappeared from time to time as clouds scudded across the face of the moon. A large cardboard box came bouncing towards me and then lifted in the air. I didn't see where it went. I saw our flysheet stretched out along the ground, flapping and straining against one remaining peg. I flung myself on top of it as Derek emerged from the tent. 'Quick!' I shouted. 'Get some rocks to hold this down!' We secured the flysheet as best we could and turned our attention to the tent. Then the rain came.

Our line of tents stood at the foot of a steep and rocky hill. It was probably the protection of this hill that saved our tent. Others, further away, had been flattened, ripped, torn out by the roots. The rain was torrential but the wind did not ease off. Rivulets and streams began to run down the hillside. Like children on a beach, we attempted to channel the stream around our tents, making dams, diverting streams, digging with anything we could lay our hands on, tin plates, bits of wood.

'Where the hell is Geoff?'

'The bugger's still in bed!'

We spent the whole night trying to secure the tent, piling rocks on to tent pegs and ropes and every now and then screaming at Geoff to get up, but he did not even stir. Perhaps he's been on the booze. He was always a heavy sleeper but this was ridiculous. Nothing would wake him, neither thunder, lightning, nor torrential rain or our loudest and foulest insults. We began to wonder if he had died.

In the morning the camp looked like a battlefield, tents down, some missing altogether; beds standing in strange isolation, the whole area strewn with the wreckage and debris of the storm. The great cook-house tent, an enormous marquee, had gone, blown into the sea. And there was Geoff, rubbing his eyes and asking, 'What's happened?'

Suddenly, it's England, green, green, incredibly green England.

1957. Demobbed, it was good to get home, to listen to my mother's stories, go to Mass, meet the family. Nothing seemed to have changed, except me. I felt removed from reality, everything was happening around me but I did not feel part of it, I felt like an observer, an outsider. To my amazement, I realised that I was feeling homesick. The realisation filled me with horror. I was missing the camaraderie of men on active service. I was missing the trucks and my sten gun, the awful food, the feeling of being on the edge of danger and the daily possibility of deadly adventure. God knows, I'd been a reluctant warrior, but now, in my twenties, I was a retired veteran and I felt that I had lost something. Or could it be that I had found something? A sense of proportion? A realisation that life was too short to waste, and short or long, fullness depended on meaning and purpose and a certain amount of intensity, a sense of adventure, to give it quality? One did not need to risk one's life for a doubtful cause, but the element of risk seems to be a necessary ingredient to being fully alive. Thank God I was home, but I was not home to hibernate, that was very clear. I did not intend to wake up in forty years' time, rubbing my eyes and asking, 'What's happened?'

'Another cup of tea love?' My mother waved towards the eternal teapot. 'It's fresh.'

'Hmm?'

'Another cup of tea and a penny for your thoughts.'

'Oh, I was just wondering if the Cypriots will ever find a use for my concrete stage.'

3   From Ironing Boards to 'Treading' the Boards

A shag is perched on a stake in the river, wings outstretched like a marine scarecrow. The stake is one of a line of withered and rotting timbers, remnants of a crumbled coal-barge jetty. The wake of my boat ripples along the wooden stakes. The shag watches my progress, but does not move.

I launched my boat early this morning, not long after seven. When I woke the sun was shining on crisp, frost-laden grass. I rode my bike down to Keyhaven, about half a mile from the cottage, and parked behind the Hurst Castle Sailing Club. The club is a wooden building that, in another part of Hampshire, could have seen service as a cricket pavilion. It is surrounded by sailing dinghies, some upturned, some covered, some with loose halyards tapping against the masts.

A little gate leads to a car park and the West Solent Boatbuilder's yard. I keep my dinghy here, bright yellow hull and white foredeck, a scow, called *Ginger Kelly*. I always enjoy walking through boatyards, looking at the hotch-potch of craft, so many variations, different hulls and coachwork, idiosyncratic embellishments by inventive owners, bowsprits, bumpkins, ladders against transoms, pots of paint and the smell of varnish, half painted, highly polished or abandoned and derelict. Overhead, seagulls squeal and everything is permeated by the seaweedy, salt smell of the estuary, and all of it captivates me.

There was nobody about when I hoisted sail and began my glide down the river. Bright and cold, winter is giving way to spring. The tide had been flooding for about an hour. Wading birds, dunlin and redshank, were making thin, sharp, claw-marks in the mud. Curlews cut the air with their plaintive cry, and of course there were gulls and terns.

A crested grebe, paddling slowly along the edge of the marsh grass, suddenly upturned and disappeared for a long time, to emerge fifty or sixty yards from where it had dived. There was a quick shake of the head and then it resumed the slow paddle as if pretending it had never dived.

And there is the shag standing on the stake, bedraggled wings outstretched, glistening, bottle-green plumage drying in the sun, head lifted, one eye fixed on me. It is very still and slightly sinister.

How do you get a job in the theatre? I don't know how you do it now, I can only say how I did it in 1957.

There is a magazine called *Contacts*, published by *Spotlight*, the actors' directory. Amongst other things, *Contacts* lists all the theatre companies in Great Britain. I managed to get hold of a copy, wrote to nearly all the repertory theatres listed, and waited. Meanwhile I had to earn a living, so I started looking for local work.

Bowaters, who make paper, took me on as a Super Calender Operator No. Three. A Super Calender is a huge roller machine which presses paper in the process of refining.

When I was shown into the factory in which I was to work, I could hardly believe my eyes. It was an enormous room with lines of rolling presses, each about as tall as a two-storey house and the lines were as long as a battleship.

The Super Calender stood at one end, with massive roller upon roller reaching towards the roof. The Calender was operated by three men. Number One operated the controls and switches. Number Two was responsible for feeding paper from each gargantuan new roll to the top roller of the Calender. Number Three, me, worked at the back of the machine and was required to feed the paper, while the presses were rolling very slowly, from the top, in and out of the various rollers to the bottom, then to run to the front, catch the paper coming through and feed it on to an empty spool situated beneath the full spool.

The moment the paper was secure, I had to flatten myself on the floor as Operator Number One pressed the high-speed button and the paper began to fly over my head at a terrifying speed. I was then required to crawl out from beneath the flying paper and to wait until the reel was completed or when, like a rifle crack, the paper broke, to dive into the resulting mess and sort things out. When it broke, it would take only seconds to stop the machine but in those seconds, paper would be forced into a mountainous heap. We would then drag the flawed paper out and push it down a well in the factory floor, where it would fall on to a conveyor belt that would take it back to the beginning of the process to be repulped.

The heat in the factory was extremely oppressive but, for me, the noise was far worse than the heat. Nowadays, I imagine people wear earphones, but nothing so sophisticated was available in 1957. To speak to someone you had to cup your hands around the listener's ear and shout at the top of your voice.

After my second day in the paper mill, I arrived home mentally drained and physically exhausted. That evening I told my mother how much I dreaded the thought of going to work in the morning. To my surprise, she said, 'Don't go. Ring them up and tell them you've finished. There's no point in doing something that is making you ill. You look terrible.'

'But if I don't give a week's notice, I won't get paid.'

She shook her head and said, 'So what? It's only money.'

The following day I asked for my cards.

My brother, Joe, who was working for an oil company in Ellesmere Port but wanted to be self-employed, suggested that we buy some socks from a wholesaler and sell them door to door.

'Socks?' I said. 'Sell *socks* door to door?'

'Why not?' said Joe. 'Everybody needs socks, in fact you can never have enough socks. It's a very popular gift, a pair of socks. There must be millions of people who get socks for Christmas every year. You can't lose with socks!'

It was my first and last attempt at door-to-door salesmanship. They were wonderful socks but nobody wanted them, not from a suitcase at the front door anyway. We trudged up and down street after street. Perhaps there was something wrong with our technique. We did not sell a single pair of socks.

'Look at it positively,' said my optimist brother. 'We won't need to buy another pair of socks for years, and not only that, but we've solved at least half the problem of what to give people for Christmas.' It was amazing how quickly those socks disappeared, helped by a certain largesse on the part of Mother.

'Hello, Peter.'

'I can't stop long, I mustn't miss that bus!'

'Sit down for a minute, Peter. Have a cup of tea and a pair of socks.'

The next project was more fruitful. Joe invested in a set of ladders, buckets, leathers and 'scrim' cloths for polishing and we were in business as window cleaners. At least I was in business; my brother was the sleeping partner. He still worked for the oil company on shift work and, despite various attempts to join me on my 'round', he never quite made it. You need to clean a great many windows to support two people financially. Although I was building up a round and the work was reasonably congenial in good weather, I felt that I had to try for something that was a little more substantial.

I eventually got a job in Liverpool as a salesman in a large store in the John Lewis Partnership, working in their kitchen furniture department. Whilst I was doing this, Joe had started to run a Saturday stall at the Birkenhead Market, selling sweets. By the time I moved to my first job in the theatre, Joe had moved into selling second-hand cars from a patch of land in Liverpool, but that really is another story, his story.

Of all the theatres that I had written to, only one responded positively. I received a letter from Hazel Vincent Wallace of the Leatherhead Repertory Theatre. She invited me to meet her in London to discuss the possibility of working for the theatre as an Assistant Stage Manager, with the possibility of the occasional small part in a play.

I arranged for a day off work and travelled down to London full of excitement, high hopes and wild dreams. The interview went extremely well and I was offered the job, but to my dismay the salary offered was only £5 a week. As a kitchen furniture salesman I was earning around £9. I did not think that I could live on £5, especially in expensive Surrey. I did not know that £5 was a reasonably good offer for an ASM at that time, nor did I realise what an excellent Company was working together in Leatherhead. Perhaps foolishly, and certainly with a great deal of genuine regret, I turned the offer down and returned to Liverpool to think again.

Selling kitchen furniture in a large store in Liverpool was proving to be quite entertaining. I observed other salesmen at work, how they approached a customer, and steered them in a particular direction; how customers were assessed, the time-wasters who would keep you occupied for a long time and then leave without buying; the people who were uncertain and hovered over the selection, and those who knew exactly what they wanted, had the money and bought. I decided quite early on that I could not bring myself to adopt the attitude of the professional salesman. I tried to put myself in the shoes of the customer and decided that if I was a customer I would want a salesman who was pleasant, helpful and above all honest about the goods he was selling. To my surprise 'honest' salesmanship paid off. If there were flaws in a particular product I would point them out. If I thought one item was better value for money than another I would say so. Eventually I found that people were coming to the shop and waiting for an opportunity to be served by me in particular.

'My mother said be sure you speak to the young man with the red hair.'

'My sister-in-law said to see you especially.'

'Er, excuse me, but did you sell a sink unit to a Mr Evans from Hoylake last week?'

The Ultimate Ironing Board was the ultimate test for shop salesmen. It was advertised in the local papers before we had unpacked them from the stock room. It was indeed the ultimate ironing board. It had everything, an extension for ironing sleeves, an extension to keep large items such as sheets off the floor, an attachment for keeping the electric flex of the iron out of the way, a ratchet for altering the height of the board, an attached swivel stool and the whole affair could be folded flat for storage. They were still unopened in the stock room when the first customers, a young couple, asked for a demonstration.

I confessed that I had never unpacked or assembled one of these wonder ironing boards before, and attempted to put the thing together. Everything that could go wrong went wrong. The sheet attachment pulled out and then fell off. I put it right. I couldn't find the flex holder until I pulled a lever and it flicked up in my face. There was a cry of consternation from the customers, but I laughed and said, 'Well at least that works, and you know what to look out for.' I levered the ratchet and the board lifted up. I leaned on the board and it collapsed. Several more customers had gathered round and a roar of laughter greeted my latest indignity. I then discovered that there was a locking device for the ratchet. That secured, I swung out the stool, sat on it and slowly descended to the floor, amidst even more laughter. The young couple were wiping their eyes, no longer able to control their mirth. Eventually, I got the whole contraption erected with everything made secure and in working order. I almost expected a round of applause, but instead someone said, 'You're bleeding, son, you've cut yourself.'

I had too; at some point during my fight with the Ultimate Ironing Board, it had won battle honours by drawing blood. I think the ratchet had got me. To my amazement, not only did the young couple buy the infernal instrument, but for weeks after, people were seeking me out with requests for 'a demonstration'. If it was laughs they wanted, it was too late. I'd mastered the brute.

About a month after my interview for the Leatherhead Repertory job, I received another letter from Miss Hazel Vincent Wallace in which she said that as I had been trained as a radar operator in the RAF, would I consider the post of Stage Manager, Electrician, and Assistant Carpenter at the theatre. They were now offering £7 a week. I had had time to consider things since my first interview. I did not hesitate. I wrote accepting the post.

There was a certain irony in my being offered this job, in that apparently the theatre company was unaware that you did not have to know anything about electricity to be a radar operator and I knew next to nothing. In the few days I had before departing for Leatherhead, I consulted John Gorman, who had been at St Anselm's College with me and for a short time had been at the same RAF camp in Yorkshire. He knew about electricity. He had converted my mother's house from gas to electric. John was later to achieve fame with a singing/acting group called The Scaffold. Several of their songs made the charts including 'Do, Do, Do, Do, Do You Remember' and 'Lily the Pink', but at this time he was working for the GPO as an engineer.

I took him to the little theatre used by the Co-op Drama Group and asked him to tell me the basics of what I needed to know. Basics is the word. He taught me about male and female plugs, how to mend a fuse and gave me some information about circuits and rheostats. There wasn't time for much more. Armed with this minimal training, which must have been all of two hours, I set off for my first job in the theatre as Stage Manager, Electrician and Assistant Carpenter at the Leatherhead Repertory Company.

I arrived at Leatherhead on a Saturday afternoon in the autumn of 1957, in time to leave my gear at the digs before going to the theatre.

At the appointed time, I presented myself before Hazel Vincent Wallace who invited me to see the last performance of Arthur Miller's *A View from the Bridge*. The theatre had filled almost to capacity, but a seat was found for me in the back of the stalls. I watched the play unfold, entranced. At last, I was here in the theatre, the place I had always wanted to be, not as a member of the audience, but as a member of the company.

Saturday, November 2nd, 1957, was the day I first saw June, the girl I was to marry. There she was, outside a tenement building on the Brooklyn waterfront, screaming abuse in Italian. When the curtain came down I was taken backstage and introduced to my new colleagues. It had been a long day and yet they still had another four or five hours' work ahead of them.

Every Saturday was a marathon for the stage-management team. There were, of course, two performances on Saturday, matinee and evening, and the final performance was followed by 'the Strike', that is the 'striking' of the set, in which the scenery was completely dismantled, props put away or packed for return to the theatrical property hire companies, along with the furniture and additional lighting equipment. Within minutes of the last member of the audience leaving the auditorium, the curtain would be raised and the stage would come to life again; only this time it was alive with the ordered commotion of hammers banging, scenery joint bandages being ripped off, furniture being manhandled, ladders being erected, voices shouting. By the time the stage had been cleared, the air would be full of dust and everybody would look grey and ghostly, which was also how they felt. By now it would be about midnight perhaps, and time for a cup of tea before erecting the new set for next week's play. It was usually well into the early hours of Sunday before the team could stagger off to their various digs or bed-sits.

On my first Saturday, in the dust-filled atmosphere, amongst all those grey and ghostly faces, there was one face that stood out, one magnificent smile, and it belonged to the girl whom I had heard screaming in Italian earlier in the evening, a girl called June Berry. Out of her role she did not look in the slightest like an Italian virago. On the contrary, she was fair and blue-eyed and bursting with the energy that contributed to her nickname, Buster. It does not require much detective work to deduce that the nickname is also related to the title of the song, 'June is bustin' out all over'. A reviewer, writing about her performance in the thriller, *The House by the Lake*, said, 'June Berry's District Nurse enters the atmosphere of suspicion and horror with the force of spring air into the fug of a badly ventilated night-club.' It was a description that fitted June as much off-stage as on it.

Actually everybody seemed to gain a second wind after the midnight teabreak. We would retreat to the tea bar in the foyer. The foyer was small and intimate, and sitting round on chairs or on the floor, we enjoyed our own private, late night review of the play that had just finished. It was also a time for swapping stories about the adventures of the week. Ken Turner, our set designer, could always be relied upon for a juicy tale embellished with nudges, winks and double-entendres that would set us all roaring with laughter. Then, refreshed, we returned to work with as much of a will as we could muster.

My fears about being able to do the job of Stage Manager, Electrician were not allayed by the sight of a huge Strand Electric lighting console. Nowadays, everything is silicon-chip small and computer neat. This lighting console was an enormous affair with rows of dimmer bars and lines of circuit sockets, plugs and an unbelievable mass of extension cables. I had never seen anything like it in my life.

The fact that I knew nothing about this infernal machine must have been evident to the departing lighting man, and I think it afforded him some amusement and perhaps not a little satisfaction to realise that his presence was very definitely going to be missed. I never learned the reason for his departure so early in the season, but he clearly had no intention of passing on any of his experience or knowledge of 'The Beast' to me.

As I stared at the monstrous machine (the beast in the prompt corner) I determined to go down fighting. There were at least two things I could do. First, as a stage manager, I had a key to the theatre which meant that when everybody had gone home I could return and experiment with the equipment. Secondly, I could ask for the assistance of an assistant stage manager, preferably one who had some experience of helping with the lighting, because anybody who knew anything about this lighting console knew more than I did.

The first three plays in which I was responsible for the lighting were not complex as far as lighting was concerned. The plays were *Emma*, *My Three Angels* and *Plaintiff in a Pretty Hat*. Alan Judd produced *Emma* and *My Three Angels* and I shall always be grateful for his quiet, gentle and patient approach to his work. He gave me a breathing space which I used to get to grips with my lighting console. Night after night I would say 'Cheerio' to the company as we locked up the theatre and went our separate ways. When the last footsteps had died away, like a thief in the night, I would return and, using my stage manager's key, re-enter the building.

An empty theatre is an eerie place. It is as if all the confrontations, the re-enacted murders, the screams, the music, the laughter, the applause and all the passionate voices that have electrified audiences have been trapped within its walls. Theatres are, by their very nature, haunted houses.

Alone in the empty theatre, I practised and experimented with the equipment. I was not alone every night; sometimes I had an accomplice, the assistant stage manager who had volunteered to help me, the girl with the flashing smile, June. June had helped the previous lighting man from time to time. She had no specialist training or knowledge, but she had helped, watched and remembered and now she was happily sharing her gleaned information with me.

Plaintiff in a Pretty Hat was directed by John Barron who was to be a great success in a variety of TV series and plays, including the much loved *All Gas and Gaiters*, in which he played the formidable Dean of St Oggs.

During these three weeks, June and I got to know each other perhaps more quickly than can be easily imagined. I cannot think of many other walks of life in which two people might be thrown together with such intensity. Most boy and girl friendships develop over months, if not years, of evening meetings and weekend dates. In our case, we were working together during most of our waking hours. Because of day-time rehearsals, evening performances and Saturday night to Sunday morning set strikes, we saw each other at our best and worst; relaxed or under tremendous pressure, wide-awake or exhausted, sometimes almost literally dropping with fatigue. We overcame technical problems together, faced a variety of those minor crises that continually crop up when you are involved in live theatre performances, we talked, argued, laughed, lived and worked side by side, day in and day out. In three weeks, we probably knew as much about each other as other young couples might discover over a much longer period of time. No doubt to many people it must have seemed like a whirlwind romance, others perhaps saw it as hasty and unwise. Whether or not we had consciously identified those aspects of character which each required from the other for a lifetime's partnership I don't know, but deep down we must have recognised something special. Perhaps it was a shared sense of adventure. Perhaps it was the realisation of reliability, a recognition that in each other we saw the one person who could be trusted absolutely if we found ourselves with our backs to the wall. Perhaps we made the right decision for the wrong reasons, I don't know. I do know that I began falling in love with June the first time I saw her smile.

During the week of *Plaintiff in a Pretty Hat*, alone together in the theatre, late at night, sitting on the stage furniture, I asked June if she would marry me. To my amazed delight, she said she would. Three weeks' courtship, and next year we will celebrate our thirty-fifth wedding anniversary. Somehow, we seem to have gone on having adventures and crises with the same speed and intensity that we experienced during our first three weeks together. Perhaps that is part of the secret.

In retrospect I can see that the first three productions represented the calm before the storm. The next production hit us with the force of a hurricane. It was *Teahouse of the August Moon*: ten scenes, a very large cast, a complex set in which the Teahouse is actually built on stage during the action of the play, special effects, sound effects, a goat from Chessington Zoo and one hundred and twenty lighting cues, all of which added up to a stage-management nightmare.

On the first night the opening scenes seemed to work reasonably well, but somewhere in the middle of the play things started to go wrong.

In the prompt corner, just offstage in the wings, the person 'on the book' sits with the script alongside a small desk of electrical switches, each with its own colour light code. There is a row of red switches and a row of green switches. The reds are warning lights and the greens are cues for action. Following the script, the prompt corner sends out signals, known as cues, to people in the wings, the flys, to the music and sound effects operator and to the lighting console, who each have a script marked with their own numbered cues, which should correspond to the numbered cues in the prompt book. In the prompter's script, at the top of a page, a pencilled instruction would say 'STAND BY LIGHT CUE 23', and the prompter would press the red switch, activating a light by the lighting console, to warn the operator that a change in lighting was coming. Then an arrow would point to the exact line or word in the prompt script and the prompter would use the green switch to instruct, 'GO – LIGHT CUE 23'.

In this production the prompt script had a multitude of pencilled cues and arrows; if you add the one hundred and twenty light cues alone to the cues to the actors and to stage management in the wings, the flys and the sound operator crouched over a gramophone, you will understand that the cue markings, underlinings and pencilled arrows made the script look as if it had been attacked by a crazed, pencil-wielding chimpanzee.

Not surprisingly, with only one complete run-through before the first performance, the system broke down; a fact that was slowly recognised as in various parts of the backstage, people stared at red warning lights waiting for a green that never came. In the prompt corner a pathetic figure was sobbing silently but hysterically and gradually we realised that the nerve-centre of our operation, the prompt corner, appeared to be occupied by someone in an advanced stage of mental or nervous breakdown.

Somehow the play was continuing. The actors were valiantly ploughing on, making the best of things. They began to give cues, hidden cries for help, from within their speeches. A desperate Sakini, staring into the wings, was willing the lighting man to respond to his cue. 'Soon – soon the moon will rise!' I searched along the row of dimmers. 'Moon, moon, oh yes, dimmers 3 and 7.' I brought the moon up and gave a thumbs-up sign to the struggling actor. All around the stage and on the stage, people began to operate by feel, by ear, or by any other instinct that was alive to what was needed. The sobbing in the prompt corner continued, but somehow, by some miracle of silent co-operation, so did the play.

As far as I was concerned, the breakdown in the prompt corner was extremely fortuitous. It acted like a smokescreen. Undoubtedly, if you will pardon the mix of metaphors, that production was my baptism of fire in which my feet of clay should have been revealed. As it happened, my contribution to the chaos was seen as merely one black spot amongst umpteen others.

In the dreadful post-mortem the following morning, it was

discovered that two lighting cues in my lighting script were completely missing from the prompt script, which meant that even if the cues had been given as scripted in the prompt book, the lighting plot would have been disastrously out of sequence. June and I meticulously checked every cue in the prompt script and that night the whole complex system ran like clockwork. Amazingly, the first night review in the local press was warm and favourable, with particular praise for the stage management. As is often the case, the play that we had witnessed from the wings bore little resemblance to the play viewed by the audience. When you are very close to something, every little mistake is magnified, whereas those seeing it for the first time have nothing to compare it with and may reasonably consider that many of the 'mistakes' are intentional and amusing.

June had a room in her grandmother's house in Leatherhead. Her grandmother, Flora Yates, was a Scot who had lived most of her life in England but had not lost any of her Scottish accent. She was a lively and animated talker and I greatly enjoyed her stories.

She had four children, two daughters and two sons. June's mother, also named Flora, was the eldest. The second daughter had been nicknamed 'Mimi' and was known only by that name all her life. The sons were Joe and Victor. Joe became a teacher who worked and raised his family in Kent. Victor, a musician, was Head of Music at St John's School, Leatherhead. Victor is a very fine pianist and had been an organ scholar at Oxford.

When the Leatherhead Repertory Theatre organised a theatrical ball at the Burford Bridge Hotel, I had rashly agreed to perform in the cabaret. Victor accompanied me at the piano and gave my somewhat naive performance a touch of sophistication. My act consisted mainly of an imitation of Danny Kaye and a song, 'It Was Just One Of Those Things', performed with allegedly comic asides. I had wanted Victor to stop whilst I made my asides. Victor insisted that it would be funnier if I made all my jokes coincide exactly with the rhythm of the music. He was, of course, absolutely right because people were, at the very least, amused by the precision with which the lines were delivered regardless of their actual content. If the line was also funny, then the laugh was proportionately bigger. It was an important lesson that proved itself again and again, in later years, in the West End.

June and I were married at Leatherhead Methodist Church on April 15th, 1958. Most of the company attended both the church service and the reception at the 'Rising Sun', taking off precious time from rehearsals. June and I were given the whole day off, which was not because the management was ungenerous, it was simply the way of things. That week we were in rehearsal for *The Summer of the Seventeenth Doll*, which was quite a complex production and in the evening we were presenting an Agatha Christie play, *Towards Zero*. We were in mid-season and as June and I represented at least a third of the stage-management team, we hardly expected more than a day away from the dream factory. We planned to have a honeymoon holiday in the summer break.

Methodists are used to robust singing, but in a small church with a congregation that was predominantly thespian, the word 'robust' would hardly do credit to those who sang at our wedding. The service was conducted by the Reverend Derrick Greeves, who was then the minister at the Westminster Central Hall opposite Westminster Abbey in London. Derrick came with his wife, Nancy. I hardly knew them at that time, but we were to become lifelong friends.

In the evening June and I were driven by Jorgi Jorgensen to the Burford Bridge Hotel. Jorgi was the regular taxi-driver for the theatre. We dined in splendid isolation in an almost deserted dining room. I don't know if the hotel staff knew that we were newly-weds, or if the attention they gave us was their usual standard, but I remember that their service was extremely warm, courteous and immediate. Sometimes it felt like one of those ritzy films in which the heroine has only to slip a cigarette into a holder for a figure to glide from the shadows and an elegant flick of the wrist produces a flame at the end of an expensive lighter.

At the end of the evening Jorgi drove us to our new home, a large, elegant − or so it seemed to me at the time − bed-sitting room at East Lodge, in Leatherhead. East Lodge is a house I remember for its timed light switches in the hall, which meant running up the stairs and trying to get the key in the lock before the light went out. It was a lovely big room with a high ceiling. There was a curtained-off kitchen area, a fireplace, armchairs and a double bed. Outside the room across the landing was a bathroom with an enormous bath and as we seemed to be the only people to use that bathroom, we felt that we had a flat rather than a bed-sitting room. East Lodge was also within walking distance of the theatre, so what more could we ask?

I could hardly believe it. It had all happened so fast. We had known each other for less than six months and here we were – married.

The Noël Coward play, *Nude With Violin* was a kind of turning point for me as an actor. June had played a considerable variety of parts from old ladies to school matrons and revolutionary char-women, whereas I had only occasionally made up the numbers by being a ghost and dancing in the chorus of the annual pantomime. Also, from time to time, I played policemen, the kind of policemen whose only spoken line was uttered as they made their exit.

'Right you are, Guv.' (*Exits through French windows looking earnest and slightly perplexed.*)

My part in *Nude With Violin* was almost as small as the statutory police constable; the difference was that this part, George, an American press photographer, had a brief exchange with the actor playing the lead, Nigel Davenport, and an exit line that was intended to get a laugh.

The play had a large cast and, in the scheme of things, my part was simply a device for bringing down the curtain on that act. At rehearsals when the producer gave 'notes' to the cast, I waited for a comment about my 'cameo' role. Alan Judd either felt that what I was doing was adequate, or that I was beyond help, but, whichever, he said nothing. I experimented with my line and in rehearsal used a variety of American dialects, but whatever I did, I was never included in the production notes. Perhaps the producer thought, 'Poor lad, he can't manage the same accent twice running, I'd better not worry him.' More likely, he simply hadn't got time to worry about a one-liner;

provided he was on cue and spoke clearly the producer was satisfied.

On the first night, a new idea dawned on me. Being a Noël Coward play set in a studio in Paris, all the characters were extremely suave and sophisticated. The press photographer is brought in in order to get an unsophisticated opinion of the painting called 'Nude with Violin'. It suddenly occurred to me that the most unsophisticated American dialect that I was capable of was a comic Brooklyn, not unlike the voice used by the American comedian, Jerry Lewis.

When my big moment came, in the last scene of the last act, I made my entrance and delivered my line in a pretty fair imitation of Jerry Lewis. After an evening of European suavity and sophistication, my dialect came as such a shock to the audience that they roared with laughter, a huge laugh that was practically a show-stopper. Off stage, actors joked with me, 'Get back to your electrics corner!', 'You've got one line too many, you have.' When the curtain came down, I waited rather anxiously for a comment from the producer – would he be angry because I had done something different from rehearsal? Would he think that my contribution was too vulgar for the play and ask me to use a different voice? I saw Alan Judd approaching me as I stood in the passage by the dressing rooms. He was smiling. As he passed me he nodded and said 'Very good' and then disappeared into a dressing room.

The experience was obviously far more important to me than it was to anybody else, but at least I'd got my laugh. Clearly no one had any intention of letting my one-line success go to my head, but it did have a marked effect on how I was used from then on. In future productions, if there was a small character role that required a dialect, I seemed to be given it – Americans, Cockneys, Lancashire soldiers, a French jockey – and when the company was invited to take part in a season of repertory plays at the Royal Court in London, I was cast as Krishna, an Indian immigrant in Notting Hill.

The play that we presented at the Royal Court in London, *Dear Augustine*, had three 'Indians' in the cast; mine was a small role, again with a comic exit line. The play required the entire cast to eat a meal of goulash on stage. June and I, as stage managers, were the cooks. June was also playing 'an old lady' as well as providing the production with its theme music 'Oh, Du Lieber Augustine' performed on a mouth-organ. The other actors who were playing Indians went along to Leichners for detailed instruction about make-up. I was far too busy with stage management to attend the Leichner session. Before the dress rehearsal, I began to apply my make-up in good time to get it finished and get on with the stage-management tasks. Halfway through my make-up preparations, one of the other 'Indian' actors, George Cooper, came in and said, 'What are you doing? You've got the base colour all wrong, what you need is . . .' and then he began to reel off a variety of directions for my make-up. My time was running out, so instead of wiping it all off and starting again I tried to mend what I had done. As I was doing this the other 'Indian', Gareth Davies, came in and said, 'What on earth are you doing to your face?' I told him that George had made some suggestions. 'Ah,' said Gareth, 'George would need a different base because he is darker than you. You're very fair, like me, what you need to do is . . .' I tried again. I was making a great mess. Then to my horror I smudged the white gauze at the front of my black wig. The gauze from which the hair-line begins is supposed to disappear on top of the completed make-up; it would never match now. I decided that the only thing I could do was to make my face at least as dark as the smudge. By the time I had finished I felt I had put the entire contents of my make-up box on to my face in an indiscriminate order. 'God, what a mess,' I thought. There was no time now, I'd just have to make the best of it.

At the end of the dress rehearsal, Jordan 'Bill' Lawrence, our producer, said, 'Oh, one final thing, George and Gareth! Have a word with Frank about make-up.' That didn't surprise me. I felt a mess and had no doubt that I looked a mess. And then, to my surprise, Bill added, 'Because Frank is the only one of you that actually looks like an Indian.'

Back in the dressing room, George and Gareth asked 'What did you use?' I pointed to my make-up box. 'All of it! Hopeless, isn't it?' The 'Indians' nodded and I said, 'I think that the only thing we can do is to have a good look at my face and then try to reproduce it.' Solemnly, three 'Indian' faces stared into my dressing-room mirror.

Leatherhead Repertory Theatre did not have a resident company of actors, but there were regulars such as Gareth Davies, Christine Pollen, Basil Moss and Louisa Vaughan who were booked fairly consistently. Some actors were engaged for particular productions, such as Nigel Davenport in *Nude With Violin*.

Flicking through a handful of programmes from those days, I am amazed at the vivid images that spring to mind: the scenery dock, the smell of sizing glue and the mysterious atmosphere of the prop room, with its sleeping relics of plays and players.

The old programmes conjure up the faces of a host of people, many of whom were at the beginning of distinguished careers. Here is Richard Briers playing an American tough guy, a 'G-Man' in a New York thriller. Next week he is Father Ambrose in *Waltz of the Toreadors*. Here is Vanessa Redgrave slapping her thighs as Colin in *Mother Goose* for the pantomime season, and immediately after the pantomime she is a Goddess in *Hippolytus*, a play by Euripides. Familiar faces in unfamiliar roles. Peter Bowles as 'Horse' Wagner in *Mrs Gibbon's Boys*, and there he is as Alfred Tubbe in *Dry Rot* with me playing the French jockey. Carmen Silvera is Grace Winslow in *The Winslow Boy*. It is a fascinating list; I wish now that I had kept all the programmes.

June and I were involved in over fifty productions from classics to pantomime, from farce to Greek tragedy. Drama school had been fun, but at Leatherhead I learned so much about so many aspects of theatre, from lighting and stage management to production, and perhaps most of all about acting.

It is not an exaggeration to say that for all practical purposes June and I lived in the theatre. Managing on a very tight budget, we cooked economy meals in the prop room, usually a minced meat concoction. I have often suggested to June that she could easily write a book called *Making the Most of Minced Meat*.

Christine Pollen was a regular name on the Leatherhead cast lists. She had a dog called Marcia. One day we saw Christine throw down before her dog what appeared to be thick and succulent pieces of meat, which Marcia snuffled and snaffled before our unbelieving eyes.

'Good heavens, Christine! It must cost you a fortune having to buy meat like that.'

'Not at all,' she replied. 'That was only six pen'orth of bits for the dog.'

'Sixpence!' We were amazed. 'All that meat for only sixpence? Where did you get it?'

'From the butchers in the High Street.'

Now Christine is a very attractive woman with a slightly husky voice. Perhaps she could achieve a more generous portion for sixpence than we could. 'Christine, will you do us a favour and get six pen'orth of "bits for the dog" – for us?'

One morning we were taking our coffee break in the coffee bar in the foyer of the theatre, when Ken Turner, our scenery designer, staggered down the steps from the street, burst through the foyer doors and fell at our feet, red-faced and struggling for breath, clutching an enormous boxer dog. Ken, a natural comedian, was always good for a laugh.

'Oh!' he gasped. 'I've had a terrible time trying to catch Marcia. I saw her trotting down the road and I realised she must have got loose. She's led me a merry dance, I can tell you! She went right down by the bridge!'

He started to straighten his jacket and smooth his hair, whilst the boxer sat staring at him balefully. We were laughing and trying, unsuccessfully, to conceal our laughter.

'It's all right for you to laugh, but have you ever tried to catch a boxer that doesn't want to be caught? And do you realise how heavy they are? I swear Marcia must weigh about ten stone! – I should know! – I carried her right up the high street and she struggled every inch of the way!'

The boxer in question was listening to this with that expression of combined sadness and hurt feelings that only a boxer can muster. We were still clutching our sides, laughing.

'I don't know why you're laughing. Christine would have been in a terrible state if Marcia had been lost.'

Gently, someone tried to break it to him.

'Ken, Marcia is a *bitch*.'

'You don't have to tell me that!'

'But Ken, this animal . . . *is a dog!*'

4   A Jack of all Trades

There is a very big loft in the cottage crammed with boxes, suitcases and the collected clutter of nearly thirty years. There are family jokes about people getting lost, disappearing in the darkest reaches of the loft. I am hoping that one day we will be able to convert the space into a study. We speculate from time to time whether or not a dormer window in the roof would enable us to see the Isle of Wight. In a recent loft safari, I came across some old theatre programmes and photographs. It really is amazing how much one forgets, but there they were, undeniable evidence of the fact that after leaving Leatherhead in early 1959 and a short spell as a night watchman on a building site, I toured with *Doctor in the House* to the New Theatre in Hull and the Empire Theatre in Edinburgh, and who knows where else; I can't remember. Sunderland rings a bell. And there is the photograph of Trever Richins as Mr Rochester in *Jane Eyre*, remonstrating with his servant, John. I can just recognise that the servant is me, with a lot more hair than I remember. That was at the Grand Theatre, Wolverhampton, where in 1959 I had signed up for another season of repertory theatre, and once again was playing a series of character cameos.

Trevor Richins, who played a number of leading roles at the Grand, was a great raconteur and something of a practical joker.

Trevor played Hercule Poirot in the Agatha Christie play, *Black Coffee* and I played Treadwell, the sinister butler. Honestly, that was the butler's name. At one point in the play, Poirot announces that he is about to summon 'Cesare Borgia'. He rings a bell and the sinister butler enters to say, in sepulchral tones, 'You rang,

Sir?' The butler entered through an upstage door. As he did so, Poirot, downstage, turned his back to the audience and said, 'Ah! Treadwell.' The audience could only see Poirot's back. What I was faced with was a Poirot who was crossing his eyes and sticking out his tongue in a grotesque manner. Naturally, I was required to keep a straight face. As the week progressed, Trevor presented me with a variety of distorted faces. There was nothing I could do, or was there? On the last night, after suffering one of his best contortions, I made my next entrance carrying a tray, a gin bottle and two glasses, as required by the script. What Trevor did not know was that I had 'fixed' the bottle, by filling it with boiling water. There was a sharp intake of breath when he put his hand on the bottle. He then drew out a pocket handkerchief and folding it with all the meticulous care that one would expect of Hercule Poirot, he used it to remove the bottle top. Having poured out the drinks, the only suggestion that something was wrong was in the raising of a slightly quizzical eyebrow as he said, 'Your drink, *mon Colonel*'. and handed his fellow actor a glass that was gently steaming. When Trevor next came into the wings, and saw me, he smiled, gave a low sweeping bow and said, 'Touché, Treadwell, touché.'

June was expecting our first child when we went up to Wolverhampton. In our last season at Leatherhead, we had moved from East House in Leatherhead to another bed-sitting room in Ashtead, the next village. We had now become mobile, having bought an ancient, twenty-five-year-old Riley Monaco. One of the chief reasons for its longevity was its rust-proof, aluminium body. It really was a wonderful old car with huge headlamps on a bar and spoked wheels. In its heyday this model had been used for racing, which is why it had a lightweight aluminium body. We had a tremendous amount of fun with that old car. We used it for our belated honeymoon, touring the South Coast and up to Wales with a tent in the boot.

Our belated honeymoon was really the first opportunity for us to be alone and discover more about each other. June had originally trained as a specialist teacher of Physical Education and after qualifying had worked at the Wakefield Girls High School. She had studied Drama as a secondary subject at her college. The theatre was, is and probably always will be an insecure way of life and it was perhaps for this reason that she qualified as a teacher before venturing into the theatre.

After Wakefield she moved to London and began teaching at Southfields. She was fortunate in this, because the Drama teacher at Southfields was Maurice Copus, whose vision and enthusiasm for drama in education was to earn him an OBE.

June became involved in his productions and attended drama classes at the Marion Naylor Stage School. It was from these classes that she graduated to Leatherhead Repertory Theatre.

June's mother and father were Methodists, her father having been educated at a Wesleyan school. I think they must have worried about their daughter's marriage to a young lapsed Catholic actor whose prospects looked decidedly uncertain. June's mother, Flora, was a woman of great kindness. A keen worker for the Church, her commitment was evident in both her life and personality. I never heard her speak an unkind word about anyone. She was a great joy to be with, bright, smiling, singing, and if ever the waters of family life were troubled, she was the oil that soothed them. It used to be considered amusing by some to make 'mother-in-law' jokes. Personally, I can only be grateful to my mother-in-law for her patience, understanding and constant good humour, which I believe reflected the depth of her faith. She was a jewel who still shines brightly in our memories and we miss her very much.

I was a very mixed-up young man at that time. I had not so much lapsed from Catholicism as deliberately ceased to practise. The first time I consciously decided not to go to Mass I half expected a thunderbolt, or the ground to open beneath me.

One of the things that pushed me away from the Church was the requirement in a mixed marriage, i.e. Catholic and non-Catholic, to agree to the children being educated as Catholics. I knew that I did not have sufficient conviction even to attempt to persuade June. Looking at my own Catholic education, not only was so much of it unadulterated misery, but it also seemed to be closed and inward looking. The expression, Catholics and non-Catholics seemed to sum up a policy of religious isolationism; there were only two kinds of people, those in and those not in. Within the Church there seemed also to be another division between those ordained and those not ordained, a paternalistic hierarchy and a meekly obedient laity. These attitudes have changed now, but they were very much in evidence then.

I had great doubts about transubstantiation being the only acceptable interpretation of the Eucharist. The idea of indulgences, a specific number of days' remission from purgatory for the recital of indulgence prayers seemed a childishly simplistic misunder-standing of the mercy of God. It also implied an idea of salvation by works, in which some kind of celestial score book is constantly being marked. The doctrine of the bodily assumption into heaven of the Blessed Virgin Mary seemed simply unnecessary. All this was, of course, before the Second Vatican Council, which was to alter attitudes enormously, including mine.

Another difficulty about being a cradle Catholic is that it is almost like being tattooed. Not only is it impossible to remove the tattoo, but part of you does not want it removed no matter what extremities your love/hate relationship may reach. In that sense I will always be a Catholic. In spite of all that I have said about my Catholic schooldays, and my doubts, I will always be grateful for the accident of being born into a Catholic home, into a great heritage. No matter how much I protest, I am aware that I enjoyed a great blessing. Leaving the Church, for me, was akin to emigrating to an unexplored continent. Many years have passed but every now and then I still feel a pang of homesickness. As they say, 'Once a Catholic . . .'

June's approach to her faith appeared to be less complicated and far more pragmatic than mine. She would not be drawn into arguments about theological niceties. Once, in reply to some convoluted question of mine, she said, 'All I know is that when I worship my life works better than when I don't.' I couldn't argue with that.

June continued to attend her Church, without fail, despite my apparent agnosticism. Once or twice I went with her and felt extremely ill at ease and out of place.

Worship might be described as the natural response of mind,

body and soul to the love of God. Few of us can disentangle our theological convictions from our psychological conditioning, and we would be pretty cold fish if we could. From a religious and cultural immersion as total as mine all other denominations were inevitably seen as splinters off splinters from the great parent tree of Catholicism. At that time, I could not have embraced Methodism even if I had wanted to. I was, of course, suffering from the delusion that faith could be embraced. I had yet to learn that you do not embrace faith, it embraces you. It is no more and no less irrational than falling in love. Love frequently defies, even triumphs over rational advice and current wisdom. Love often does the right thing for the wrong reason. I had yet to discover that faith has more to do with love than with reason.

Armed with an estate agent's leaflet, I searched the Stafford road on the way out of Wolverhampton, looking for an address that did not seem to exist. The nearest place I could find was a fish and chip shop, a strangely squat building out of keeping with the other shops. I went into the fish and chip shop and asked for directions.

'Oh yes, the place you want is through the gate next to us. In fact this shop used to be the lodge to that house.'

I went through the gate, along a driveway bordered by untidy clumps of trees. There was a great deal of litter lying on either side of the drive. It was not very encouraging and I could still see no sign of the house. Then the driveway turned sharply to the right. A more formal avenue of trees now lined the driveway, rising slightly. There, at the top of the drive, was Oxley House, a once grand but now tired mansion.

The drive led to an imposing façade. Four great columns stood at the entrance. Beyond the columns was a double door. Through tall windows on either side of the door I could see a large and bare hallway.

To the side of the house a conservatory overlooked a lawn from which steps led to a lower lawn. A tree-clad hill rose up beyond the house. It was an extraordinary find. A few hundred yards away, yet almost inaudible, traffic pounded down the Stafford road and housewives went about their shopping along a row of typically suburban shops. Oxley House was an unexpected oasis, a relic of another age which had somehow survived the developers, overlooked, forgotten perhaps.

I was greeted by a small, comfortable man in a British Rail uniform, complete with cap. He spoke with a rich Midland accent.

"Elio Mr Toppeeng, ma name's Bing. Everybody joost calls me Bing. Would you loike me to show you over the flat?"

He led me through the front door and into a hall with a floor of black and white marbled squares. There was a huge fireplace to one side. Opposite the fireplace, a sweeping stone staircase that would have satisfied a Hollywood film producer curled its elegant way to a balustraded balcony.

'Thiz 'ud be yer frunt door,' Bing said, closing the double doors behind us. 'The flat iz oopstairs reely. Ah mean, thurz not a lot you could do with thiz 'all, iz theer?' I looked at the space and concluded that it would be possible to hold a dance for about fifty people or perhaps rehearse a small orchestra, but I said nothing.

The rooms upstairs were in proportion with the entrance hall. It was a wonderful house, simply crying out for someone to bring it to life.

'Eetz a beet expenseeve,' said Bing with a worried expression. When he broke the price to me it was no more than we had been paying for a single room in Surrey.

As we came down the stairs I saw an old limousine parked on the far side of the drive, against the trees. The wheels were down on their rims, grass was growing up through the bumpers. I wondered how many years had passed since its chauffeur had parked the car on that spot. And then I saw something else, a silhouette of someone sitting in the back seat, holding on to the old-fashioned looped steadying strap.

'Bing, is that an old lady sitting in the back of that car?'

'Yiz, eet eez, eets ma muther. She loikes seeing theer.'

We furnished the flat mainly with pieces from the Wolverhampton Theatre furniture store, on the understanding that if a particular item was required the scenic designer would come and take it.

Ken Turner, the designer from Leatherhead, was now at the

DEK TON

A Professional & Trustworthy Service

D E K T O N

S h i p p i n g   L i m i t e d

Door-to-door services to Ghana

Decker
07875651841

THEO

Tony
07536095333

25 Brunswick Street
Luton - Bedfordshire
LU2 0HG

Website: www.dektonshipping.co.uk
Email: dektonshipping2010@yahoo.com
sales@dektonshipping.co.uk

Wolverhampton Grand Theatre, and with his help the flat was furnished quite elegantly. It was a happy time. We were looking forward to the birth of our first child. Our main bedroom enjoyed the luxury of a separate dressing room and we had a lot of fun preparing this little room as a nursery.

My instincts about dancing in the hall must have been right. At Hallowe'en, we held a party for the company. Lanterns were hung in the trees in the drive and a borrowed candelabra lit the hall. The night was loud with music, song and stories. Oxley House was alive again, or at least our part of it was.

On December 6th, 1959, Anne was born. She was fair-haired, she had great blue eyes and even allowing for parental pride, she was a very beautiful baby.

The arrival of Anne stirred my still warm Catholic embers. I did not 'agonise' about my beliefs, or the lack of them. My mother had often conjured up images of people who had 'lost their faith', as being souls in torment. With a marvellous mixture of faith and devout superstition she once said of another 'lapsed Catholic', 'He'll never have a day's luck until he comes back to the faith.' However, I was not in torment. I had not stopped going to Mass for long, when what little prayer life I owned also dried up. I was not discontented or worried, I simply didn't think about it. I just got on with living. But now, with the arrival of Anne, questions arose about our religious obligations to her. I was aware that I had not come to terms with the questions raised by my experience in Cyprus. What was the point of survival? What is the struggle for?

For the first time it struck me that my faith had been displaced not only by doubt, but by a good deal of cynicism. My attitudes were negative. I had replaced Catholicism with an unargued agnosticism.

I needed to talk to someone but I had no confidence in the idea of talking to yet another Catholic priest. I wanted an open, no-holds-barred discussion. What I did not want was a recital from the only too familiar catechism. So, because of June's faith, I decided to approach a local Methodist minister. I expected that he would arrange a meeting, but apparently he was very busy at the time. He said he would drop me a line soon. He did.

He sent me a printed, folded, single page questionnaire, which began, 'Now that you are about to leave Sunday School . . .' I tossed it in the waste-paper basket and shelving the questions, got on with living.

Rosemary Towler was an actress in the Wolverhampton company and her father was the works manager of a light engineering factory in the Midlands, Newey Brothers. One night towards the end of the Wolverhampton season, in the 'Duchess' bar, the actors' Green Room, Mr Towler suggested that as June and I now had a child, and as unemployment was my most immediate prospect, perhaps it would be a good thing if I took a job that offered a little more security than the theatre. More to the point, he could offer me a job as an assistant manager of a department in his factory.

June and I discussed the offer and the more we talked about it the more sensible and attractive it became. Perhaps messing about in the theatre was frivolous and irresponsible now that I had a wife and child to support. I decided that I ought to give it a try.

The department I joined was called the pin shop. Newey Brothers made every conceivable type of straight pin, from the stout and specially treated furrier's pin, through dressmakers' pins to wispy, thin lepidopterists' pins. For several months, I learned about how they were made, chromed, coppered or galvanised, and how they were packed under a variety of trade names and finally dispatched to the customer. It was not difficult to learn, the work was not arduous and I had a key to the management loo! I was existing quite happily until someone came to talk to me about pensions. The thought of staying in a pin factory until I retired jerked me to life and made me face up to the fact that I was not travelling even vaguely in the direction of my talents. I could see how easy it would be to become trapped by the security the firm offered. I was seized with a sudden panic, a fear that if I stayed a moment longer I would never get out.

That night I talked it over with June and the following day I resigned.

Getting another job in the theatre was not going to be easy, in fact, getting any job in the theatre is never easy. To keep me going until I could find theatre work, I applied for a post, advertised in the local paper, as a hospital porter at the Wolverhampton General Hospital. It proved to be an experience that I would not have missed for all the proverbial tea in China. I could have been tempted to follow a career in the hospital service far more easily than ever I could in industry.

A hospital is a community within a community. Once you enter its doors, you enter an intense and complex world. In some ways, a hospital is more real than the so-called 'real' world. Outside, it is easy to live behind façades; it is not so easy once you pass beyond a hospital reception desk. Illness is indifferent to race, creed or politics. Nerves, sinews, tissues, arteries, tumours or blood clots are unimpressed by status. Fear lies close to the surface and courage emerges where you least expect it. In this world within a world, patients, doctors, nurses, porters, cleaners and visitors rub shoulders, sometimes willingly, sometimes reluctantly, with fundamental issues: birth, joy, suffering, anger, healing and compassion, death and bereavement. Nor is it a monotonous repetition of the same experiences. There are as many variations as there are people. Perhaps one of the greatest healing factors is an optimistic sense of humour. I remember once, talking to a Liverpudlian who had suffered a number of heart attacks. On each occasion, his numerous family had gathered round his bed and his jokes and cheerfulness had sent them away reassured. After his most recent attack, I had asked him how he was feeling. He was very ill but a long way from surrender. With just a glimmer of a smile he said, 'I'm all right, Frank, for a fella with one foot in the grave and the other on a banana skin.'

Initially I felt a little guilty about taking a job which I would continue with only for as long as it suited me. I need not have worried. At that time, hospital porters came and went with such rapidity that by the time I left, having worked there for three or four months, I was one of the longest serving porters. And those who came and went were a curious breed, indeed. I don't know if hospitals attract hypochondriacs or whether the environment brings out latent hypochondria, but some of the porters I met at that time seemed to have almost no topic of conversation other than physical ailments, particularly their own. Some limped along corridors. 'It's me feet, y'see.' Others stood, continuously massaging their bad backs. 'I can't do no liftin' – Doctor says.' Yet the crippled brigade moved with remarkable alacrity when a dirty or unpopular job presented itself. They simply vanished and could only be found after an exhaustive search which might end in a boiler room where a man whose 'nerves' gave him 'gyp' might be seen examining a temperature gauge with commendable intensity, or in a linen store where one who is convinced that 'Nobody knows the pain I've suffered' is bravely counting sheets as if his life depended on it. It would seem almost wrong to interrupt them were it not for the stale smell of cigarette smoke hanging in the air.

In contrast there was an old boy whose dedication had earned him the nickname of 'Creep', for the simple reason that anybody who finished a job and actively went in search of another could be called nothing else. He was unconcerned about his nickname, in fact he seemed to be amused by it. He was a lovely, uncomplicated man. He told me that his father had been a Methodist Lay Preacher and that he had wanted to be a preacher, like his father, but he had not been able to cope with the study and examinations that were required. However, his father had told him that preaching with his life was more important than preaching from a pulpit. Living the gospel, he said, was the best way of preaching it.

I doubt if I have ever met anyone who came so near to that ideal. The day was not long enough for Creep, lifting people out of beds, pushing them on stretchers or in wheelchairs, pulling dinner trollies or heaving laundry baskets, Creep went from one job to the next as if he was trying to win some curious hospital obstacle race of his own devising. Of course everybody knew him and he knew everybody in the hospital. He even knew the visitors on their way to the wards and would greet them with some word of encouragement. He frequently said 'God bless you' to people. From anyone else it might have sounded sanctimonious but when Creep said it, people felt that somehow they had indeed been blessed. I never knew him to criticise any of the Artful Dodgers or to complain about either his work or his health. He was one of the few people I have met who appeared to be happy not only in their work, but within themselves. His approach to life seemed almost childlike, naive. He seemed to be either unaware or incapable of recognising intrigue or innuendo. He was a breath of fresh air and he probably influenced me and perhaps many others more than he would ever know.

In my free time I wrote to various theatre companies. Eventually there was a response from the company with whom I had toured in *Doctor in the House*. After a quick trip to London, I returned with a contract to tour as stage manager and understudy with a thriller called *A Clean Kill*.

I left the hospital with some regret. I had become part of the community and it had been an instructive and happy interlude. However it was 1960, I was twenty-three, a husband and father and I had a career to continue.

As is usual, the touring company knitted together as a little community. The senior member of the cast was Garry Marsh who had played Mr Brown, the father of William in the films of Richmal Crompton's *Just William* stories. Helen Christie, who was later to enjoy a long run in London in *No Sex Please, We're British*, was very kind in sending an abundance of baby clothes to June. I also shared a lot of time with Liane Aukin, who played the young heroine. At the end of the tour I spent a night at the home of her parents in their beautiful Regency house in Queen Anne Street in London, a few minutes from Portland Place and BBC Broadcasting House. Liane eventually became a drama producer for the BBC. The house in Queen Anne Street was demolished some years later to make way for a car park development. A few years ago, when I met Liane in the BBC, she told me that all that remained to her of that house was a privileged parking space. I doubt if she saw the parking space as a 'privilege' so much as a bitter reminder of happier days.

I don't know if anyone has compiled a book of experiences associated with 'digs', the touring actor's temporary lodgings. If not, it is waiting to be written. The stories are legion.

One of the tasks of a touring company manager is to scout ahead to find suitable accommodation for the company. One way of doing this is to telephone the stage-door keeper at the next theatre. The

stage-door keeper usually has a list of tried and tested addresses
of homely landladies.

When we took *Doctor in the House* to the New Theatre in Hull,
in 1959 a number of us booked into the house of a landlady who
had assured us that she could accommodate at least eight of the
company. The trouble with making this kind of arrangement is that
by the time you arrive at the digs, usually on a Sunday evening, it is
too late and you are too tired to go looking for alternative lodgings
if the one you have booked into proves to be disappointing. In
Hull, I found myself having to share a bedroom with the company
manager. This loss of privacy was bad enough, but imagine how
we felt when we discovered that the only way we could get to our
room was through the bedroom of a lady ventriloquist who was
playing at a local variety theatre. The lady ventriloquist was not
only a regular to these digs, but apparently this was her favourite
room or, as she put it, 'It's the most desirable room in the house,
love, honestly, I love it!' The imagination struggled to cope with
the idea of what a less desirable room might have to offer.

It was also an interesting juxtaposition of professions. The
'legitimate' actors – I've never understood that description, but
it meant us, our company – were inclined to rise as late as
landladies would allow and to start the day as gently and as
relaxedly as possible, lounging about in old clothes, sweaters or
well-worn and much-loved elbow-patched jackets, saving elegance,
if it was required, for the evening performance. The variety artists,
at least the ones in our digs, seemed to be perpetually on the brink
of a performance. They burst into the breakfast room, nudging,
winking, cracking jokes and laughing, so bright-eyed, bright-faced
and so endlessly cheerful as to make all the 'legits' appear positively
jaundiced, which, indeed, in comparison we were. We settled into
a fairly amicable fellowship in which the variety artists assumed
the role of hyperactive children and the 'legits' became the tired,
and for the most part, tolerant parents. Their schedule did not
allow them to come to our play but we were able to catch their
mid-week matinee, where a comedian with Eddie Cantor eyes
introduced us to the audience as 'the distinguished company of
Thespians currently playing in their smash-hit play, *Doctor in the*

House at the New Theatre.' He asked us to 'Stand up and take a bow.' If our tour had been a smash-hit perhaps we would have felt less embarrassed. As it was the houses at the New Theatre were indifferent and only recently, in Edinburgh, we had experienced playing to an audience, which had consisted mainly of a wedding party crowded into a box. However, 'Eddie Cantor' had meant well and perhaps he did influence the size of our audience. From that night on, our audience did increase and by Saturday night we were playing to an almost full house.

I have just remembered why Sunderland rings a bell in my memory. It was a bitterly cold Sunday night in Sunderland, when I arrived at my digs for the week. I was shown into a reasonably comfortable, but distinctly chilly room. The landlady said that supper had been served over an hour ago and that the 'dining room' was closed. This, despite the fact that she had been informed in advance exactly when our train would, and did, arrive. 'The best I can do,' she said with the air of one who had long suffered the irregularity of actors, 'is bring you a sandwich and a cup of tea on a tray.'

When she had disappeared to carry out her threat, I noticed that the makings of a fire had been laid in the tiny Victorian fireplace. Beside the fireplace was a coal scuttle, so small that it looked as if it had been made principally for decoration rather than use. However there was some coal in it, and paper and sticks waited in the fireplace. I was by now cold and hungry. As it did not look as if my hunger would be satisfied, I thought I might as well be warm, so I lit the fire.

The landlady returned, the promised tray in her hands. As she crossed the room she caught sight of the fire and gave a little shriek. 'Oh, oh,' she said, 'you've used *all* the coal.' Clearly she was concerned that I would need more before the night was out.

'Oh, don't worry about that,' I said, 'just tell me where you keep your coal and I'll refill the scuttle.' She put the tray down with a rattle. 'You'll do no such thing,' she said. 'You must think I'm running a charity.' Failing to understand her, I raised my eyebrows. 'That coal,' she said, her eyes almost popping out of her head with indignation, 'that coal was meant to last the *week*!'

5   *Coronation Street*, **Muggeridge and the Almighty**

It has been dry and windless for the last few days, a good time to varnish boat woodwork. On the grass, outside our cricket pavilion-cum-clubhouse, I have fixed up a couple of trestle supports for my dinghy mast.

The only threat to a mirror-glass finish on my mast is the suicidal tendency of the midge. Midges have a fanatical devotion to dive-bombing glistening wet varnish in kamikaze swarms. When that happens there is nothing for it but to wait until the paint dries and to start again with the glasspaper.

However, the last coat of varnish has been applied and the old timber has taken on a new, vibrant, 'ready for anything' look. The mast is gleaming and sparkling in the sunlight and with any luck it will dry before twilight, which is when the midges start their death or glory mission in earnest.

I'm sitting on the veranda of the 'pavilion'. A breath of wind has just ruffled the pennants on the club flagstaff and in the dinghy park halyards are clinking against masts. Beyond the masts, about two miles away, is the dark outline of Hurst Castle. In one of its towers Charles I was imprisoned before being transferred to the Tower of London, where he was beheaded.

A warden of Hurst Castle used to make a macabre joke when showing visitors around the dungeons. He would point to a sign over the low cell door and say, 'That was put up there for Charles I.'

The sign reads, 'MIND YOUR HEAD'.

June and I have been hopelessly in love with wooden boats for years. We keep telling ourselves how sensible it would be to buy a glass-fibre boat, so much less maintenance to do, but we always end up buying a wooden one, mahogany on oak for preference. I suppose we are just incurable romantics really.

Our first little shallow draught cruiser, *Wildcat*, was mahogany on oak, lots of varnished wood, latticed doors to the tiny cabin, wood-capped rails around the cockpit, brass portholes, a little ship's bell, a rakish slant to the transom and a stout bowsprit for a flying jib.

Her livery was quite dramatic too. The hull was black above the waterline, a thin band of white 'boot-topping' separated the black from its bright red bottom.

It was a Finesse, one of the first boats built by Alan Platt of Thundersley in Essex. Despite the fact that without the bowsprit she was only twenty-one feet long, June and I, and our three small children, spent a month aboard her in the glorious summer of 1976.

Originally there had been only two adult berths and a child's berth in the fo'c'sle, but June built a second child's berth up forward and slung a canvas pipe-cot over one of the adult berths. 'Snug' was the kindest word for it, but nevertheless, it supplied us with some of our most cherished memories.

I suppose our stage-management years of 'make do and mend', building scenery and even furniture was a good preparation for the practical skills required if you are foolish enough to start messing about in wooden boats.

There was another period of having to be ingenious with bits of wood, when I worked for Granada TV's Zoological Film Unit in Regent's Park in London.

The tour of *A Clean Kill*, was marred by two things. The first cause for concern was that every now and then we had no theatre in which to perform, yet our contracts required us to stay with the tour. None of us had been aware of this until the week we played Streatham Hill, when we were informed that the management had been unable to book a theatre for the following week. The company was outraged but our storm of protest was silenced when we were advised to read the small print in our contracts. If I remember rightly, the small print promised us a minimum of three theatres in every four weeks. This meant that we had to be very careful with our wages because one week we might be earning and the next we might not.

Secondly, somewhere on the tour, our company manager did a flit, 'disappeared', 'scarpered', never to be seen again. He had not become the kind of missing person that the police are interested in, there was nothing suspicious about his disappearance. He had simply packed his bags and left. The police certainly wouldn't be interested in the fact that he had broken his contract with a theatrical touring management. The actors however felt completely stranded. It was as if a party of schoolchildren had been abandoned by their teacher in the middle of a day trip to Boulogne.

We were at the Leeds Grand Theatre and Opera House when his absence was discovered. I was elected by the company to telephone the management in London to tell them what had happened and to ask them what we did next.

I remember being very excited and reeling off a long string of questions, such as, how did the company get to the Oxford Playhouse? What happened to the scenery? How did we get paid? Who did we contact about digs?

There was a long silence after my recital of woes, and then the voice in London said, 'Stay by the phone, I'll ring you back.'

Ten minutes later the telephone rang. Surrounded by the company I picked up the receiver, listened, and then said,

'Er, well, I don't know. I've never – er – can I think about this and ring you back? – You'll ring me? In ten minutes? – Okay.'

I hung up. 'They've asked me to take over as the tour's company manager.'

We debated. I knew next to nothing about the job, but none of us could afford to be out of work. It would mean a bigger wage packet for me, but I would be doing two jobs at the same time. In the end, with much encouragement and promises of help from the rest of the company, I agreed to do it.

The experience opened up a whole new world of logistics. It

involved such things as paying the wages, booking a scenery-carrying wagon from the railway to be hitched to the train taking us to the next town, arranging scenery transport from the station to the theatre, checking the takings and percentages with the local theatre manager, distributing gratuities to the local stage management and scene shifting crew, keeping the accounts generally, and liaison with London. In short, general factotum and a shoulder to cry on for the whole company.

It is amazing how quickly responsibility changes one's perspective. One of my duties was to call rehearsals whenever I thought a particular scene needed refreshing, and to direct the rehearsals. Possibly, I may have been the youngest on the team, but the mantle of my job gave me a different stature, not so much in my eyes as in the eyes of my peers. Suddenly, I had become the person who answered questions, held the purse strings, made decisions. It was like role playing, only for real. It involved being two personalities. At one moment I was a laughing, joking member of the company, and the next I was the one who said 'Yes' or 'No' and whose ultimate decision was final. I was one of the gang, but I was also 'Management'.

To my surprise, I managed to manage quite well.

In one North Country town, to my amazement, we were met at the station by a horse-drawn removal van.

I was told that the owner of the removal firm lived in faded glory in a crumbling mansion on the edge of town. Apparently, in his father's day it had been a thriving business, but the present owner of the firm, the third or fourth generation in this family business, had been unable to face changing his beloved horses for motor vehicles and had simply refused to move with the times, a decision with which I was not wholly unsympathetic. The local theatre was one of his last regular customers. Because of the horses, long-distance removals never came his way, yet he still behaved and dressed like a Victorian merchant prince of the removal trade. He wore leather leggings and a bowler hat. A gold watch and fob chain hung across the ample belly of his waistcoat. Even his whiskers were in period, long sideburns and a heavy moustache. He looked like an actor dressed for a part in *Hobson's Choice*. But, he was courteous and efficient, his only difficulty was that he belonged to the wrong generation.

Trying to keep body and soul together, and send money home is not easy on tour, especially if there is the possibility of a week in which you do not have a theatre to play. However, at the Streatham Hill Theatre, I had shared my problems with the local resident stage manager. He immediately offered me a job for the following week. Apparently a touring production of an Ivor Novello musical was coming to the theatre, and extra stagehands would have to be taken on.

'Are you a member of NATKE?' (The National Association of Theatrical and Kinematographic Employees.)

'No, I'm Equity.'

'Ah well, never mind, we'll soon fix that, mate.'

Within minutes two NATKE members had proposed and seconded me and I had become an instant member of the stagehands' union. It was a tremendous help to me, not only for that week, but also in the not too distant future.

At the end of the tour, back in London, as I mentioned earlier, Liane Aukin kindly invited me to stay the night at her parents' house in Queen Anne Street.

The tour had left me with very little cash to spare. This is a masterly example of British understatement. I had sent my last wage packet to June, who was still in the Midlands with Anne, our firstborn. I had ten shillings (in old money) in my pocket, and no job, or even the prospect of a job. However, an actor, Douglas Livingstone, with whom I had been on tour in *Doctor in the House* had generously offered me, at the very least, a couch to sleep on if ever I was desperate. As it happened, I never took up the offer, but it was certainly in my mind that Sunday as I walked away from Liane's house.

With my ten-bob note in my pocket, I made my way towards the centre of town. It occurred to me that I could go to the Westminster Methodist Central Hall. This idea was sentimental rather than religious. The minister at Westminster was the Reverend Derrick Greeves, the man who had conducted our marriage service. I was lonely, missing June and Anne, and going to a service conducted by Derrick Greeves would be a kind of link. I'm afraid I don't remember much about the service, except that there was a wonderful organist who played a breathtaking Voluntary which was so thrilling that the congregation stayed in their seats long after the service had finished. Later I was to learn that the organist was Dr William Lloyd Webber, the father of Andrew and Julian. (We still have a pair of Lloyd Webber vases bought at a church jumble sale.)

On my way out I saw Derrick standing in the hall below the two magnificent sweeping staircases, now thronged with the departing congregation. Derrick was surrounded by people, tourists, American Methodists bringing greetings from their home churches. I was intending to slip past the crowd and make my way out into the street when I heard Derrick shout my name.

'Frank! Hang on a minute, would you?' I was amazed that he had remembered me. I had not seen him for nearly two years and even then, apart from the wedding, I had only met him a couple of times to discuss the marriage preparations.

I waited until the crowd had dispersed and Derrick came striding over to me. 'How are you? Where's June? How is the baby?'

I told him of our situation.

'So you are actually free at the moment. Where are you staying tonight?'

I told him about Douglas Livingstone's offer of a couch.

'Look, if it is a casual arrangement with your friend, could you opt out? You see, I was just wondering if you could do me a favour. Nancy and I are looking for a babysitter for tonight, and we could offer you a bed. Do you think you could help us?'

He did it so well that it did not actually occur to me that he was helping me, I really thought I was stepping into the breach and helping him. I realise now that had he but lifted an eyebrow, umpteen willing babysitters would have been at his command.

On Monday morning Derrick gave me a lift into town in his old taxi-cab. He and Nancy had convinced me that I would be doing them an enormous service if I were to babysit for them again that night. So, assured of a place to lay my head for another night, I started off on my round of agents.

In those days it was possible to be represented not by one agent but by several on a 'Keep in touch' basis. And true to form one after another greeted me with the traditional, 'Nothing at the moment, old chap, but keep in touch.'

I began to lose count of the tawdry wooden staircases, the shabby name-boards and the tiny reception areas outside equally tiny offices which claimed to be the headquarters of international agencies of theatre, film and television.

Wandering around central London, Soho Square, Wardour Street and Charing Cross Road, looking for work in the theatre can be a very depressing occupation. I experienced a very intense feeling of being an 'outsider', of not belonging in London. All about me were people who belonged, who walked purposefully, had jobs, homes and families in or near London. I also knew that to 'get on' in the theatre I had to establish a base in London, but how? I had a wife and daughter in the Midlands, a ten-shilling note in my pocket and the promise of somewhere to sleep. But where did I go from here?

I kept touching the ten-shilling note in my pocket as if it were some kind of talisman. I even conceived a daft notion that I had to get a job, any job, before I could break into that note. Perhaps it was not so daft. I had to start earning, but I so much wanted it to be a job in the theatre, or related to the theatre, no matter how humble.

Sometime around midday I remembered that as a member of NATKE I was entitled to go to their London office which also acted as an employment agency for West End theatre staff. I thought I might as well try my luck there.

I can't remember exactly where their office was, somewhere near St Martin's in the Fields I think. It didn't seem important at the time, but what happened at that office changed the direction of my life.

'Do you fancy a job at London Zoo, my son?'

'The zoo?' (I liked the 'my son' bit; it felt like 'Family'.)

'Yeah, Granada TV have got a zoological film unit there. They want a stagehand in their studio at the zoo. It's flat rate, I'm afraid, no overtime. Nine till five. Have you got transport?'

'No.'

'Well, it's an awkward place to get to without transport. Anyway, interested?'

A telephone call was made, an interview arranged for the afternoon, late enough for me to be able to walk there. I did not want to break into my ten bob. Anyway, a walk up Regent Street, along Portland Place, and into Regent's Park would be very pleasant.

By four o'clock it had been agreed that I should start work the following morning. It did not register at the time, because I really thought of this job as a temporary post, but in fact, my career in television had started.

After the interview I had walked as far as Oxford Circus before the implications hit me. I had got a job in TV, in London! I now had as much right as these people bustling around me to walk purposefully into Oxford Circus tube station, slap down my ten shillings and buy a ticket for South Kensington. However, I was no longer depressed or tired. I was bubbling with energy. There was no reason to spend my ten bob talisman, not yet anyway. So, I stepped out for Chelsea and the home of the Reverend Derrick Greeves.

In the evening I shared my news with the Greeveses. They seemed to admire my willingness to move from being a company manager one minute to a stagehand the next. Derrick also told me that he had a friend who was the warden of a Toc H hostel in Camberwell who could offer me a room, if I wanted it, and I would not be required to pay in advance.

I realised that although I could now survive, the next thing I had to do was to find a place of my own, so that June and Anne could join me. To do that I needed to earn more money than a stagehand's flat rate. That night I laid my ten-shilling note on the bedside table, lay down, hands behind my heaad, and did some serious thinking.

During the lunchtime of my first day with Granada TV, I

changed my ten-shilling note into coins, walked out of the zoo and found a telephone box.

'Hello. Is that the NATKE office? I'm the chap who went for the job at London Zoo yesterday. They said they would telephone you . . . They did? Good. You were right, it doesn't pay much. Look, I'm grateful about getting this job, but I have a wife and child in the Midlands. I've got to find a place to live and bring them down here. I know I can't do it on this money, but I've been thinking. I finish at five o'clock, so I could easily work in the evenings, in theatres, as a stagehand, props – anything. Can you help?'

A longish pause followed.

'Just a minute, my son, can I call you back?'

I gave the telephone-box number, hung up and waited. Actually I didn't hang up the receiver, I just kept my finger on the receiver key. There was a man pacing up and down outside the box, and I wanted to look as if I was still talking.

Minutes ticked by, then the telephone began to stir, and before it could ring I released the key and said, 'Hello. Is that NATKE?'

There was a pause, and then a slightly surprised voice said, 'Yes, but you must have been quick off the mark. Your number hadn't even started ringing. Anyway, there is a job going. Props, at the Criterion in Piccadilly. Six nights and a matinee on Saturdays. Can you get there by six-thirty?'

'When?'

'Tonight. Stage door is at the back of the theatre in Jermyn Street. Ask for the stage manager. Okay?'

'Yes. That's marvellous. Should I ring and tell them I'm coming?'

'No, I'll do that.'

'Well, thank you very much. I can hardly believe it.'

'That's okay. And er . . . good luck, my son.'

The show was a revue, with songs and sketches based on the writings of Vladimir Nabakov. Its stars included Edward Woodward and Graham Stark. For several weeks, as soon as the curtain was down on Saturday night I hitchhiked up the M1 to visit June and then back down again on Sunday. Then I found a little flat in Wood Green, very small, the ground floor of a back street terraced house.

At last June and Anne were able to join me. Somehow I had done it. I had my two girls with me, two rooms and a kitchen in Wood Green and two jobs.

Granada TV's Zoological Film Unit was tucked away in a corner of London Zoo, between the Great Birds of Prey and the Exotic Birds' House which contained the mimic birds, the parrots and the best mimic of them all, the mynah bird. His 'pièce de résistance' was a prefect reproduction of the incredibly loud call of the South American bell bird.

The building in front of the film unit contained the home of the wapiti deer, a stag, who at rutting time made a great bellowing roar. He did it consistently until the sound engineer approached him with a microphone, at which moment he would become utterly silent. But the second the sound man left the house, the roar would start up again.

The film unit itself was housed in a small building that contained offices and sound and film editing suites. At one end of the building was the zoo's lost children's office and the zoo's carpenter-cum-inventor's workshop, where Wally, the carpenter-cum-handyman-cum-inventor, spent his days. Wally was always good fun, always ready for a chat and a laugh about any subject under the sun. One of the great excitements of the week was selecting Wally's syndicate football pools. We didn't have a system. We did win every now and then, but it never amounted to more than a few shillings.

At the southern end of the film unit was a separate building called the 'Den'. This was the film studio and my domain. I was not only a stagehand, but also carpenter and, in effect, scenic designer. In fact I was the entire stage scenery department. It was my job to design, construct and paint the background scenery for filming in the Den, and then sweep and mop up afterwards. (Animals get nervous under studio lights, and in front of cameras, just like people.) That was not how my job was described but it was what I did. I did not then, nor do I now, complain, because this was a tremendous opportunity to learn about a new discipline. Filming is a complex process and I was happy to be involved, to be learning about the techniques and the tools of the film-maker's art.

The stage consisted of a coved cyclorama at one end of the studio; that is, a curved wooden wall painted sky blue, and separated from the rest of the studio by a very large reinforced glass screen. There was a door in this screen through which the animals and the presenter could enter the set. There was also a 'hatch' in the door for animals that might be dangerous. A dangerous animal could be brought up to the hatch in a crate or cage and then hatches of both the crate and the glass door would be opened, allowing the animal to enter the Den, untouched by human hand.

The presenter was Dr Desmond Morris, and the series we were working on at the time was called *A to Zoo*.

If we were filming arctic foxes, whose fur turns white in winter, I would create an arctic scene by constructing papier-mâché rocks, covering the floor with polystyrene 'snow' and arranging for a polystyrene 'snowfall'. On other occasions it could be rocks and sand for desert creatures, or greenery for forest animals.

Once, I had to construct a 'tunnel' from the studio door to the stage, strong enough to constrain a tiger. The double doors of the Den were at the opposite end of the studio from the stage. Naturally, the truck containing the crated tiger could only reverse up to these doors and getting the tiger from the doors to the stage was my job, hence, the 'tunnel'.

I built the tunnel with angle iron and wire mesh, high and wide enough for the tiger to walk through, but not to turn around. When the tiger arrived I said to the keeper, 'Well, there it is. All you have to do is lift the hatch.'

The keeper raised his eyebrows and then looked hard and long at the tunnel. He walked along its entire length, inspecting its construction. He took his time; I think he must have checked every nut and bolt. Then he walked back to the truck.

'Yes, well – I'll tell you what I'll do. I'll open the crate.' Then he grinned and said, 'As for the tunnel, you made it, you can open it.'

This last remark produced several sidelong looks from the waiting filmcrew and I cannot deny that a shiver of apprehension ran through me. However, I did not think, for one second, that he would release his tiger if he did not have one hundred per cent confidence in the tunnel. At least I hoped he wouldn't.

In the event, it worked. The tiger did not spring out of his crate, but came out very cautiously. And far from being upset by the lights in the Den, when he reached the brightly lit stage area he lay down and stretched himself luxuriously, like a domestic cat that has found a warm place in the sun.

They say that cameramen can get so locked into the picture they are framing that they often lose touch with the reality and the danger of their actual situation. There are classic examples of this, such as the news cameraman in a warzone who continued to film the soldier who was shooting him, even after he had been hit. Our cameraman, Norman Langley, belonged to this breed.

The Kodiak bear, named after the Alaskan island from which it comes, is one of the biggest bears in the world. Fully grown they weigh 1,500 lbs, that is about 107 stones. When they stand on their hind legs they can be as much as fifteen feet tall.

I have a vivid memory of Norman Langley filming a Kodiak bear in London Zoo. I can see him now, with a hand-held shoulder camera, walking backwards away from a fifteen-foot bear, which was shambling towards him on his hind legs. Eventually Norman came up against the bars of the cage, and was forced to stand still. But the Kodiak bear kept coming towards him. We were anxiously awaiting the intervention of the keeper, to distract the bear away from Norman. Before this happened, to our amazement, Norman, with his camera still running, shouted at the bear, 'Stand still, blast you. I can't keep you in focus if you come any nearer.' The bear, obligingly, stood still.

On another occasion, in the Den, we were filming an Indian hooded cobra, one of the deadliest of snakes. We were trying to prove a point about snake charming. The snake was in a basket of the Indian snake-charmer variety, and we were playing various kinds of music to see if the snake would respond more to one kind of music than another.

Broadcasting to HM Forces everywhere.

My mother Dorothy

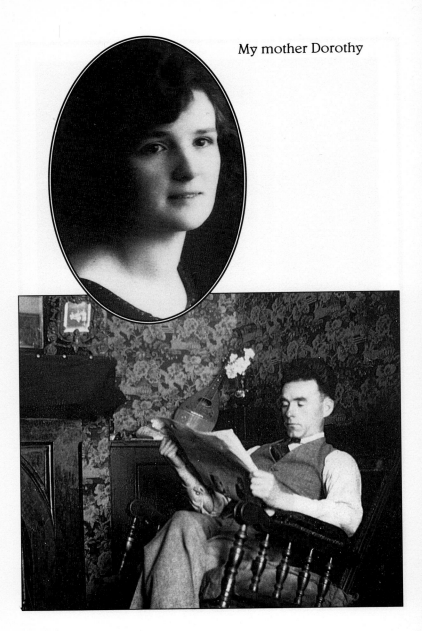

My father Frank

Top left: My identity card photo - aged 16.
Top right: Aged 19 in Cyprus.
Bottom: Aged 16 in the CADS production of
Juno and the Paycock.

My brother Joe's wedding to Stella, 1955.
My mother is second from the left.

The same occasion. The boy in short trousers is my
brother Tom.

June and me at our wedding, Leatherhead Methodist Church, 1958.

June, Leatherhead Repertory Theatre, 1958.

Harvest Festival at Woodingdean.

June in *Diamond Dust* at the Congress
Theatre, Eastbourne, 1970.

Top: Sailing the *Flora* off the Isle of Wight - one of our favourite photographs.
Bottom: The launch of the *Stubblechin Jones*, Keyhaven, Easter 1973.

Traditional Indian snake-charmer music produced no reaction whatsoever, neither did Blues, Beethoven or Bach. The fact is that when a cobra's hood is extended it can't hear anything anyway. No, the trick lies not in the music, but in movement. The snake-handler, a very large and rotund man, began to wave a forked stick over the basket.

I can't remember why, but we were filming this in the body of the Den, not behind the glass screen. The sound engineer, director, production assistant, electrician, grips, Norman Langley and me were standing in a semi-circle around the snake basket when the cobra began to rise. It rose slowly, as if mesmerised, swaying in a rhythmic movement, synchronised exactly to the movement of the forked stick.

They say that when a cobra strikes, the speed of the strike does not fall much short of the speed of a bullet. For no apparent reason, and without warning, this cobra struck. I don't know if the snake was attempting to strike the snake-handler or the forked stick, but I have never seen such a large man move so fast before or since. There were screams and people running everywhere. The only person who had not moved was the cameraman, Norman Langley. He was the only member of the filmcrew who actually saw the snake-handler catch the snake with his forked stick, return it to its basket and slam the lid on.

The great grey kangaroo has a massive tail with which it is said to balance when making its great leaping run. In order to illustrate this point I was filmed jumping like a kangaroo. If you are fit enough, try it. It's not very dignified and you will find that after three or four jumps you end up on your face.

When this episode was transmitted on TV we received letters from Australians who rather colourfully informed us that they did not set much store by this theory of the kangaroo's balancing tail. Kangaroos who had lost their tails in some accident or other had been seen on several occasions and they seemed to be able to run without falling on their faces. Whilst this might be true, it is also true that a three-legged dog is able to walk, but it does it much better with four.

Because we were such a small and intimate company, I was able to learn a great deal about filming. The crew were all friendly and willing to share their knowledge and did not seem to mind my constant stream of questions about how, when and why certain things were done. The mysteries of camera lenses, reflection sheets, dollies, tape recorders, microphones, continuity, tricks of film editing and sound dubbing were all grist to my mill.

One of the advantages of working in any capacity for a television company like Granada is that every week internal advertisements go up on noticeboards about vacancies and training schemes within the company, for studio managers, cameramen, directors, engineers, and so on. I had applied for a number of these, but regularly received the standard rejection, '. . . we regret to inform you that you have not been shortlisted for this vacancy. However, this does not preclude you from applying for a similar post in the future . . .'

So, I kept on trying.

I don't know why, but there seems to be a tradition in 'Wild Life' programmes that if you are filming a chimpanzee you will conduct an experiment to demonstrate the intelligence of the chimpanzee. I suppose it is not all that surprising; after all, an animal that appears to have human qualities is quite fascinating.

At that time, in London Zoo, there was a chimpanzee that had been found, as a baby, in a cave with a baby mountain gorilla. In captivity they had been kept together. Eventually they would have to be separated because the gorilla grows into a much larger adult than the chimpanzee, and a playful swipe from the gorilla might seriously damage the chimp. However, at the time of my story they were still together.

Everybody knows what a chimpanzee looks like, but perhaps not everybody is familiar with the difference between a mountain gorilla and a lowland gorilla. The gorilla is the largest of the apes. Lowland gorillas usually have short brown hair, immensely powerful shoulders, and flat faces with very prominent ridges over the eyes, which give them a permanent air of brooding menace. They usually walk on all fours, with the knuckles of their long forearms just touching the ground. Upright, the adult stands about six feet tall.

The mountain gorilla has the same characteristics except that he has long, black hair, with black eyes set in a black leathery face, all of which seems to add to the look of brooding menace. In the wild, they pair for life and live as a family with their own offspring. In fact, they are shy vegetarians, who would much rather be left alone, which is probably why they are far less lively exhibits in zoos than chimpanzees, who appear to be gregarious and comical show-offs.

On this particular occasion we wanted to film the young chimpanzee and the idea, not perhaps the most original, was to demonstrate how intelligent he was.

We fixed a pulley and string to the roof bars of the cage. There was a hook at one end of the string to which we attached a banana. We hoisted the banana to the roof and tied the other end of the string to the wall bars. All we had to do was teach the chimpanzee that if it untied the string, the banana would come down.

The chimp was slightly more intelligent than we were. It took him about five seconds to work out that he could reach the banana by swinging across the roof bars, so, undoubtedly, he reasoned, 'Why should I bother with fiddly bits of string when I can achieve my objective in a manner far more congenial to my natural abilities?'

My job was to keep the hook supplied with bananas.

Whenever you take a film or television camera into a public place, you can guarantee that it will arouse the curiosity of passers-by and this case was no exception. Beyond the bars of the cage there was a rail to keep the public at a safe distance. The camera crew were between the rail and the cage and behind them, at the rail, a large crowd had gathered. I was the only idiot actually inside the cage.

Chimpanzees can devour bananas at an incredible rate. Every time I put a banana on the hook, this chimp would swing hand over hand across the roof of the cage and neatly remove the banana. Hanging by one hand, he would unzip the banana with his teeth, and about three seconds later the empty banana skin would hit the floor.

I must have been attempting to attach the sixth or seventh

banana, I'm not sure which, when the chimp, who by now was correctly anticipating the sequence of events, swung over me and grabbed my head with both of his feet. To the watching crowd this must have looked very funny, and there was a roar of laughter, but I can tell you that the grip of a chimpanzee's foot is like an iron vice, and if it is your head in the vice, the experience is not quite so amusing.

The chimpanzee, however, enjoys an audience, so his response to the roar of laughter was to start chattering and bouncing up and down on my head without releasing his grip. The crowd hooted, small children screamed with delight. I suspected that my skull was about to crack at any minute.

Now all this noise upset the mountain gorilla, who had, until this moment, been brooding quietly in a corner of the cage. He shambled out of his corner and began to circle me and the bouncing chimpanzee, huffing and grunting, and obviously unhappy about having his peace disturbed. Clearly, I was in a somewhat tricky situation. The thought passing through my mind was, 'What a stupid way to go.'

It was at this moment that the keeper opened the gate at the back of the cage and uttered the time-honoured phrase of all zoo keepers, 'Git-aht-of-it!'

To the further amusement of the crowd, and to my amazement, the chimp and the gorilla shot into a corner of the cage and sat there hugging each other. I staggered out, convinced that there must be a better way of advancing one's career in show business.

Some people, politicians for example, seem to be able to keep minutely detailed diaries recording back-room conversations, and accounts of who said what to whom in the canteen at Westminster. I've never been able to keep that kind of diary. My diaries consist of terse notes, such as:

9.30 – Studio B15
3 pm – Editing. H4

What I was doing in B15, or what I was editing in H4 has been lost for ever. Up in our loft there are stacks of cardboard boxes filled with folders, files and bundles of letters. Perhaps, if I were to start exploring these boxes I might find a clue as to what happened when, where and with whom during the years I worked for Granada TV. But you know what happens once one embarks on that kind of quest. Hours can be spent, quite happily, saying things like, 'Well, well fancy that', and 'Isn't that fascinating?'

After several hours, somebody misses you, or perhaps a distant voice can be heard shouting, 'I've just made a pot of tea. Anyone interested?'

That's when you realise that your 'research' (the reading of yellowed newspaper cuttings, the perusal of sixteen packets of black and white snapshots, two school reports and an appalling student essay) has produced absolutely nothing in the area you are supposed to be researching.

There is no order in a loft, everything is stored haphazardly. All one can do is choose a box at random and dip into it, which is the method I will have to adopt whilst raking through my four years with Granada TV, the first four years of the Swinging Sixties.

Does your name influence your character? If, for instance, you name a child Rambo, will that affect his estimation of himself, or does the naming of children simply tell us something about the parents? I once knew an actor called Tristram Jellineck. It suited him. But not all actors are happy with their given names and many change them to what they imagine might be a more attractive sounding name.

I remember meeting an agent, who, once upon a time, would have been considered the archetypal actor's agent, reminiscent of George Cole's television character, Arthur Daley, whose first words to me were, 'Topping? – Frank Topping? It's a good name. I like it. What's your real name?'

'That is my real name.'

'I know it's your real name *now*, but what was your given name?'

'Frank Topping, that *is* my given name. My father's name is

Frank Topping, *my* name is Frank Topping. I've never had any other name.'

The agent mused on this for a moment, sniffed, and then said, 'Right. Well, don't change it!'

When I transferred from the Zoo Film Unit to Granada's TV studios in Chelsea, like it or not, I was known to the stagecrew as 'Ginge'. I had enjoyed every minute of my time at the zoo, but it was good to be working with actors again, though not necessarily in plays. As a stagehand, I could be working on quiz programmes, variety shows, current affairs, documentaries, or the making of TV commercials.

Many of the stage scenery crew had moved from Pinewood or Ealing film studios into television work. They had been in the film industry since the end of the Second World War and through the fifties. Not surprisingly, they spent a great deal of time recalling their adventures in what many consider to have been the 'heyday' of British films.

Granada's Chelsea studio was in the King's Road, opposite the Chelsea Town Hall. It had been a theatre, known to several generations as the 'Chelsea Palace'. Because it was a theatre, the stalls and circle seating made it ideal for audience participation programmes, comedy series, variety shows and quiz games. The stage had been extended over the stalls almost as far as the dress circle, the floor had been given a smooth surface to enable the pedestal TV cameras to glide without bumps and probably the lighting had been quadrupled.

When I arrived, *The Army Game*, with William Hartnel, Alfie Bass and Bill Frazer, was coming to the end of a long run. William Hartnel was soon to become the first 'Dr Who'. Albert Finney who had already achieved international success in the film *Saturday Night and Sunday Morning* made a guest appearance in one of the last programmes. I had the impression that it was an unofficial appearance for old times' sake, because he did not have a speaking part, but simply appeared in uniform among a crowd of soldiers.

An offshoot of *The Army Game* was in the process of being made, in which the adventures of the characters created by Alfie

Bass and Bill Frazer, 'Bootsie' and 'Snudge', were continued in Civvy Street.

Quite soon after arriving at Chelsea I was shortlisted for a job as a trainee studio floor manager, and got the job. The method of training was simple: the trainee was assigned as an assistant to an experienced floor manager. It is a good method. The best way of learning any job is by doing it. I was assigned to the floor manager of *Bootsie and Snudge*, which was the beginning of a friendship with Alfie Bass.

Alfie and his family lived in North London at the time, as we did. One summer he asked June and I if we would like to live in his house whilst he and his family went on holiday. When Alfie was showing us around his house he pointed out a cupboard which contained the children's toys.

'I made that,' he said, not without a little pride.

'Did you really?' I said.

'Yeah, that was my trade, I was trained as a carpenter.'

At this precise moment our daughter, Anne, who had just started to walk, but who spent most of her time exploring the world on all fours, opened the cupboard door, which promptly fell off its hinges and crashed, embarrassingly, to the floor.

There was a slightly stunned silence and then Alfie said, 'Yeah, well, I'd been thinking that cupboard would probably be more useful without doors.'

Running an ancient Riley Monaco is fun but it requires a dedicated enthusiast with engineering skills, capable of fashioning replacement engine parts that are no longer manufactured. Happily we found just such an enthusiast and so she went 'to a good home'.

Being devils for punishment and rather slow to learn about things mechanical June and I acquired a rather ancient motorbike and sidecar, or a motorcycle 'combination' as it was called in those days. It was a 500 cc. Ariel, with a two-seater sidecar. To get to Alfie's house meant driving some distance up the Great North Way, along a stretch of dual carriageway. Whatever the time of day, the traffic on this road was usually quite heavy and fast moving.

One day I was driving along the outside lane on my motorcycle combination when the ancient engine appeared to seize up. It simply stopped for no apparent reason. As usual there was a lot of traffic in both lanes. It was an awful moment. The motorbike and sidecar was losing speed rapidly. I started waving my arm frantically up and down, to indicate to those behind me that I was stopping. Just as I seemed to have lost almost all forward motion, I kicked the gear pedal into neutral and then jumped off and started running, pushing the bike as hard as I could and waiting for the crunch of the car behind me as it hit the combination.

The car behind me managed to stop, but the car behind him did not, nor did the car behind that one, nor even the one further back. In fact there was a whole series of smashing sounds.

'Crash – tinkle tinkle!'

'Crash – tinkle tinkle!'

'Crash – tinkle tinkle!'

A truck in this lane skilfully swung over into the inside lane. Unfortunately, another truck in the inside lane had slowed down, perhaps to see what was going on in the fast lane, I don't know, but one truck ran into the back of the other and both lanes of the Great North Way came to a halt.

I was completely untouched. I pushed the combination over to the kerb, some yards ahead of the truck that now had another truck trying to reverse away from its shattered rear. People were getting out and starting to shout. Nobody seemed to have been hurt, but there were a lot of smashed front and rear lights and a lot of very angry drivers.

Then the driver of the nearest truck called to me. He seemed to be controlled, resigned perhaps, as a professional who had seen it all before.

'You'd better come and give us your insurance details, mate!'

To my surprise I heard myself saying, 'I'm sorry, I'm not involved. I haven't been touched. The car behind me stopped in time. Any car that ran into another must have been driving too close.'

There was a momentary silence and then the truck driver, perhaps realising I had given him his own line of defence, turned to the others and said, 'He's right. You're supposed to drive at a speed at which you can stop without hitting the car in front of you.'

There were a lot of aggressive responses to that, and there were one or two faces in the gathering group that looked as if they were within an ace of becoming exceedingly ugly.

The truck driver turned back to me. 'What happened, son? Why did you stop?'

I looked at the bike and said, 'I don't know. The engine seemed to seize up.'

I do not know whether it was out of embarrassment or what, but without any real hope of anything happening, I put my foot on the kick starter and kicked it down. Immediately, the engine roared into life. So without further ado, I swung my leg over the seat, flicked the gear pedal into gear and the bike began to pull away. I looked back, and with an apologetic shrug, called out, rather feebly, 'Sorry!'

I think I heard one or two shouts being hurled after me, but I could not be sure, because an ancient 500 cc. engine is terribly noisy. I suppose I should have stopped, but I had sensed amongst the crowd the beginnings of a rather nasty form of aggression, not perhaps surprising, you might think, but as the means of departure had suddenly and unexpectedly been presented to me, I must have acted on a deeply ingrained inner dictum, learned years ago in the back streets of a northern seaport, that 'discretion is the better part of valour'.

However, it took a long time for the feeling of guilt to go away. For months I waited, expecting to receive a letter from someone's lawyer. I was not absolutely certain that I had been blameless in the incident, and even if I was in the clear, I should have given someone my details in case there was a court case. There had been plenty of time for someone to have noted my vehicle registration number, but in the event nothing happened, and eventually I began to sleep more easily. One thing that eased my conscience a bit was that when I had the bike checked at a garage, they could find nothing wrong with the engine, nor give any reason for its sudden stopping. As TV engineers say, 'When the gremlins are out to get you – they get you.'

Victor Borge did not want the audience to 'cool down' during the commercial break so he continued to 'work' the audience in the interval. He appeared to improvise a series of jokes and routines with which he kept the audience laughing. I say 'appeared to improvise' because one of his great skills is to make highly rehearsed and honed work appear as if the jokes and ideas had only just occurred to him.

He had arranged for a microphone, dangling at the end of a telescopic boom, to nuzzle the back of his head, like a horse. He continued to talk to the audience, ignoring the nuzzling for a while, but eventually gave in to the persistent 'horse' by producing a handful of sugar cubes and feeding the imaginary animal.

In the studio, before the programme began, Victor called me over to his piano, and in that fascinating, Danish/American dialect said, 'When we come to de end of the commercial break whaddeyer do? What warnings do you give the studio?'

'I give one minute, thirty seconds, fifteen, ten, and then a silent, five-second finger countdown to your cue.'

'Whaddeyer *actually* say?'

'I usually say, "Stand by, studio. One minute!" and so on.'

'All right, when you get to fifteen seconds I want you to shout, very loudly, "Fifteen seconds to go!" then I can do a double-take at you and shout to the audience, "Okay. Anybody wanna go! – Lock de doors!" – an' stuff like dat. Okay?'

The commercial break only happened for the viewers at home; for the studio audience the Victor Borge show was continuous.

Perfectionists are sometimes difficult people to work with but they usually set the standard by which other artists are measured, whether it is Pablo Cassells still practising his cello for six to eight hours a day even in his eighties, or Fred Astaire doing thirty-seven film takes to get one dance sequence absolutely perfect.

A television studio floor manager needs to have perfectionist tendencies. He, or she, co-ordinates everything that happens on the studio floor. The floor manager is the fount of all knowledge in the studio, from rehearsals to completed programme he is Mr I'll Beg, Borrow or Steal It, Mr It's Done, It's Coming and Leave It To Me. In other words the original Mr Fixit.

My brother Tom was once asked by a school teacher from St Anselm's, 'What is Frank doing these days?' Tom told him, 'He's a TV floor manager in London.' 'Oh,' said the teacher, 'The Army & Navy Stores or Harrods?'

In every TV drama production the studio floor manager has attended rehearsals in a rehearsal studio, where he has marked out the shape of the set on the floor with coloured tape. He has checked every move that will be made by the actors, and every script change. He has made a note of all the props that will be required and ordered them from the prop department. He has also provided rehearsal props. He is aware of any costume changes needed during the recording, any special effects, explosions, smoke or whatever. He has discussed with the director any movement of scenery that will happen, either to change a scene or to enable cameras to reach a particular position. If make-up artists are required to make someone look dirty or tearful, or change a wig, he will know about it.

In the television studio he wears 'split cans' or, in other words, earphones with two sources. This invention has a wonderful potential for bringing about a severe form of schizophrenic breakdown. In one ear he can hear the director's voice and a variety of other voices from the control room: production assistant, vision mixer and cameramen talking to the director. In the other ear he can hear programme sound and various technicians. Because he must be able to hear people on the studio floor, he pushes one earphone slightly off his ear, making absolutely sure that the one person he can always hear is the director, though any one of a dozen voices from as many different departments could be trying to speak to him at almost any time and frequently it seems as if they have conspired to ask a dozen questions or give a dozen instructions simultaneously.

If the show he is working on is a variety show or a musical, apart from anything else the sheer amount of noise in his ears is horrendous. However on a programme of such complexity he will usually have an assistant, and perhaps a stage manager to whom he can delegate, though ultimately, as far as the studio floor is concerned, if anything goes wrong, the buck stops with him. Because of the responsibility, he requires instant and unquestioning obedience from the entire studio. In a live programme, it can happen that a performer skips a whole page, perhaps because of a similarly worded cue, but whatever the reason, the floor manager has to hold it all together.

For instance, in the case of a skipped page, if he says to the stage crew chargehand, 'Move the saloon door off the set now,' the one thing he does not want is an argument from the chargehand.

Supposing the chargehand says, 'No, mate, we do that on page seventeen,' by the time the floor manager has explained why he wants the saloon door moving immediately, it could be too late for that course of action to help things, so the chargehand will respond instantly, whether or not he thinks you are right or wrong.

Apart from the director, the studio floor manager is usually the only person who knows what everybody, in every department from actors to call-boy, should be doing at any point of the production; not only is the floor manager required to be omniscient but, occasionally, omnipresent. Part of my training included spending some time in Granada's Manchester studios, home of the longest-running soap opera in the history of British television, *Coronation Street*.

At that time the cast included Violet Carson who had created a 'larger than life' character called Ena Sharples, caretaker of the Coronation Street Mission Hall. Ena was a gorgon, a never to be crossed harridan who, with a tilt of her terrifying chins and a single, knife-like glance, could put the fear of God into anyone who had the temerity to cross her path. That was the television character. The actress, Violet Carson, offstage, was charming and gracious, though it has to be said that she could be a little intimidating even in the Green Room. Well, she was to me at any rate.

To me she was a legendary figure. I had grown up listening to her perform as a pianist and singer on BBC radio, or the 'wireless', as it was more commonly known in those days. In *Children's Hour*, I had, as it were, sat at her knee and sung such favourites as 'Me and my Teddy Bear' and 'The Teddy Bear's Picnic', both of which were particularly poignant songs, having secretly nursed an unrequited longing for a teddy bear. Amazingly, somehow, I had met a fictional character, I had come face to face with my radio Nanny, and I knew my place.

In rehearsals, I had been dutifully addressing her for some time as 'Miss Carson'. One morning, just as our rehearsal was about to begin, she called me to one side and inclining her majestic head, said, as one bestowing a great privilege, 'Young man, you may call me Violet.' I was almost speechless. I did call her Violet, but with great difficulty. After all, you don't call Nanny by her first name. Nannies don't have first names and somehow 'Violet' did not seem appropriate to such a giant of the small screen and my imagination.

Certain events, days, hours, minutes, because of their intensity, sear themselves into your memory. The day an overtime ban left me with one stagehand (instead of the usual six, eight or even ten stagehands) to cope with the recording of two episodes of *Coronation Street* is just such a day. I can't remember exactly what the dispute was about but it was something to do with the company opening a new studio in Manchester and the unions saying that a new studio required a new crew, not just the same crews working longer hours. To make their point they arranged a ban on overtime. One of the effects of this overtime ban was that *Coronation Street*'s two episodes were rehearsed with a full complement of studio operators but just before we were about to begin the recording five of our six stagehands walked out of the studio.

The director asked me if I thought it would be possible to record the two episodes with a stagecrew of one. I said I didn't know but was prepared to try. After all if we did not attempt it nothing would be achieved, if we attempted it and failed nothing more would be lost, and if we attempted it and succeeded then so much the better.

The initial scenes had already been prepared, the problems would only occur as we progressed deeper into the play, when pieces of scenery needed to be moved. As far as I could see there was only one place in Episode One that might prove difficult and that was where the 'Snug' door in the pub, 'The Rover's Return', had to be moved. It was on wheels, but rather heavy for one man to move. Union rules were strictly adhered to in the studio. In those days you could not change a light bulb without summoning a fully paid up member of the Electricians' Union.

I called the cast together on the set before the recording began and explained the situation to them. Speaking as an actor I can tell you that some actors can be rather precious in rehearsal and even during the recording of a programme.

'I'm sorry to stop, darling, but there should be a cigarette lighter on the end of the mantelpiece, and it simply isn't there! I am sorry, darling, but it quite threw me.'

On the other hand, when the chips are down, actors are also capable of producing highly imaginative flights of improvisation in order to save a situation that has gone wrong.

That morning the gist of what I said was something like this. 'If you walk on to a set and there is no chair for you to sit on, then act standing up. If there is a prop missing then improvise, keep going no matter what happens. As long as there is a camera with a red light on assume that we are still recording. Now, we might get through to the end or we might not, but if we all concentrate and think ahead and help each other, it's just possible.'

There were no grumbles; in fact the situation gave the performances an edge. There was a sense of adventure and fun in the studio which I suspect can be difficult to maintain in a series that has run and run for years.

The one and only stagehand really did make an enormous effort to cover both props and scenery effectively. As the recording progressed he became the unseen star of the show. When it came to heaving the 'Snug' door off the set one or two surreptitious hands and feet came to his aid and no doubt saved him from bursting a blood vessel.

I seemed to spend most of my time running silently from one end of the studio to the other, trying to anticipate the next possible disaster. All went well until about ninety seconds from the end of the first recording. I was standing by to give the final cue to an actor who was off the set to walk through a door at exactly the right moment for him to come face to face with an actor walking down the street. I was to do this by pressing a button at the end of a long cable which would cause a cue light to flash over the actor's entry door. Suddenly, I heard the director's voice in my ear. 'Frank! The Caption Roller hasn't been rewound!'

The Caption Roller is a motorised machine which rolls the credit captions across the final pictures. The credits are printed in white against a black background. When superimposed over a picture the black disappears and all you can see is the white credits moving up the screen. At the end of the rehearsal the Caption Roller should have been rewound back to the beginning and ready for the recording. It had not been done.

I looked around for the one and only stagehand. He was nowhere to be seen. The Caption Roller was at the other end of the studio. The actor on the set began to stroll down the street.

There was nothing for it, I put the cue-light cable down on the floor and I ran. I ran leaping over camera cables, dodging around the back of cameras, ducking under microphone boom platforms until I had reached the other end of the studio and the Caption Roller. I pressed the rewind button and out of the corner of my eye saw the one and only stagehand sitting on a chair in the wings, not wearing headphones and therefore completely oblivious of the problem. I pointed a peremptory finger at him and at the Caption Roller. He would understand once he saw what was happening. I turned and began my run back down the studio, under the microphone boom platforms, around the cameras, leaping like a ballet dancer over camera cables. I had almost made it when a toe caught in the last camera cable to be cleared and I went headlong sliding over the smooth and shining studio floor. In the headphones of my radio receiver I heard the calm voice of the director say, 'Cue him, Frank.'

To my amazement, there, in front of my nose on the floor, was the cue cable. Then I heard the director's voice again, only not quite so calm this time. 'Cue him! For God's sake!'

I pressed the cue button and the two actors came face to face. 'Cue music!'

The familiar signature tune began.

'Cue Captions!'

I looked up at a studio monitor screen. The captions were rolling.

The second episode required the same amount of concentration from everybody but nothing happened that demanded a dramatic full-length dive along the studio floor. When the captions for the second episode came to an end, the studio waited in silence for the technical clearance. It came and I made the usual announcement, 'Okay, everybody, we're clear!'

At this point the camera and sound crews and the cast burst into spontaneous applause. And there, standing by his Caption Roller, was the one and only stagehand, taking a well-deserved bow.

Filming on location, in a street, or a field or a country mansion, is a different discipline and there is a different technical crew. Frequently a separate filmcrew is hired especially for the exterior scenes. On these occasions, if the television floor manager goes on location he becomes the first assistant film director. There is not much difference in the work but some of the technical terms used whilst filming are different from the terms used in a TV studio. For instance, at the end of a filming session the first assistant film director, instead of shouting, 'Okay, everybody! We're clear!' shouts, 'Okay, everybody, it's a wrap!'

One of the drama series that I worked on as a first assistant director was *A Little Big Business* with David Kossoff and Francis Matthews. Later, when I was a radio producer, I worked with David on his famous 'Bible Stories', and several other series. We became good friends.

David is a perfectionist and the scripts he writes are meticulous. He does not waste words, his stories are extremely economical. To reduce biblical sagas to four or five minutes and yet retain the meaning and integrity of the story is no mean feat.

However, the BBC is an extremely hard task master when it comes to the timing of radio programmes. After all, the Greenwich Time Signal waits for no story-teller, no matter how good the story-teller may be. Sometimes David's stories were longer than the allocated time. We had lively discussions about how we might reduce the stories still further to fit the slot. David argued, quite rightly, that the stories had already been pared to the bone, but I still had the problem of satisfying the schedulers.

One day, after we had recorded a number of stories but still had a few that would not fit the time requirement, I asked David if I might take the scripts home and see if I could possibly edit out a few seconds here and a few seconds there. David was naturally reluctant. He knew his scripts intimately, and when you are convinced that any further cuts would damage the story, it is difficult to hand over your work to another 'Word Surgeon'. Nevertheless, he gave me permission to try.

Editing an actor's script, especially one he has written, is not simply a question of reducing the number of words. The words have to fit the style the actor has adopted for this particular script and you need therefore to be very familiar with his chosen method of emphasis, his timing of a phrase, you must be able to *hear* him performing the text. One advantage I had was my ability to mimic. I spent a considerable amount of time not simply paring away words, but performing them, trying to convince myself that David would say a particular phrase in a particular way.

At the next studio session I presented David with the newly typed and edited scripts. I watched anxiously as he read them. After a while I saw him nodding his head, and then he smiled to himself, a very subtle kind of smile. When he had finished, he looked up, or rather, looked *over* his glasses, and said, 'Good. You are a very, very clever young man. Let us begin.'

He told me later that he had never allowed anybody to edit his stories before. I understood why, perfectly.

If you work for a protracted period with somebody, you get to know each other rather well. Unconsciously perhaps, each observes the other and absorbs. We worked together on the 'Bible Stories' and then the broadcasts that preceded *The Little Book of Sylvanus* and *The Book of Witnesses*.

Having virtually exhausted the Old and New Testaments, I suggested to David that it might be a good idea for him to write a series of Rabbi stories which we could broadcast. He did. He created Rabbi Mark and a whole town filled with delicious characters. Eventually the stories were published by Collins in a book called, *A Small Town is a World*.

I had never consciously imitated David in his presence. Whether somebody had told him about my ability to mimic him or whether he had simply observed the odd phrase coming from my lips during one of our many recording sessions, I don't know. But when David had finished writing the scripts, he telephoned me at the BBC and that familiar, patriarchal voice said, 'I've finished the scripts. Would you like me to record them – or are *you* going to do them?'

I once had a secretary at the BBC who was, in some respects, like a female version of the character Michael Crawford created in *Some Mothers Do 'Ave 'Em*, Frank Spenser. She not only had his charm but also a fair degree of his 'accident proneness'. In addition, there were the facial movements, in particular that way of saying, 'Hmmm', which suggested that the world had somehow conspired against her. One particular conversation that has stayed with me was the occasion when she said, 'Do you know those programmes we recorded with David Kossoff?'

'Yes?'

'Hmmm, well, hmmm, well there's been a little accident.'

'What kind of "accident"?'

'Hmmm, well – Hmmm.'

There was a long silence, and I said, 'Just tell me, I won't bite, honest.'

'Well, hmmm. They've been wiped.'

'Wiped? Erased?'

'Hmmm, yes, like I said, there's been a little accident. Do you know those little stickers we put on the boxes when we've finished with a tape, and then they get wiped?'

'Yes.'

'Well, hmmm. Some of them got stuck on the David Kossoff boxes – accidentally.'

I telephoned David.

'David, first the bad news and then the good news. The stories we recorded last week – they've been wiped.'

There was a little chuckle from the other end of the phone.

'And the good news is, you'll have to pay me to do them again?'

'Yes.'

'Another thing.'

'Yes?'

'It's your turn to buy lunch.'

Not too long ago David and I co-presented a concert at Canterbury Cathedral in aid of NCH, the National Children's Home. Afterwards, at Slatters Hotel, we shared a meal with the ex-General Secretary of the TUC, Lord Murray, and his wife, Heather. We all got on like a house on fire, and talked and laughed until quite late. It was the beginning of new friendships.

Lionel and Heather are great supporters of NCH and because of this June and I meet them, regularly at NCH fund raising events, but – but I've leapt ahead, at least a quarter of a century. Let's go back to the sixties and Granada TV.

Rootling around in the attic of my mind, looking for sixties memorabilia, proves to be just as confusing as searching in the dust-laden attic of our house, but let me poke about and pick a few things off the shelves.

Ah! Over here I can see Maria Callas. The director wants her to come down a great sweeping staircase, specially built in the studio. Miss Callas is patient during the first two or three retakes, adopting the director's suggestions that she should pause on this step, look over the balustrade at this point in the aria, and so on. Unfortunately, he keeps changing his mind. He is giving his instructions from the comparative safety of the control room and is therefore slightly removed from the tension that those of us in the studio can sense building up inside our famous singer. Various people are trying to warn him but he seems to be oblivious to the atmosphere he is creating.

He really should have known better, apart from the fact that even great opera singers cannot keep giving perfect singing performances over and over without tiring. Eventually the safety valve blew and the pent-up steam that emerged from our prima donna's nostrils would have powered the *Royal Scot* halfway to Edinburgh. She swept down the magnificent staircase. At the foot of the stairs she kicked the train of her dress behind her and marched across the stage to where her pianist sat at the Bechstein Grand. Taking up a position in the bow of the piano she looked about her, no doubt making sure that she had everyone's full attention; then, with a magnificent gesture, she pointed an operatic finger at a spot on the stage.

The entire studio was silent. We knew, without question, that whatever she was about to say, it was her very *last* word on the subject. She turned a smouldering eye toward the control room. Her voice was not loud, or filled with passion but heavy, with a dreadful, icy finality. This was an offer that could not be refused. Aspirates rasping, she declared, 'I sing from here. Send your cameras – *h*up the stairs!'

And that was how it was done.

Another singing lady of an entirely different temperament to La Callas was Ella Fitzgerald, who took part in a run of musical shows starring big American names. Very relaxed, totally at home in studios and behind a microphone, she was in some ways a very homely, ordinary person and yet everyone was aware that we were working with a jazz legend.

Some of these musical evenings are a bit of a blur. For instance, I have a very clear memory of helping the film actor, the ever suave and villainous George Sanders, climb out of a mock-up of a Turkish Bath, but I have no idea what the rest of the show was about.

Around the same period I recall being kissed by Zsa Zsa Gabor. 'Darlink – you remind me so much of my father. He had a beard just like yours, same colour, same eyes, same – everytink!'

An Evening with Johnny Mathis I recall as archetypal American star and entourage. Every time he stood up so did a small army of people, too many for me to even begin to guess what each person's function was in the Johnny Mathis organisation.

'Bigness' seemed to be important to quite a number of musical stars. I remember a huge scaffolding construction being built in a studio in order to house the screaming fans of Little Richard. I can see a youthful Bill Podmore perched behind a camera on a crane that could swoop down on an artist from a great height. One particularly spectacular effect with this camera was achieved when a very long and extended batten of wood, rigged down its entire length with electric lights, was suspended at an angle from a grand piano, painted white for this one shot. The pianist played a very extravagant descent from the top keys of the piano to the bottom bass notes, and as he did so Bill Podmore zoomed down the long batten of lights to arrive at the bass notes of the piano at the same time as the pianist.

Bill was extremely good at keeping a moving, zoom-lensed television camera in focus; this might have been something to do with the fact that he was an ex-RAF pilot. It was an extremely spectacular shot, it took a lot of time, effort and money to achieve, but in the end I suppose it was just a circus trick, a little ephemera long lost in television history now.

When people are the 'current' star performers of the day, one rarely has any awareness of their place in performing or musical history. Sometimes when the performer, band or orchestra has survived for a good number of years, or when a particular piece of music has been performed and recorded by a great number of artists, you are then aware that you are meeting someone who has become or will become legendary but, usually, it's just another working day. One musician, however, who was a living legend, was Duke Ellington.

One of the legends about Duke Ellington's orchestra was that a good number of his outstanding instrumentalists were unable to read music. This proved to be a fact. During rehearsals there were two instances when this was revealed. One was when a clarinetist was standing alone at a music stand, playing his clarinet solo and apparently following the music on the stand, when Duke Ellington looked over the musician's shoulder, smiled and without disturbing the solo performance for one second, turned the music the right way up!

The other instance was when a line of standing musicians was set up in front of, and separate from, the orchestra. Each musician had either a solo or a duet or some other combination to play and when that had been achieved the musician concerned returned to sit with the rest of the orchestra. At one point in the rehearsal the director came out to discuss shots with some of the musicians. I remember that the director, a young man, had his arm in a sling which made it very difficult for him to handle the enormous musical score he was carrying. He was trying to ascertain at exactly which point in the music each player moved to the solo stands and at which point they would return to their seats. He turned to the solo trumpeter and said, 'Do you think you could point to the place in the score where you return to the stand?'

The trumpeter looked at the score, frowned, shook his head and said, in a voice not unlike that of Louis Armstrong, 'I dunno about the "score", man, but when the band go "De-dada de- dada de- dada de- dada de- da da da" – that's when I go back to the stand.'

Being a television floor manager-cum-assistant film director meant adapting to a great variety of programmes, musical 'extravaganzas' with American film stars, quiz games with Barbara Kelly and Bob Holness, soap operas like *Bootsie and Snudge* and *Coronation Street,* experimental drama, such as N. F. Simpson's *A Resounding Tinkle,* documentaries with Bamber Gascoigne and intense debates with Malcolm Muggeridge who entertained us with his agonised teasing of the truth in his 'in depth' conversations with various religious leaders in the series, *I Believe.*

In one sense the days were too full. So many experiences poured over my head, day after day and week after week, that even now I am not able to fully appreciate them. Once again, incidents, scenes, loom out of the fog and briefly appear before my mind's eye with crystal clarity. For a few moments I can see people and places, hear voices and feel the ambience of a studio or a control room as if the incident were being re-lived. I have to look very closely because I know that within a very short time the scene will be swallowed up in the fog from which it emerged.

'Hello, Muggeridge! Good heavens! What's the matter, man? You look absolutely dissipated.'

The speaker is wearing frock coat and gaiters. It is Geoffrey Fisher, the Archbishop of Canterbury, swinging into the attack the moment he arrives in the Green Room of the old Chelsea Palace. In some ways he is a caricature of a bishop, permanently surprised eyebrows and lips not quite pursed, like somebody who was about to whistle but who has thought better of it.

Muggeridge in fact looks no more or less dissipated than he

always looks. For Muggeridge, constructing a spoken sentence is a pain-ridden exercise which tortures every muscle in his face.

'My dear Archbishop (always polite, Muggeridge), how wonderful to see you so ebullient. Dissipation of mind and body is, I fear, part of the human condition, experienced even by Archbishops of Canterbury, no less than editors of *Punch*. Unless the word you were looking for was "dissolute", in which case I probably have the edge on you. Would you like a cup of tea?'

In the studio it occurs to me that as the conversation to be recorded would take three-quarters of an hour (which would later be edited to thirty minutes), an elderly gentleman like the Archbishop might appreciate a visit to the loo. I put it to him discreetly.

'The lavatory?' said the Archbishop. 'What a good idea.'

As this involves a walk and a descent of stairs, and because the Archbishop has a noticeable limp, I offer him my arm. He asks me about my religious convictions. I tell him that my background is Roman Catholic. 'Ah ha!' he says, as if this disclosure has some significant bearing on the conversation he is about to have with Muggeridge. Then, somehow, we are talking about hierarchy and Christianity, and I find myself asking a question, which, even as the words form in my mind I am regretting it, but somehow I cannot stop myself and I can hear the words coming out of my mouth, I am asking if palaces, investments in breweries, jewelled vestments, gold and silver plate and extravagant forms of address, such as those used to address the higher echelons of the clergy, could really be found to be compatible with the teaching and example of Jesus Christ.

'Did Muggeridge ask you to put that question?'

'No, sir, it's my own question.'

'What line do you think Muggeridge is going to take?'

'I think he will talk about the things you discussed with him in the Green Room.'

The Archbishop was on the defensive. Muggeridge's brief was not to attack the people he talked to, but simply to find out what they believed. The discussion was meant to inform, not to confront, and yet here was I confronting him, but only because, somehow, he seemed to be inviting debate.

After the recording the Archbishop is once more on my arm, we are returning from making yet another descent to the loo, and now we are making our way to the stage door where the Archbishop's car is waiting for him.

'So, you would favour some other form of Church government, would you? Do away with the Bench of Bishops and the College of Cardinals, hmm?'

'I don't think we need do away with bishops, but perhaps it might be more appropriate if the higher the office held in the Church, the lower the stipend and more humble the dwelling. After all, when you are young and earthy, and perhaps with a growing family, that is when you need more pay and a bigger house, but as your spirituality increases the less need will you have for material things, like money and property.'

We have now reached the episcopal limousine and the chauffeur is holding open the car door.

'What an amusing idea,' says the Archbishop, settling himself into the leather upholstery. 'Well, it's been a very entertaining day. Thank you.' The chauffeur closes the door and walks around to the driving seat. As the car begins to move away, the Archbishop's window winds down. There is just the glimmer of a twinkle beneath the quizzical eyebrows.

'Goodbye, my boy, and Godspeed to an episcopal seat!'

We used to hire an interview studio at the Independent News headquarters in Kingsway in London, to interview politicians or people in the news and then send the tape through a GPO line to Granada's Manchester studios for inclusion in the regional news magazine *Scene at 6.30*. *Scene at 6.30* was a very lively programme presented in those days by Gabriel Byrne, a young Irishman who now presents Telefis Eire's very popular programme, *The Late Show*.

One of the regulars on *Scene at 6.30* was an Irish singer called Val Doonican. He was a relaxed, easy-going man with no airs or graces. I was to meet him years later after he had enjoyed a very long run of recording and television successes and had become, as they say, a 'household name'. To my delight he had not changed one iota. He was the same easy-going, self-effacing chap who was simply amazed at his continuing good fortune.

A group of singers, four lads from Liverpool who were to become hugely famous as The Beatles, also appeared on *Scene at 6.30*. The next time I was to meet them was in the ITN studios in Kingsway where all four of them signed my copy of John Lennon's book, *In My Own Write*. Sadly, that book disappeared from my study library on one of the many occasions that we moved house.

I enjoyed the ITN sessions simply because you never knew who might turn up. Mainly it was politicians and trades union leaders, but sometimes it would be slightly more exotic people like American epic novel authors, such as Leon Uris, or Gore Vidal, or the actors who were playing the characters in the epic film production of the epic author's novel.

I remember sharing sandwiches with George Woodcock, the bushy eyebrowed General Secretary of the TUC; and also the last visit to England of Ian Smith, the Rhodesian Prime Minister, a matter of days before he led his country in their Unilateral Declaration of Independence. The studio we hired was very basic, a control room and a studio with two chairs, two microphones and two television cameras.

I can't remember how it came about but the Rhodesian Prime Minister, Ian Smith, was alone in the little studio with a stagehand, a big chap with rolled-up shirt sleeves and a huge leather belt around his ample belly – the stagehand, I mean. The journalist who was to interview Ian Smith was having a last-minute conference with the director. For some reason I was also in the control room. One of the sound engineers, testing his equipment perhaps, faded up the microphones and suddenly we found ourselves listening to a strange conversation.

'Oh, look at this. It's just come off in my hand.'

Ian Smith was holding in his hand the wooden arm of the chair in which he was sitting.

'Do you think I could have another chair?'

'Nah, give it 'ere, mate, I'll fix it back on.'

'Well, I really would feel more comfortable with a chair that isn't broken.'

The stagehand gave his trousers a reassuring hitch and sniffed. 'Sorry, mate, no can do. 'Ere, let's 'ave a go at that arm.'

Ian Smith stood up and surrendered the chair arm. He looked a little puzzled. 'I don't think you understand. I'm not the interviewer, I'm the Prime Minister of Rhodesia.'

The stagehand had re-positioned the chair arm and steadied it with one hand whilst preparing to give it a mighty thump with the other. He looked up at the Prime Minister. 'I don't care if you're the bleedin' Aga Khan, mate. These are the only chairs we've got, ain't they?'

Which reminds me of an apocryphal story of the 'Dark Days of the Second World War', in which King Haakon of Norway was said to have arrived at the BBC in order to make a broadcast to his own country through the BBC World Service. His arrival was discreet and unheralded. Accompanied only by an aide, he presented himself at the reception desk. The commissionaire, an aged and bluff Cockney, looked up. 'Good evening, sir. Can I help you?'

'Good evening,' said the King. 'I have come to record a programme for the World Service.'

'Very good, sir.' The commissionaire picked up a telephone, 'What name is it, sir?'

'Haakon.'

The commissionaire's face showed no sign of recognition, so the King helped him further. 'Haakon,' he repeated, 'the King of Norway.'

The commissionaire's eyebrows shot up and he immediately jumped to his feet. He seemed a little confused. 'Er, yes, sir, I'll tell them you're here, sir.' He turned back to his telephone, dialled a number and said, 'Hello. There's a gentleman here from, er, – er, or dear, I'm sorry, look, er, hang on a minute.' He put his hand over the mouthpiece and turned to look at the Scandinavian Monarch.

'Er – excuse me, sir, but – er – what country was it you said you was king of?'

6   Leap of Faith: Daddy Goes
to College

We both have scows; they are wonderful little dinghies. We sailed together down Hawkers Channel this morning, each in our own boat, and out through an inlet that we call 'Spoonbill Creek', named after the first boat we bought for June to start her sailing school, 'Topping Sailing'. It was a GP14 dinghy which we had christened *Spoonbill*.

The creek is not an easy place to sail, the tide has to be right, you have to tack a great deal because there are no long reaches of water, and you need, therefore, to know where the shallow water is. For those very reasons, not many people use it. It's too easy to run aground and get stuck. It's a bit like having your own 'secret waters' as you are highly unlikely to meet anyone else using it. June knows this river as well as or better than most. Her sailing school has given her more hours on the river than most dinghy sailors and enabled her to explore all the creeks and backwaters.

We sailed out into the Solent and then along the coast and into the Lymington river, following another backwater that avoids the main channel entrance where all the big Isle of Wight ferries steam in. We threaded our way through the lines of yacht moorings and eventually tied up by the Old Quay. We did a little shopping in Lymington High Street and indulged in an ice-cream before casting off for the return passage.

Today there are not many people about. There is a moderate little breeze, the sun is shining and the shingle is glistening at the water's edge. Lying here with my head resting on a carefully arranged beach towel, I have been recalling the events that led to my leaving Granada Television in 1964 and becoming a theological student. Sometimes it is difficult to put your finger on the exact moment when a decision is made, sometimes decisions are made over a period of time and you pass the actual moment without realising that you have passed it. Suddenly, you find yourself doing something and wondering how you came to be doing what you are doing.

I am not superstitious, at least, I think I am not. I believe that most 'good luck' is the result of persistence and hard work; generally people make their own 'luck'. Nevertheless, there are occasions when we enjoy, or suffer, fortune that we neither deserve nor earn. The important thing is that when these moments occur we take advantage of them. As Brutus says:

> There is a tide in the affairs of men,
> Which, taken at the flood, leads on to fortune;
> Omitted, all the voyage of their life
> Is bound in shallows and in miseries.

Some years ago I wrote a book called *An Impossible God*. It is a study of some of the characters who shared in, or observed, some part of the Passion of Jesus Christ. One of the characters that fascinated me was Simon of Cyrene. It is his fate to turn up on a particular street corner, at the precise moment that Christ reaches that corner and falls beneath the weight of the cross. The streets are jammed with people but it is Simon who catches the Centurion's eye and Simon who suddenly finds himself playing a central role in the terrible drama of Christ's Passion. Looking back on the event Simon asks himself if he was

> Chosen, or merely ill-fated? And what's the difference?
> Is there a line between the vagaries of chance and providence?
> A division between accident and an act of God?
> Who expects his entire life to change by accident?
> No one expects, but they happen,
> These 'accidents' of time and place.
> With cruel precision, random elements of circumstance
>   converge . . .

Random elements, did I say?
Strange isn't it, how the unpredicted and the unrelated
Blend, effortlessly.

In Joseph Conrad's novel, *Chance*, one of the characters, Marlow, is talking about 'accident' and says, '. . . By accident I mean that which happens blindly and without intelligent design. That's generally the way a brother-in-law happens into a man's life.' It's generally the way most people happen into our lives. Jobs, brothers-in-law and marriages are all, to some extent, dependent upon accidents of time and place. Of the many such accidents in my own life none has favoured me more than the random elements that led to our marriage.

I would not have been surprised, nor would my wife, if an expert marriage guidance counsellor, looking at our backgrounds and circumstances, had advised against marriage. A Liverpool Irish, Christian Brother educated, guilt-ridden, Latin Mass, Altar boy Catholic, and a staunch, dyed-in-the-wool, English, hymn singing Methodist, would not, at first glance, appear to be ideal or natural partners. June grew up in Bath, I grew up on Merseyside, you would expect different perspectives in both religion and culture, and indeed there were; to some extent we even spoke a different language.

When June and I met, within a matter of days we were engaged to be married. Foolhardy, I know, but, did we send out and recognise in each other, signals? Were there subliminal clues to each other's character, recognised at a level deeper than either of us were conscious? Perhaps that's what 'intuition' is. I have read somewhere that the intuitive leap is the brain making a series of very logical and accurate assessments and deductions so rapidly that the intuitive person is not capable of keeping track of his own cerebral computing. I like to think that this is what happened when June and I met. Perhaps without knowing it all the questions were put and answered, the inner computer whirring away and storing up information.

When June and I first met my allegiance to Catholicism was, to say the least, threadbare. National Service in Cyprus had raised crucial questions for me. My experiences there had concentrated my mind wonderfully, if only for a short time. Seeing a friend die does that.

Arriving back from Cyprus my first meal in England was in an RAF mess, alongside someone whose entire military service had been spent in England. The meal was sausages and mash, and the sausages were very slightly burned. The man next to me was complaining.

'Honestly! Look at these sausages, they're burnt! It's disgusting! They're absolutely inedible!'

I had not seen a sausage, burnt or otherwise, for quite some time. I leaned across and said, 'If you can't eat them, I think I can help you out.' And then I speared his sausages with my fork.

That same evening there was another chap trying on what looked to me to be a brand new Harris tweed jacket. He was unhappy about something. He kept looking at himself in a full length mirror.

'Do you see what I mean? It's definitely longer on the left, isn't it? I mean, look at that sleeve!'

In Cyprus people were dying violently, and I was still spiritually very close to the island. I remember asking myself, 'Is this what it's all about? Is this what you cling to life for? Is this why you stay alive – to come back and worry about trivia, about sausages and the cut of your jacket? Because if that's what it's about, it isn't worth the sweat or the fear or the pain. It isn't worth the effort. There has to be more than this.'

This reflective state of mind did not last long. That is to say, I did not spend weeks or months cudgelling my brain for an answer to the meaning of existence, but it seriously affected my approach to life in general. I felt slightly out of step with my contemporaries. With demob looming ahead, I could not get worked up about what I was going to do for a living. Something had happened to my sense of responsibility. I had a detached feeling of freedom. I thought, 'The world is my oyster, I can do anything, go anywhere, all I have to do is live, to eat, drink and swallow life whole.'

At first I put it down to Cyprus, but on reflection I can see that Cyprus was just the catalyst that brought together all my questions, doubts and fears, all the late-night pillow thumping and adolescent agonising, and exploded them all by dropping a real death among them, not a contemplation of death, but an actual dying.

When I emerged from that experience, something had happened to me, but I did not immediately understand what it was. A huge weight had slipped from my shoulders, which left me shaky on my feet. With the weight gone I was light-headed, giddy, not quite sure how to walk without the burden that had clung to my back for years.

Looking back now, from a distance, I can see that the burden I left behind, wedged in some cleft of rock in Cyprus, or at the bottom of one of those lagoons where hundreds of sea urchins and crustacea fasten on to whatever lies on the sea bed, was an amorphous lump of all the superstitious, medieval, Christian-Brother indoctrinated guilt of centuries. The claws of limbo, purgatory and hell, of venial, mortal and original sin had somehow lost their fish-hook grip and sloughed off.

When I first met June, Cyprus was a recent event and I was in my carefree, unburdened and weightless state, when even the air had a fresh taste to it and a clarity that enabled me to see the honest-to-goodness, open-hearted nature of a girl with a wonderful smile. Neither of us hesitated. Thirty something years later, battle-scarred but still unbowed, the truth of that vision is still evident to me. On the other hand, you might choose to say that we are a couple of 'lucky blighters'.

The 'sloughing off' of my medieval guilt-burden brought tremendous relief. It is very difficult to describe. I suppose it must be akin to being released from prison, or someone paying off all your debts for you. I really did feel a new person, free, wonderfully free. Of course you can never wipe out the past, nor would one want to. It meant, in effect, that I stopped going to church for a long time. It's very difficult to embrace any other denomination if you have been a Catholic. After all, to a cradle Catholic, what are the other denominations anyway, but mere splinters, off splinters, off the great Mother Church. They all have their peculiar emphases about not baptising babies or having two sacraments instead of seven, or in some cases no sacraments at all, about liturgy and vestments, religious statues or no statues, but nothing that I could get worked up about.

For me, the separation from Catholicism occurred when the experience of a sudden and violent death dropped like a bomb amongst my self-indulgent and adolescent navel-gazings. Questions and issues such as transubstantiation, indulgences, the Assumption of the Blessed Virgin Mary and how many angels could stand on a pinhead, struck me as being incredibly irrelevant. I could not believe that Jesus Christ gave up his life in order to settle issues such as these. All this was thundering about in my brain during my last few days in the RAF. The thunder subsided when I threw myself into the world of theatre and television.

So, I had stopped going to Mass and found that the ground had not opened up and swallowed me, and then what little praying I may have done ceased altogether. I settled without difficulty into the life of a happy agnostic. I say 'happy' because my mother used to draw a picture of the agonies suffered by those who had 'lost their faith'. This was not so for me. I was not suffering. I was not 'agonising' about my lost faith. I was, quite simply, going about my life and enjoying it.

The clouds are beginning to gather and the sun has disappeared. It's getting a little cold here on the beach. June thinks we should get back before the weather begins to deteriorate seriously. It does look a bit nasty and the wind is increasing. Hey ho! Up with the sails and off we go!

Phew! That was an eventful sail: a sudden thunderstorm with fitful bursts of wind, claps of thunder and streaks of lightning, and then a cloudburst which gave the sails a nice wash. We are back home. We've showered and towelled briskly. The sun is out again and everywhere feels fresh. A piece of toast is filling the room with its fragrance and a pot of tea is just about ready to pour.

The thing is, I had thrown the baby out with the bath water. I had rejected various Roman Catholic doctrines, and Catholic interpretations of some pretty esoteric and peripheral theological questions. With them I had also thrown out the really important and fundamental questions, such as, 'Do I really believe in God?' and 'Who was or is Jesus Christ?' Life in Granada Television was fascinating and absorbing, indeed fascinating enough to keep me from facing up to the questions that had grabbed me by the throat in Cyprus, and so I had not made any progress in discovering whether or not there was any meaning or purpose in anything. In fact there were quite a number of questions that I had pushed to the back of my mind. Intellectual cowardice, I suppose. 'If at first you can't work it out, forget it.' But do you really forget it?

Have you heard of 'Sleep Problem Solving'? The theory is that if you have an unresolved question in your mind and you sleep on it, your brain sorts things out while you rest. I remember one night, before going to sleep, I prayed an agnostic prayer. I said, 'If there is a God, then show me, somehow.' The reply was not immediate but in time I have come to believe that Pascal was right when he said, 'To seek God, is to find him.' I suspect that once ultimate questions make their mark in your brain there is a limit to how long you can either suppress or ignore them. Eventually they thrust themselves into the foreground. Perhaps my unconscious mind had been wrestling with the issues all the time. Certainly the speed and clarity with which my brain eventually announced its findings were odd, to say the least. Whatever the psychological theories, this is what happened.

The carefree and penniless young man that had swept a young lady off her feet and married her within a very short space of time gradually became less carefree. By now he was earning a good living and beginning to carve out a television career for himself, and his character was changing with his ascent of the career ladder. In addition to Anne, Simon had also arrived. Simon was born at the Bearsted Jewish Memorial Home in Stoke Newington, May 4th, 1961. (Mark was born at the Salvation Army Mother's Hospital in Hackney on July 21st, 1963).

One night June and I were having an argument. I can't remember what we were arguing about, but it was something to do with the fact that my character was changing and not necessarily for the better. At what proved to be the high point of the row I said, in a somewhat sarcastic manner, 'So what do you want me to do? Become a parson?'

We both looked at each other and started laughing. I heard myself saying, 'That's it, isn't it? That's what I've got to do.' I have no idea how we both made the same intuitive leap at one and the same time, but we did. We both knew, there and then, that somehow this was the direction I had to take. I know it sounds crazy, but somehow my brain had worked out the equation that I had been struggling with for several years. At the beginning of our argument I was an agnostic, then in the middle of a sarcastic jibe, I knew there was a God, a God whose nature was love and that Jesus Christ was the revelation of that nature. It's backwards, I know, but I have spent the intervening years between that day and this, working out how I reached that conclusion. I am not trying to persuade anybody about my beliefs; these are just statements of fact about my personal experience. People ask me, 'How did it happen?' Well, that's how it happened.

We talked it over and decided that perhaps a good person to discuss it with would be the Reverend Derrick Greeves, the minister who had married us, and had helped me when I had been looking for work. He was the minister at Westminster Central Hall, opposite the Houses of Parliament and Westminster Abbey, and his manse was in Chelsea, off the King's Road, a few minutes' walk from where I was working at the Granada Studios in the old Chelsea Palace.

The following morning I was being welcomed into his house.

'Frank! How marvellous! How are June and the children?'

'Er, fine, very well, thank you.'

'Good. And how's the job at Granada?'

'Great, it's going very well.'

'It really is good to see you. Let me give Nancy a shout and we'll have a coffee. Nancy! It's Frank! Frank Topping!'

I had a bit of a problem with the ensuing conversation, because what I really wanted to ask him was, 'How do I become a minister?' But as I did not even go to church and therefore was not a member of any denomination, it seemed rather a precocious question to put to him. So instead I asked him,

'How do I become a member of your Church?' So that is what he told me.

I was on a terrific 'high' all day. I was very excited, but not being able to tell anyone about it was incredibly frustrating. It was like not telling anybody about your first-born child. I was just bursting to tell someone. In the evening June said, 'Why don't you ring Derrick and just get it off your chest?' I rang him and said, 'Look, this morning when I came to see you I asked about how I became a member of your Church. What I really wanted to ask you was, "How do I become a minister?"'

There was hardly a pause before he said, 'Yes, I know.'

'What do you mean, you *know*?' I asked.

'Well,' he said, 'the moment you walked into my study this morning, the first thing that came into my head was, "Ah, another candidate for the ministry." Simple as that really.'

I don't think I really had any idea of what I was letting myself in for, but it moved us on to a new stage in our relationship with the Greeves family. When someone becomes a candidate for the Methodist ministry they are 'sponsored' by a minister. Clearly that minister must believe in the candidate's call and suitability for the life. The sponsoring minister becomes the friend and advocate of the candidate and can appeal against any decision or criticism that is made against the candidate at any stage in the long process that leads ultimately to rejection or acceptance for ordination. Indeed I have witnessed a passionate appeal by a sponsoring minister that reversed the decision of a district synod. (A Methodist district synod is about the size of five or six Anglican dioceses put together.)

Derrick and I had to get to know each other. In spite of his inner conviction about my call, he had to know for certain. He had to know the details of my life, the experiences, the thinking and the potential, so that he could be my 'Father in God' and my friend at court.

We began to meet once a week before breakfast to study the Bible and discuss theology. He was a considerable scholar, who wrote an excellent study of St Paul, called, *Christ in Me*. He found it very difficult to discuss texts without going back to the

Greek, so it was not long before he began to introduce me to the Koine, the Greek used in the Holy Land at the time of Our Lord. I very much enjoyed these early-morning sessions, which were really rather convenient as his manse was just around the corner from Granada's Chelsea studios.

I said that I did not know what I was letting myself in for, which was true. I had no idea, for instance, that I could have become an Anglican priest in a much shorter period of time. Methodism is a preaching order and they are extremely methodical in making sure that their preachers are, how shall I put it, 'well versed'. There are much shorter routes to ordination nowadays, particularly for older candidates.

When someone declares that they believe that they have a calling to the Methodist ministry, it can take up to seven or eight years before that person is actually ordained. You cannot become a ministerial candidate until you have become a 'Fully Accredited Local Preacher'. That procedure takes at least a year, sometimes two, during which examinations are taken in Old and New Testament Studies, Theology, Worship and Preaching.

The ministerial candidate then moves on to the year of candidature in which further examinations are taken, and 'Trial Sermons' are preached. There is also a progression of interviews at meetings representing the Church at local, regional and national levels, and a very comprehensive 'Book List' has to be presented, that is a list of the complete range of books read by the candidate in the past and those books that his sponsoring minister advises him to read and add to the list.

Book lists are required at so many stages they become obsessive. After one has spent a year as an accepted candidate, three years at college and three years as a probationer before ordination, the ordinand, by this stage, has become totally addicted to checking his current book list and life without a book 'on the go' would be unthinkable.

On November 1st, 1961, All Saints Day, in the small chapel in Westminster Central Hall, I was received into membership of the Methodist Church. In December 1963 I became a 'fully accredited local preacher'. The next year took on a rather hectic pattern of studying for my Minister's Candidate's examinations whilst carrying on my television career. I remember one exceedingly tight piece of time-tabling which involved passing an oral exam at night in Manchester whilst working on *Coronation Street* during the day, and then flying down to London in Lord Bernstein's Executive aeroplane, an eight-seater De Havilland Dove, to sit written examinations at Westminster Central Hall the following day.

In June 1964 I knew that I had been accepted as a Methodist ordinand. The July Committee, which is a little Methodist joke because it never meets in July, and 1964 being no exception it met in June, is virtually the final examination of candidates for the ministry. It's a bit like a military 'Officer Selection' procedure. It takes place in one of the colleges; at that time there were five Methodist theological colleges dotted about the country in various university towns. That year the committee met in Bristol.

The candidate stays at the college for a few days, has medical (and more recently psychological) examinations; meets members of the teaching staff from the various colleges and finally goes before the 'July Committee'. The committee is large enough to be divided into two committees, Committee 'A' and Committee 'B', which meet at the same time in different rooms. The 'half' that I sat before must have consisted of a dozen or more people, (it felt like twenty, perhaps it was?) mainly in clerical collars, with the exception of a few statutory laymen.

What happens is that the candidate's examination results are discussed, the reports on his preaching, his health, his wealth, his wife, his family, his general knowledge, his involvement in society, his understanding of current affairs, his call and of course his 'Book List'. This can take some time. What he says in this committee, what his records and reports say, in fact everything that has led to this moment will be assessed and reduced to a 'score'.

After your session with Committee 'A' or 'B' you are thanked and told to return to the hall and wait with the other candidates. Eventually, the committee sends out a messenger. You are not given the committee's decision, or told your 'score'. You are told that you may go, which means they are unanimous about you, for or against; or they say that they would like you to meet the full committee, that is committees 'A' and 'B' when they sit together, which means that you did not have a unanimous vote.

Now I have to confess that my feelings at this stage were somewhat ambiguous. I really was enjoying myself in television. I enjoyed the variety of programmes from drama to documentary and to add a little spice I was even moonlighting and doing 'voices' for commercials. Deep down I had a secret desire to be honourably rejected. Then at least my conscience would be clear. I could say, 'I put my call to the test, and was turned down. Right. What more could I have done? Nothing. Therefore, I can now get on with my career.'

I was called before the committee rather late in the day, I think it was about seven o'clock in the evening. I was tired and I really did think it went rather badly for me. For some reason whenever I answered a question everybody laughed, and as my own self-esteem at that moment was not exactly brimming with confidence, I thought they were laughing at me rather than with me. It began when one committee member trying to relate to my life in the arts, asked, 'What do you think is the message of Harold Pinter's plays?'

Ignoring the fact that all of Pinter's plays could not possibly have the same meaning, I thought I could see what the questioner was getting at. As it happened, I had worked on a play by Pinter called *The Dumb Waiter* that he had specially written for Granada Television and I heard myself saying to the July Committee, 'It's funny you should ask that, because not long ago I asked Harold Pinter a similar question.'

I was not prepared for the roar of laughter that followed my answer. I suppose it sounded like name dropping, but if every day of your life you are working with politicians, playwrights or film stars, it is not name dropping to you, they are simply the people you work with.

When the laughter faded the questioner pursued his question, 'And what did Mr Pinter say?' he asked, flicking an amused eye towards his colleagues. (I wonder why people think you can't see their little eye signals?)

My mind floated back to the studio. I could see the Australian actor, Harold H. Corbett in his Pinter character arguing in typical Pinter style about whether or not it was permissible to say, 'The kettle is boiling' when in fact it is the water that boils and not the kettle. I remembered the naivety of my question and very clearly Harold Pinter's reply. So I told them what he had said.

'He said, "If you can find a message, mate, let me know."'

There was another roar of laughter. I began to feel a slight surge of panic. Here was I playing this scene as seriously as I could, whilst all these people thought they were at a farce. But somehow, I could not stop answering according to their growing expectations.

Kenneth Grayston, a biblical scholar later to take the Chair of Theology at Bristol University said, 'I see from your book list that you do not appear to have read many commentaries on the Bible. Would you like to comment on that?'

'Well, I have to admit that I haven't read the Bible either.'

Another uproarious outburst. Then I heard myself saying, 'I thought perhaps I ought to read the book, before I read the reviews.'

The mirth continued. One of the committee was quaking with a handkerchief to his face. I killed that laugh by jumping in before it was finished to rapidly explain that a few years ago I had not been a Methodist. Nor had I been brought up in a tradition of Bible study. And apart from those bits of the Bible that are quoted in the Catholic Catechism, the Bible was a relatively new book to me. I do not remember many more details of that interview except that it seemed clear to me that I was no doubt being deservedly assessed as a bit of a buffoon.

By the time I left the committee room I was convinced that the interview must have gone down as one of the worst on record. I sank into a chair and began to console myself that at least I had tried and now I could get on with the rest of my life. As if to confirm my suspicions a message was sent out almost immediately. Obviously they had not needed to waste much time arriving at their decision.

'Mr Topping,' the messenger said, 'the committee feel that you can go home now. Thank you and goodbye.'

So that was it, unanimously against. All over. Still, it had been a good experience.

June was with the children down in Hampshire, at her parents' home near the Solent. It would be very late by the time I got down there. They would probably all have gone to bed. I think it was after midnight when I arrived. I let myself into the kitchen and on the table there was a note from June. It said:

FRANK DARLING, DO WAKE ME. DERRICK RANG. HIS SPY ON THE COMMITTEE SAID YOU WERE WONDERFUL AND THAT YOU HAD BEEN GIVEN AN A1. DERRICK SAID YOU WOULD KNOW WHAT THAT MEANT. J XXX

I did know what it meant although I could hardly believe it. It is amazing how people sharing in the same event can have totally different perceptions of what was actually happening. In my more jaded moments I put the whole thing down to it being so late in the day when I met the committee. They no doubt had seen a succession of very worthy and serious candidates and suddenly this clown arrived. The vote was unanimously in my favour because someone had said something like, 'Oh, we must have him, at the very least he'll brighten up a few synods.'

In September 1964 I resigned from Granada Television and we moved to Bath, where June's twin brother, John, had a house. For the next three years I was a student at Didsbury College, now called Wesley College, Bristol. At first June lived in Bath with the children whilst I lived in the college but in the final year we were able to move to a house that backed on to the college grounds.

Going to a Methodist college as a mature student was comparatively rare in the early sixties, though my year was something of an experiment because it consisted of a group of mature and married men. Methodism only ordained men at that time, the ordination of women was some years ahead. In fact Methodist theological colleges had until this time been run rather like celibate Catholic seminaries. There is an apocryphal story told about a principal of Wesley House, Cambridge. Apparently, the chairman of the student body at Wesley has been daring enough to ask for permission to hold an end-of-term dance. To his surprise the principal had agreed. However, as the end of term approached, the student chairman wanted to sort out a few practical arrangements and asked the principal which lavatories did he think should be demarcated 'Gents' and which 'Ladies'. The principal's eyebrows became airborne.

'Ladies? What ladies?'

'Well sir, do you remember my asking you permission to hold a dance?'

'Yes, of course I do. But nobody said anything about ladies!'

Our year had a total of twenty-one children, an unheard of thing in those days. We were a motley crew including an ex-farmer who had been an artillery captain, a trades union convenor, an accountant, a teacher and of course me.

Among the people whom I was to get to know quite well, as a result of producing Harold Pinter's play, *The Birthday Party*, at college were Robin Hutt and Mike Walling. After college Robin and I were not to meet again for nearly twenty years until we found ourselves together at a Catholic/Methodist Conference in Belfast. Mike Walling I have met and meet 'en passant' at various synods and conferences. We are both in the same synod. In my own year I struck up particularly close friendships with Tom Summersby, the ex-Artillery captain, an exceedingly tall chap, about six foot six; and a Midlander called Alf Austin, who was the only chap I ever knew who when he was broke would go out and buy a second-hand car, put right anything that was wrong with it, perhaps make some minor improvement and then sell it for a profit.

The principal of the college was the Reverend Dr Frederic Greeves, the brother of the Reverend Derrick Greeves. There was a third Greeves brother called Trevor. They were all Methodist ministers who were sons of Methodist ministers going back, at least, I think, to the eighteenth century. Derrick's son Roger, is also a Methodist minister.

Fred Greeves taught Theology. Rupert Davies taught Church History and Religious Philosophy. Kenneth Grayson was the New Testament Studies and Greek tutor, although the first year of

Greek was usually taught by an assistant tutor, a bright young man straight from college usually. In our case John Curnow was the assistant tutor. He must have done a good job because that year I won a prize for New Testament Greek, largely I suspect because of Derrick Greeves's early-morning breakfast sessions and because among the questions (which were mainly passages to be translated), the Greek to English translation was from the first five or six chapters of the Gospel of St Mark. Having worked on the chapters for some time, unconsciously, my actor's brain had learned them, so I found that when I came to the Greek translation questions the moment I recognised a word or two in Greek, I could remember the entire chapter in English. I still use my Greek Bible when working on scripture passages. Going back to the original text has become something of a habit.

First-century Holy Land Greek has proved rather useful on a holiday in Greek islands. I have only recently begun to attempt to learn some modern Greek, but a few years ago I struck up a friendly relationship one afternoon with an elderly Greek priest who realised that although I appeared unable to speak much modern Greek, I was clearly quite happy reading the New Testament texts written on his church wall. He excitedly concluded from this that I was a brother priest. He made June and I sit down in his quite empty church and then dashed behind the sanctuary screen. Now, whether or not our visit coincided with the time of a normal service I do not know, but to our surprise and delight he emerged from behind the screen robed in his ornate vestments and began to recite an office, apparently solely for our benefit; there was no one else in the church. After one of his many disappearances behind the screen he emerged with an incense thurible and, with much solemn bowing, he incensed the sanctuary, the altar, the nave and us. It was charming and I think his way of saying that even if we had a language problem we were united in our faith. It was one of the most truly ecumenical moments of my life.

I don't know if it was because I was a mature student, but I relished the work at college. I loved research and reading. Looking back, I see to my surprise that I collected several prizes. Curiously, I don't think prize-winning registered all that much when I was at college. It was probably considered bad form to allow such things to register. Anyway, I forgot about it until a few years ago when our boys, Simon and Mark, began to read Theology and, borrowing some of my books, discovered labels inside declaring them to be awarded with this, that, or the other prize. Old Testament studies – Theology and History – was taught by David Stacey, who one year awarded me the annual Old Testament Theology Prize, writing on my paper, 'Despite your obvious scorn for things like facts, this paper scores highly for its theological originality'.

In my third and final year I won a prize for Religious Philosophy. I remember when we began to study Philosophy, Rupert Davies took us through a short course in basic logic. I took to it like a duck to water; so much so that during Rupert's lectures, if he asked the class to work out some problem in logic, before I could even open my mouth he would point at me and say, 'Not you, Frank.'

At weekends we would be sent out to preach in the Methodist chapels in Bristol and Somerset and in the valleys of South Wales. The Severn Bridge had not been built then so it involved a long detour through Gloucester. On one of those trips, with four of us squeezed into Robin Hutt's little car, I remember listening to the radio and hearing a description of the return to England of Sir Francis Chichester after his epic solo voyage around the world. I little thought that one day in the future I would be making radio and television programmes with epic sailors such as Chay Blyth and Clare Francis.

One of my memories of preaching in South Wales was arriving one evening at a little village in which every other building seemed to be a chapel, Baptist, Strict Baptist, Elim, Congregational, Presbyterian, Church of Wales. However I couldn't find the Methodist chapel, so I stopped a passer-by.

'Excuse me. Could you direct me to the Methodist chapel?'

To my surprise he screwed up his face and replied, 'Methodist? English or Welsh?'

On the other hand, there were at that time two rival Methodist chapels in Bristol which stood alongside each other, separated only by a narrow side road. The noticeboard of one chapel read, 'Come and worship on the site where John Wesley preached.' And on the noticeboard of the chapel next door it said, 'Come and worship at the *friendly* Methodist chapel.' Ironically at that time the Church of England and the Methodists were having 'conversations' about Church unity. The Almighty's answer to the Methodist Synod's prayer about this local embarrassment was to drive a motorway through both chapels and have a splendid new chapel built with the compensation purchase money. 'The Lord moves in a mysterious way his wonders to perform!'

Everyone at college had to be attached to a 'Mission Band' and I was attached to the group that visited an approved school every week. Other Mission Bands went to churches in the town or visited hospitals, but if you were on the approved school team you had to stay on it all the time, simply because it took such a long time to win the confidence of the boys.

Lads used to boast about their crimes; the bigger their crime the higher their status. So one learned to take what they said with a pinch of salt. I once asked a lad with whom I had taken a long time to build up a relationship, 'What are you in for, Charlie?'

Without batting an eyelid he said, 'I killed my grandmother with an axe.'

'Oh yeah?' I said, whilst thinking, 'That's a bit over the top. I've heard a few boasts in my time but that's ridiculous.'

That night I asked casually in the staff room, idly flicking through the local paper, as one who is not taken in by the wild boasts of teenagers, 'By the way, what's Charlie here for?'

'Oh, him,' they said. 'He killed his Granny with an axe.'

The family are coming down this weekend. Anne, Robert and Suzannah, Simon and Jane; and Mark and Rachel. If the weather is fine we will use the scows. We've booked one of the club boats so that we can all sail down to the Camber, mess about on the beach and perhaps have a cup of tea at Hurst Castle. All the children can sail. Well, our granddaughter Suzannah is only three, but she's a jolly good member of the crew.

June and I came down here as honeymooners, we came when our children were younger than Suzannah, and we were down here that summer before I took up my first post as a probationer Methodist minister. For my first Church appointment, in September 1967, I was sent to Sussex to work with the Reverend Frank Thewlis, a wonderful man, a 'Central Mission' preacher, one of the specially gifted ministers who ran the Methodist Central Hall Missions that had been established in major cities and towns throughout the country. I was to be his assistant, but primarily I was to work as a Chaplain at Sussex University, and to be the Methodist Chaplain to the teacher's training college and the art college and, as it turned out, to student nurses in Brighton.

Our manse was just over the Downs from Falmer and Coldean, where the university is situated, on the seaward side, in Woodingdean. I also had pastoral responsibility for the Methodist Church at Woodingdean. The 'deans' abound in this area: Coldean, Woodingdean, Bevendean, Ovingdean, Saltdean and Rottingdean. It's not too surprising that the famous local girls' school is called Rodean. From the bedroom windows we could see the sea.

It was an odd house, built on the side of a hill. The drive from the road led to a garage which was on the first floor, so that if you walked from the garage into the house you found yourself on the bedroom landing. It took us some time to get the place straight or at least the way we wanted it, because the previous minister, a bachelor, had been ill and had left early, so the house had been shut up for a bit. The decor to a certain extent reflected the nature of his breakdown: there were rooms with ceilings painted black, the bathroom was predominantly purple. The lightbulbs of the wall-lights in the living room were green, blue and red. The breakfast room/kitchen had a divider which made you feel that you were imprisoned in a bamboo cage. It was made of bamboo poles cemented into place. (I hacksawed these very early on.)

The kitchen had a large Rayburn solid fuel cooker that didn't work. For some strange reason its firebox was stuffed with eggshells. The Rayburn that didn't work was supplemented by a one-ring electric cooker and a two-ring Baby Belling cooker, one ring of which did not work.

How June managed to cook meals for a family of five in these conditions I do not know. However, we redecorated and got a proper cooker and put our own untidy but comfortable mark

on the place. Eventually June got a job teaching at the Rudyard
Kipling Junior School in Woodingdean, the school our children
had started to attend, and a very agreeable lady called Mrs Grevatt
came in regularly to make sure that we were never quite overcome
by our homely untidiness.

My work with the students was very enjoyable. Every Sunday
evening they would fill our house with their laughter and their
singing and their conversation and argument. Sussex University
at that time was self-consciously 'avant-garde' and some students
were very actively engaged in politics. The 'Methodist Society' may
not have contained any political activists, but they certainly enjoyed
the debates. The MethSoc students became very actively involved
however with the Methodist Church in Woodingdean.

When I had first arrived at Woodingdean I had been told by a
prominent layman in the area, 'Don't worry about Woodingdean
church, it's a bit of a white elephant. It never has taken off the
ground, and I expect it never will. But never you mind, your job
is taking care of the students really.' I don't know if he said it
deliberately to stimulate me, but his remark was like a red rag to
a bull to me. 'White elephant? Never taken off and never will?' I
immediately wanted to know 'Why?' And more particularly, 'What
could I do about it?'

The students helped me to conduct a 'mission' to Woodingdean.
Looking at the church membership lists I saw that there was a
church member in almost every street in the area. I arranged for
there to be a week of morning coffee or afternoon tea parties,
hosted by the members for anyone in their street who wanted to
come. With the help of the students, we visited the people street
by street, telling them of the coffee or tea parties, and telling them
it was being organised by the Methodist church. The object of
the meetings was to discuss what the church could do that would
help to improve the quality of life in Woodingdean. Ultimately
this led to the church starting creches and mothers' and toddlers'
clubs. We started a youth recruiting campaign, which involved me
parading around the estates one Saturday morning at the head of
a Boys' Brigade band, inviting children to 'Follow the band!' to
the church hall for free films and lemonade! And like some latter

day Pied Piper I led a great swarm of children into the hall where they could see films about the Girl Guide movement and about the Boys' Brigade. In time all this activity led to the formation of two youth clubs, a Boys' Brigade Company, a Girl Guide and Brownie Company and a waiting list to join them.

On the first Sunday of every month we held a Family Parade Service in which the Guides, the Brownies and the Boys' Brigade presented their colours, supported, of course, by their parents. The end result of all these youth and community activities was that at the very least the Sunday Family Parade Services packed the church to the doors.

During this time the BBC introduced the first eight local radio stations, and one of them was Brighton. I was invited to attend the preliminary discussions held by the local Council of Churches about how the churches could make a contribution to a local radio station. This involvement led to the first church service ever to be broadcast on BBC Radio Brighton being transmitted from Woodingdean Methodist Church. All of this helped to make the local people feel that they were part of a lively and active community and church people were at the heart of it.

I personally had no particular skill in running either youth clubs or Sunday schools. In fact the prospect of having to do either of those two things sharpened my determination to find the best and most skilled people possible to run them for me and thus ensure that I would never have to attempt to do them myself. June does have gifts and skills in work with young people and she was an enormous help and strength during these campaigns and the ongoing work of the church.

The result of getting good people to run all the youth activities was that the work among young people and their families took off rather well. Where I did have some skills was in producing shows. The Methodist Association of Youth Clubs – the MAYC, which is the largest association of youth clubs in the country – presents an annual Youth Weekend in London which involves rallies in Trafalgar Square, debates and fashion shows in theatres, pop concerts, a huge display or show at the Royal Albert Hall and frequently a televised Sunday morning service from the Royal

Albert Hall. I wrote and produced items for the Albert Hall show and in the process was co-opted on to the production team for the whole show.

Another result, which I found somewhat embarrassing, was that I achieved a reputation for being some kind of expert in youth work, and was proposed for the office of Vice-President of the Methodist Association of Youth Clubs in the South East. It was a well intentioned but misguided idea because my skill lay in getting other skilled people to do the job rather than me. When I tried to explain this to the people making the proposal they smiled benignly and no doubt attributed my protestations to modesty, and in due course I found myself at a ceremony in which I was invested with a chain of office as Vice President of the MAYC in the South East District of the Methodist Church.

My work with university students presented me with another problem. How do you preach to a community of students, university lecturers and their families? In other words, where do you 'pitch' your sermon? At which level do you aim? Do you say, 'Well, this is a university, I must preach with a regard to the fact that a large part of the congregation are academics', or do you say, 'There are a good number of lively and radical young students here. I must speak to them', or do you say, 'There are a lot of children and no Sunday School at the university, I must have something to say to them.' Where do you pitch it?

People may be highly qualified mathematicians, or scientists or historians, but the likelihood is that their formal theological education came to an end when they left school. This means that to present the latest theological debate in the language of theologians from the pulpit, even in a university (even supposing I was capable of it), would simply not be fair. It would be like giving a lecture in French to an audience who have only schoolboy French or speak Miles Kington's 'Franglais'.

If on the other hand one were to preach solely to the children present in terms of being kind to each other and not kicking the cat, that would very quickly become a sickly and inadequate diet.

I decided to attempt to preach as to children but not childishly, to attempt to deal only with the heart of the Gospel, worthwhile

Sailing the *Stubblechin Jones* in the Solent.

Top: With June, Anne and Mark, preparing to move to North Wales, 1983.
Bottom: Failand Lodge Farmhouse.

Top: With Donald Swann on a Thames barge at Battersea, 1980.
Bottom: Rehearsing in Battersea with Donald.

Top: The first ever Junior Paraplegic Games,
Stoke Mandeville, 1982.
Bottom: With Father John Arrowsmith and Brian Blessed,
backstage at *Cats*, 1982.

Top: With Richard Briers at a charity concert in aid of
National Children's Homes at the Royal Albert Hall.

Bottom: Meeting the Queen at another Royal Albert Hall
NCH charity gala, 1986.

Top: Mark and Rachel's wedding: (left to right) Simon and Jane, me, June, granddaughter Suzannah, Mark and Rachel, Robert and Anne.

Relaxing in the sun in Bristol.

Hard at work in the Dordogne.

As John Steinbeck in *Once There Was A War*, 1986.

In the New Forest.

subjects, major issues, even if controversial and difficult, and to 'pitch it' in language and story accessible to children. It is an extremely difficult ideal to aim for but occasionally inspiration breaks through and when it does both child and professor are satisfied.

One day I was walking down the stairs that lead to the reception area in Radio Brighton (which is now called Radio Sussex) when I was met by a producer, Keith Slade, who was running up the stairs clutching a pile of long-playing records. As he passed he said, 'Frank, can you spare an hour?'

'When?' I asked.

'Now,' he said. 'Right now.'

Wondering what I might be letting myself in for, I said yes.

'Follow me!' he shouted and carried on running up the stairs.

I followed him into a studio where he explained that he was about to present a 'Phone-in' record request programme. He said that there was just too much to do because he had to put the records on the turntable, check the decibel level, answer the telephone and talk to the listeners all at the same time. If I could answer the phone or talk to the listeners, or do anything that would take the pressure off him for a bit, he would be grateful. It was the start of a great partnership. Every now and then two performers 'gel' together and we did.

The programme developed into a very popular two-hander called *Flat Spin*. We pretended that we shared an apartment, a flat in Radio Brighton, not unlike the apartment that Arthur Askey and Richard Murdoch pretended they lived in on the roof of Broadcasting House in London, in the early days of radio.

It started off as a joke. While I was talking to a listener, Keith began to play a record, not music but a sound effect, 'gurgling plumbing' or something like that, and I made some weak joke about the last time Keith mended the plumbing we got Radio 4 on the gas stove and had to boil our eggs in the kitchen sink, and suddenly the 'flat' had come into existence.

Responding to a record, a sound effect or a piece of film music became an integral part of the programme. We played 'Western

Scenes' to music from the *Big Country* or re-enacted *War and Peace* to music from *Dr Zhivago*. Both of us were actors with a wide range of dialects so there seemed to be no limit to our improvisational games. We had a series of sound effects that we could play when we wanted a scene to end, like an explosion or a burst of machine-gun fire or someone dropping a screaming one-man-band entertainer and all his equipment down a sewer.

A great deal of the programme involved light-hearted banter with the listener who had telephoned. At times we made rude comments about people's names or the name of the people for whom they were requesting a record. It did not put people off, it simply encouraged them. Keith told me that when he was doing the programme on his own he spent a great deal of time begging people to telephone. Once the two-handed *Flat Spin* was under way the telephone switchboard became jammed with calls within minutes of the programme starting.

One of the interesting side effects of that programme was that I received more letters that were pastoral enquiries after the comedy record programme than I did after the overtly religious programmes that I broadcast. We never hid the fact that I was a local parson; in fact Keith would make jokes like, 'Watch your language, the Vicar's here!' or 'I hope you noticed I polished up your halo for you. It's amazing what Brasso will clean.'

I realise now that I was broadcasting to a large audience who, in the normal course of events, simply would not dream of listening to a religious broadcast, but here was a local man who was a parson who seemed to laugh and joke. He sounded warm and kind and accessible, maybe they could talk to him . . . ? It was a lesson I was to remember.

Another job which Keith gave me was editing and reading short stories. The editing started when he gave me a story to read, which I thought had missed its own punchline. I pointed it out to Keith and told him that I thought the story would finish better at a particular line on the penultimate page.

'You are absolutely right,' he said. 'Here,' he passed me another script. 'What's wrong with that then?'

I quickly skimmed through the script and said, 'Cut out the

first two paragraphs, bring the introduction of the heroine from page two to the beginning and, well, the final paragraph needs rewriting.'

Keith looked at the script. 'How would you rewrite the last paragraph?' I told him and he said, 'You can do this a lot better and a lot quicker than I can, mate. Do you want to earn a little pocket money?'

I was earning a little pocket money with Keith one day when I persuaded Clive Dunne who was appearing in pantomime at the Theatre Royal to come and be interviewed for the radio. I had worked with Clive on a good number of television programmes when he had been in the Granada series *Bootsie and Snudge*.

He came to Radio Brighton and told me about a new series that he was just beginning. 'You must see it,' he said. 'It is *very* funny, we just know that it's going to be a *huge* success.'

Hmm! Well, as they say, 'If I had a pound for every time an actor has said that . . .'

'What is it called?' I asked.

'*Dad's Army*,' he said.

June and I arranged to go for a meal with Clive and with Bernard Bresslaw and a few other members of the cast of the pantomime, to a Greek restaurant in Brighton called 'Zorba's.' It turned out to be an hilarious evening with Clive entering into the spirit of a Greek 'plate smashing' dance, until he realised that he was paying for the plates. Bernard Bresslaw requested the traditional Greek band to play the Beatles number, 'Ob-la-di, ob-la-da, life goes on . . .'

'Sorry, honly play the Grick music!'

'It's very easy,' Bernard said, and proceeded to sing it to them, accompanied by our theatrical crowd and eventually by the entire restaurant. The band quickly learned the tune and were enjoying adding Greek flourishes to it. By now it had passed the licensing hours to sell wine, but the proprietor clearly did not want the evening to end too soon so he replenished the wine on our table as a gift. When eventually we did begin to make our way home he invited us all to come back next week, 'On the house!' So we did.

I met another old friend from the Granada days while I was at

Sussex University, Malcolm Muggeridge. He had come to preach for the CC, the Christian Community, the ecumenical grouping of the various denominational societies at the university like AngSoc, CathSoc and MethSoc. I was there, as one of the chaplains, to welcome him.

Muggeridge greeted me with the words, 'My dear chap. You're a priest!'

'Well, actually I'm a Methodist minister.'

He screwed up his face into his famous agonised 'seeker after truth' expression. 'A Methodist! But why? Dear boy, why?'

As he was visiting on a somewhat tight schedule we were both aware that this was neither the time nor the place to begin a discussion of any depth.

'Will you come to lunch at Robertsbridge?' he said. 'Give me a ring and we'll fix it up.' And we did.

After his sermon, when the service was over a young man with a tape-recorder requested an interview. Muggeridge agreed and the young man began his interview not with a question but a curiously phrased statement.

'Mr Muggeridge,' he began, 'I believe you had some connection with the magazine *Punch*.'

Muggeridge raised his eyebrows, pursed his lips and said, 'Yes, dear boy, for five sad years I was its editor.'

'Why sad years?'

Muggeridge smiled a sad smile and then launched into vintage Muggeridge humour. 'Because, dear boy, all humorists die of melancholia. Can you imagine the dilemma that confronts the editor of *Punch* every Monday morning. His task is to produce something funnier than reality, and there on the front page of the *Guardian* is a photograph of Quintin Hogg. How can he compete? To face this dilemma, week after week and year after year can only serve to plunge the poor humorist ever deeper into terminal melancholy. Hence, "five sad years". I only just got out in time, dear boy.'

David Wayne had been the programme organiser at BBC Radio Brighton and when he was appointed to be station manager of one of the larger new stations, BBC Radio Bristol, he suggested that I might consider applying for a post as a producer in Bristol. After various consultations with the chairman of the district and the committee that considers applications From Methodist ministers to become 'Sector Ministers' which is Methodism's equivalent of French 'Worker Priests', I applied for the post; along with the two thousand other people who had applied for the five 'General Producer' vacancies.

In due course I learned that I had been shortlisted and was invited to attend an interview selection board. Eventually I was appointed, but there was a very long delay between the interview and the letter telling me that I had got the job. I don't know the details of the debate that delayed my appointment, it was not to do with me personally but a principle that was being argued between the trades unions and the BBC management. The end result however was that I was appointed after everybody else had finished the special training course that had been arranged for all the production staff of the new radio stations.

I was appointed, in August 1970, only a matter of weeks before we went on the air, which did not give me a great deal of time to learn about the operation of the newly designed studio desks. If you have never seen one of these desks, imagine the flight deck on Concorde and you will have some idea of what they look like. They are very special control desks that enable one person to present his own programme, doing everything from playing jingles, records, cassettes or reel to reel tapes, to opting in and out of national news bulletins, weather forecasts, Greenwich time signals or national programmes, linking up with unattended studios in a variety of locations, or with the radio car or another studio in the same building. I also missed the 'Radio Car Training' and the 'Tape Editing, Sound Mixing, Music and Special Effects Training'. Nevertheless, by launch day I had to be able to navigate my way through the airwaves using any or all of this 'state of the art' equipment. In other words, I was about to launch into the deep without a lifebelt.

As a general producer, I was given responsibility for a weekly farming magazine, a music magazine, a religious magazine, and a daily religious 'Thought'. I was also the short-story editor, producer and presenter of a comedy record programme on Saturday mornings and the continuity newsreader and announcer for the weekends. So there I was, a one-man-band radio producer. It was terrifying and wonderful.

Other wonders included the quality of the team that David Wayne had selected. He had set out to pick a very special team. As a member of that team I hope it doesn't sound too conceited to say that I believe he succeeded. He certainly made us feel that we were special, that we were the exact and only team that he required for the job of scotching for ever the anti-local radio jibes about 'Toy Town Radio' and establishing a standard that would make BBC Radio Bristol a flagship in the local radio venture.

Among the Radio Bristol pioneers were several people who were to become either publicly acclaimed or professionally renowned in the not too distant future. Looking after the equivalent of the Woman's Hour programmes was a girl called Kate Adie, and in the newsroom there was a young reporter from the *Guardian* called Michael Buerk. The education producer was an ex-teacher called Ken Blakeson who was to become a very successful radio and television playwright. The arts producer was Johnathan Fulford, who moved on to become a producer of national television arts programmes for the BBC. David Wayne himself later became the head of the BBC Midland region.

One of my first problems was to find very quickly somewhere to live that was convenient and affordable. I had made arrangements to live in some quarters in my old college but at the very last minute these arrangements had fallen through. On the actual day of my arrival in Bristol I was told that the rooms we had planned to live in were no longer available. We had even arranged which local schools the children should attend. I drove to the BBC office that I was sharing with Kate Adie and Ken Blakeson and announced my problem.

'Not only have I not got anywhere for June and the children to live when they come, I do not actually have anywhere to lay my head tonight.'

Kate immediately sprang into action. She said, 'I have just rented a wing of a farm house. I'm sharing it with Jane Kelly (one of the production assistants). It's not too far away. It's a village out on the Portishead road. I have got a feeling that there is another wing available. Would you mind living out of town?'

'No, it sounds wonderful.'

'Shall I find out if it's still available?'

'Yes, please.'

'Okay. I'll ring the farmer now and see if we can have a look at it.'

'We?'

'Yes, I'll drive you there. It'll be quicker than you trying to find the place on your own, especially on that contraption of yours.'

I had left our vehicle, which was yet another van, in Brighton with June and the children and I had brought with me to Bristol a very small motorbike that June used in Woodingdean for local shopping.

Five minutes later, in Kate's car, we were heading for the Clifton Suspension Bridge and Failand Lodge Farm.

The farmer was called Mervyn Down. He ran a mixed farm of about three hundred acres, market gardening, beef cattle and pigs. We found him, not in the house but out in a field of sprouts.

We talked for a while standing in the field. He was being a bit vague about the availability of the wing, referring to other enquiries he'd received and other people who were interested in it. He was clearly, and not surprisingly, assessing whether or not I was the kind of person he wanted living next to him on his farm. He appeared to like the idea of a young family and a wife who was a teacher, and was amused that I was going to be the local radio farming producer. We started laughing about something and then he suddenly seemed to make up his mind.

'Well, I haven't actually let it yet. Perhaps you had better have a look and see if it's what you want.'

Failand Lodge is a three-winged Georgian building. Kate had rented the north wing, Mervyn Down lived in the central section and it took me about five minutes to decide that I wanted to rent the south wing. The rooms were wonderfully spacious, the living room, at the western end of the wing, had three elegant windows, two facing south and one west and there was a huge fireplace across a corner. The dining room was in proportion to the living room and so was the kitchen. In a passage near the kitchen there were several small service rooms, a scullery, a pantry and a store room. The rooms upstairs were as generous in their proportions as the living rooms. Naturally one had access to the entire farm, but there was also a small concealed garden that went with this wing. It was deep Somerset countryside and yet only about ten minutes away from the Clifton Suspension Bridge and Bristol. I loved it immediately and knew that June would.

June was not able to join me straight away because of having to finish a school term teaching in Brighton. So at first I was living in a very bare house with hardly any furniture, more or less camping in the place until June came with the children.

I decided that as I did not have enough time even to begin building up the contacts I would need to run a religious magazine programme, certainly not by the first week, I would make a dramatised religious documentary instead. From Brighton I had brought with me tapes of interviews that I had recorded with various people, and I thought it might be possible to weave some of these together to create a documentary on a theme.

I had learned that living in the Bristol area was an ex-China missionary called the Reverend Vernon Stone, who had been the last Methodist minister to leave mainland China when the Communists took over. He had been arrested and imprisoned for a considerable time. During his imprisonment an attempt had been made to 'reform' him. It was a fascinating story. Vernon Stone's story also related to two of the interviews I had on tape. One was an interview with Richard Wurmbrand who had been imprisoned in Roumania for fourteen years and who had spent three years in solitary confinement before being brought to 'trial'. I also had on tape a conversation with Frank Gibson, a lifelong friend of June's family, who had been imprisoned in Changi Jail by the Japanese during the Second World War and had been interrogated by the Kempetia, the Japanese equivalent of the Gestapo, at the same time as Bishop Wilson of Singapore was being interrogated and therefore was a first-hand witness to the suffering of that very brave Bishop.

Vernon Stone's story was the pivotal point of the programme. These stories were not local stories, but he was the man living 'down our way' whose story made the documentary valid for a local station. I visited Vernon Stone and he very kindly allowed me to record our conversation for the programme. I now had on tape three very vivid, first-hand accounts of men in different parts of the world being brought to physical and mental breaking point, who not only survived the experience but emerged spiritually stronger. The one thing they had in common was their Christian faith. I called the programme, *Christians under Stress*. I weaved the interviews together with a tightly written narrative mixed with music which I thought would highlight or intensify the telling of their stories.

I was very excited about the programme but a little worried about my lack of technical experience to actually put together the effects and ideas that were in my mind. While I was working on it, David Wayne, the station manager, came into the studio and overheard the opening section of the programme which I had just mixed together. When I stopped the machine he said, 'Where's that from?'

'What do you mean?' I asked.

'Well, it's a soundtrack from a film or something, isn't it?'

'No, I've just made it. I've just cobbled it together.'

He threw back his head and laughed. 'Really? Huh! And you never went to any of the training courses. God knows what you would have made if you had.' He grinned. 'You're going to do all right, Frank.'

The programme was first broadcast on a Sunday, the station's first Sunday, at midday. Not long after the broadcast the telephone rang and someone in the newsroom took the call. As I was duty continuity for the weekend the reporter who took the call rang down to the studio. 'Hello, Frank. I've just had an amazing phone call about the programme that's just finished.' Apparently the caller was a barman from a pub near Bath. The radio had been on in his bar when one of his Sunday lunchtime regulars asked him if he could get the new radio station, BBC Radio Bristol. The barman said he could and tuned the radio to our station at precisely the moment that I had said, 'You are listening to BBC Radio Bristol' and then started the *Christians under Stress* tape.

'Well,' said the barman, 'that was it! Halfway through the programme I looked around the bar and all my regulars were sitting there with empty glasses! And what's more, nobody asked for a refill until the programme ended! I've never seen anything like it,' he said. 'Sunday lunchtime in the regulars' bar with nobody talking and nobody drinking! That's why I phoned,' he said. 'I thought you'd like to know about something like that.'

It was in the first few weeks, before June and the children had joined me, that I had my little accident on the Clifton Suspension Bridge. It happened in the early hours of a Saturday morning.

At the weekends, as the duty continuity announcer, it was my job to arrive at the station in the very early hours of the morning, switch on the transmitter, go up to the newsroom, tear out the 'Rip and Read' news from one machine and the weather forecast from another; sub the news, go down to Studio One, switch on the control desk, put the station identity cassette into its machine and, at the appropriate moment, play our station signature tune, open a microphone and say, as brightly as possible, 'Good morning. You are listening to BBC Radio Bristol. The time is six a.m. and here is the news!'

That Saturday morning, at about five a.m., I was crossing the Clifton Suspension Bridge on my way to work, riding my small motorbike. On the Bristol side of the bridge, near the toll collector's kiosks, there are some public conveniences. Parked outside them on this particular morning was a motor car. At that time in the morning the streets are deserted and there is hardly any traffic whatsoever. If it had been a crowded, busy time of day the accident might have been more understandable, but as I was the only thing moving at that time what happened is more surprising. 'Chance' again, I suppose.

At the precise moment that I passed the parked vehicle, the driver's door opened. It could not have been timed more perfectly. I drove straight into the door. The motorbike crashed against it and I flew over the top. I landed face down, sliding for a few feet on what was a newly gravelled stretch of tarmac. My crash helmet saved my head and face. I was wearing a reasonably new pair of motorcyclist's gauntlets, although these were ripped to shreds by my slide, so that my hands showed through them, my hands were not even scratched. My left knee however was a different story; an ordinary pair of trousers was no protection.

It takes a few seconds to assess the damage after a sudden and violent accident. You make your physical explorations very carefully. Are my fingers working, my toes, arms, legs? Ah! All is not well with my knee, my left knee, but I don't want to look, not sure if I could look even if I wanted to.

Where did the people come from at that time in the morning? Did they rush out of houses? Crawl out of the earth? Come down from the trees? Wherever they came from, there was a complete circle of faces looking down at me and all talking at once.

'It's all right, son, someone's ringing for an ambulance. You'll be all right.'

'Here, put this coat under his head.'

'Don't move him! He might have broken his neck!'

The circle breaks open suddenly and a face with a helmet appears. A policeman's helmet. The face begins to speak but I can't believe what I am hearing. I can feel a pulsing in my leg, I suspect because I am bleeding rather heavily. I know a bone is exposed, I haven't looked because after the remark about the possibility of my neck being broken I don't want to risk moving my head.

'Have you got your driving licence on you, sir?'

I am aware of very quietly making a suggestion about what I think the policeman ought to do. I am also aware that the language on my lips is not exactly becoming to a Methodist minister. The assembled crowd is as incredulous as I am.

'Oh, for God's sake!'

'Would you believe it?'

I don't remember the ambulance coming, I don't remember the ambulance men or the ambulance journey. When my next conscious thought broke through I was in a bed in the Bristol Royal Infirmary. So I suppose I must have passed out.

When I was eventually discharged and delivered to Failand Lodge, Kate Adie insisted that I convalesced in her wing. She said, 'You are supposed to be lying down for the next few days and as I have seen your "camping" arrangements next door and as I am the one with the instructions from the hospital about changing the dressing on your leg, it makes far more sense if you stay here and Jane (Jane Kelly) and I can look after you.' It was most generous and very typical of her. Not only did she take me into her part of the house, she even sacrificed her own room for the purpose of my recuperation.

Lying in Kate's huge double bed, I began to plan a religious production for Lent and Easter. I wanted to do something special, something different. I turned over a number of ideas in my mind and in the end I wrote a play, with songs. In local radio programme budgets are small, everything is done on a shoestring. On the other hand if you had an idea you just went ahead with it. It didn't have to be submitted to and passed by several committees. You could make a mistake, get up, shake off the dust and start again, which is not so easy to do in national radio.

I had asked David Wayne and Bill Salisbury, the programme organiser on Radio Bristol, how much it would cost to employ professional musicians to perform original music. The answer was quite simple. In local radio terms, prohibitive.

On the other hand, the use of local amateur musicians was a different proposition altogether. Arrangements could be made. One of the newsroom reporters, Roger Bennett, was, in private life, a jazz musician, a clarinetist who led a traditional jazz band called 'The Bluenotes' who played and were very well received at local 'gigs'. He agreed to help me with the music I needed for my play. So, largely because of cost and because of the availability of a jazz band the songs that I wrote for my play were written in a blues style. Though when you come to think of it, you could not get a better subject for 'blues' than the Passion.

The play needed a cast of thousands and practically everybody on the station provided voices, including Kate, who gave a fine cameo performance as a 'woman of easy virtue'. I certainly could not afford a cast of thousands, therefore I had to create the 'feeling' of great crowds, the feeling of an 'epic'. To do this I built up the crowd scenes in 'layers' of sound: voices dubbed over voices and mixed with sound effects, 'echo' or 'space' ambience created artificially. When Pontius Pilate spoke it sounded like a voice speaking in the open air across an amphitheatre. 'Waves' of voices shouted abuse, until suddenly one, harsh, clear voice broke through like a jagged knife, so abrasively, yet with such cruel clarity, that it sent a shiver down the listener's spine. 'Crucify him!'

I recorded the play in hundreds of short 'sound bites'. I dragged people in from the corridors to say or shout a particular line. Jesus was played by Ken Blakeson, the education producer who had a good sensitive voice, warmed by Yorkshire earthiness. I spent days working into the early hours of the morning, editing, dubbing, re-recording, taking a few notes of music from one of the songs and making a thematic loop of sound so that I could thread through and draw together the various scenes. It was like trying to put together a patchwork quilt of sound. It was also written so that you moved from the present time into the past and back again and sometimes you were not quite sure which time you were in. This was a very deliberate attempt to catch the timelessness of Christ's sacrifice, the eternal nature of a drama that is complete and yet is still being played.

The play was called *On the Hill* and it formed a very crucial part in my future career. A few years later, after a very slight reworking of all this material, the play was broadcast on Radio 3 and entered for an Unda award. The Unda Seville Festival is an international religious radio festival, 'Doves' are awarded according to categories of programme. *On the Hill* won not only an Unda Dove but also the Grace Wyndham Goldie Award for the best production of any category in the UK Festival of 1975.

7   A Rose in a Bottle

Sailing into Yarmouth on the Isle of Wight in a little dinghy can be a bit of a nightmare in summer, what with the Lymington Ferry threatening to swamp you and three-decker gin palaces sweeping out as if they were manoeuvring around Hyde Park Corner; and sails flapping and cracking as they are lowered or raised outside the harbour entrance; and the Harbour Master standing in his little launch waving his arms like a waterborne *gendarme* on traffic duty. All in all, to have tied up your scow to the dinghy pontoon and to have walked up the gangplank so that you can stand on the quay and survey the motley goings on, is to have successfully run the Yarmouth gauntlet.

And after your Solent crossing it is very pleasing. You can stride along the quayside with the same air of windbattered but noble satisfaction as those heroes who arrive at the same place after crossing the wider channel from Cherbourg.

Perhaps I am an incurable romantic but I find sailing my own boat into a port, any port, is always exciting. I enjoy the curious feeling of arriving in a foreign place, no matter how many times I have been there before. Then to walk into, say, the George Hotel in Yarmouth, and to take a cup of coffee out into the hotel garden is to feel like someone who has returned to civilisation after an encounter with the wild and untamed elements of creation. Which is of course exactly what one has done, no matter in how small a way.

I don't know why it is, but June and I seem to have a deep-seated wanderlust. We were in Bristol for only eighteen months before moving to Manchester in 1972 where I was to be the religious broadcasting assistant for the North Region of the BBC. I was now to be responsible for all religious radio programmes emanating from the North Region, and that region covers a lot of ground. It extends from the west coast to the east coast and from the Scottish border to Stamford in Lincolnshire, which is only ninety miles north of London. At that time there were no motorways crossing the Pennines and I soon learned that most religious programmes from the region were 'outside broadcasts'.

One of the first locations I had to travel to was in Sunderland, where some years ago I had spent a week with *Doctor in the House* at the Sunderland Empire. Now I was in the town to record a *Sunday Half-Hour*. I arrived in a modest little saloon to critical comments from the OB crew.

'That won't last long.'

'You'll run that into the ground in less than six months.'

'Worse, you'll run yourself into the ground in six months.'

'Yes, you're going to need something a bit sturdier than that.'

All these comments referred to the smallness of my car. Clearly they knew something that had not dawned on me. They knew that anyone whose job was going to involve regular crossings of the Pennines, with their twisting mountain roads, narrow passes and hairpin bends, was also going to need a vehicle that would be able to take that kind of hard driving and get me to my destination in a reasonably fit condition. They were absolutely right. It did not take many trips from west to east for me to realise that I would quickly become exhausted. Unless you took an extra day and travelled the night before, the job involved a long and arduous drive, at the end of which one had to leap out and start work, enthusing and encouraging others to release lots of energy into the programme you were about to record. In a very short time I had exchanged the modest family saloon for a second-hand 3.5 Rover Automatic with power-assisted steering. It made a huge difference.

When I made that recording in Sunderland a friend and BBC colleague, Father John Thompson, whose office was next door to mine in Manchester, popped in to see me.

'Listen,' he said. 'In Sunderland there is a Jesuit House quite near the church where you are recording. I stayed with them the last time I was up there and they are great fellows, marvellous hospitality, wonderful talkers. Shall I give them a ring and ask if they can give you a bed for the night? It has to be better than staying in a hotel. Believe me you'll have a great time.'

And so I did. At the end of a very entertaining supper in the Jesuits' house in Sunderland, I had to make an apologetic request. I explained that a producer's meeting had been called for ten a.m. the following morning in Manchester. To get there on time I would have to leave very early indeed. I needed therefore to ask if they would mind if I helped myself to some breakfast and slipped away in the very early morning, well before first light. They were extremely sympathetic and said, 'Make yourself at home – just go into the kitchen and help yourself to anything you want.'

In the dark early hours of the following morning I was fumbling about in their kitchen, trying to find where they kept the spoons and the bowls and the cereals and so on when I became aware that I was not alone. I turned around and saw a bearded priest standing in the doorway. He was not one of the priests with whom I had had supper the previous evening, so I did not know his name. He was wearing a black cassock. When he spoke he spoke slowly; his accent was Slavonic, Polish or Lithuanian perhaps. His voice was very deep.

'What are you doing?'

'Ah! Good morning, Father. It's all right, I'm just getting myself some breakfast, I have to drive to a meeting in Manchester this morning which is why I'm up so early. I hope I haven't wakened you with my rattling. Er, the kettle's on. Would you like a cup of tea?'

There was a silence and I thought I heard a gentle sigh. Then he spoke. 'Sit down and look at the rose. I will get your breakfast.'

I wasn't quite sure that I had heard him correctly so I said, with a slightly embarrassed laugh, 'Er, I beg your pardon, but did you say, "look at the rose"?'

'Yes. Look at the rose and I will get your breakfast.'

The conversation had taken on an element of surrealism that I was finding just a little difficult to cope with at that time of the morning.

'I'm sorry. What rose?'

There was another silence. Unfortunately, the passage light was behind his head, which made it difficult to see his face clearly. Once again I thought I heard that little sigh before he spoke.

'Precisely. You have not seen the rose. And in your hurry for Manchester, and meetings, you will not see anything more beautiful this day. So, sit down and look at the rose. That rose, on the table.'

On the kitchen table, alongside the salt and pepper, the vinegar carafe and the tomato sauce was a milk bottle with a single red rose in it. It was very beautiful. So I sat down. It was a good lesson. What's more, I have never forgotten it. I can still see my rose in a bottle. And when life is getting a little hectic, I conjure it up.

One of the advantages of living in Manchester was that we were able to have family explorations of the Lake District and Scotland in the school holidays. Sadly the Lake District becomes almost too crowded in the summer so we decided to find some 'off the beaten track' areas of the Lake District, the less well known waters and the small lakes or tarns. We made one escape from the holiday crowds by marooning ourselves on an island in a tarn called Tarn Hows.

Small islands have a fascination that amounts to magnetism in my family. The roads around Tarn Hows were heavy with tourist traffic. The grass verges were being flattened under a stream of walkers' boots, and the isolation of the small island in the tarn beckoned us. But how to get there? This was not a sufficiently big stretch of water to have rowing or sailing boats for hire so we had to improvise.

In the boot of our car we had a miniature rubber boat, a child's boat. It was capable of bearing the weight of a child, but was barely big enough to contain a full grown man and had only just enough buoyancy to support an adult. We decided to use this to get two adults and three children to the island. To propel the boat we had a pair of canvas hand-paddles. If you can imagine a glove in the shape of a tennis racket, that's what a canvas hand-paddle looks like. They are terrible things, because after about five minutes of trying to push water with them your arms feel as if they are about to drop off. However, they will propel you, slowly.

Being a keen camping family, the other thing that we had plenty of in the boot of our car was string. Nevertheless we still had to join together a variety of lengths and thicknesses (a double sheet bend is recommended!) to be able to make a single length long enough for one person to paddle out to the island, land, put the paddles in the boat and then for the boat to be drawn back to the mainland by the string so that the next person could cross the dividing water.

The operation began to attract spectators, and by the time the last person (me) embarked there was quite a crowd. When I stepped ashore on the island the crowd began to applaud, so we dutifully acknowledged their appreciation with a solemn bow.

It was in Manchester that we bought our first family sailing boat, an open boat called a Drascombe Dabber. It was a wonderful, two-masted boat, having a main mast and small mizzen. It also had a bowsprit that gave the boat a very elegant line when under full sail.

As a family we have great affection for Kerrera, a small island off the west coast of Scotland. We were on a camping holiday and came across the island more by chance than design. We had pitched our tent on the mainland not far from Oban and quite near Kerrera Sound. In fact we did not stay the night at that site because of the behaviour of a rowdy crowd of youths who arrived just after we had put up our tent. It was when one of them started throwing a large knife about, into trees or into the ground, that we decided it would be wiser, for the sake of the children, to leave. We told the camp site manager why we were leaving and left him to deal with the situation. As the father of three small children, I had no intention of confronting a crowd of beer-swilling, knife-throwing young men.

Moving from that site actually led us to finding a beautiful camp site facing Loch Linnhe, and in the process we noticed an unusual sign on the road alongside Kerrera Sound. The sign consisted of a black square board with an inner square that could be swivelled so that the board was either all black or a black surround with a white square in the middle. The board faced the island of Kerrera.

When the white square was showing it was a signal to the boatman living at the Ferry Croft that someone wished to be taken across to the island. And in the timeless and leisurely way of the islanders of the west coast, when he was ready he would come across and collect his passengers.

That first year, 1972, we stayed at our camp site near Loch Linnhe and visited Kerrera. Perhaps the main attraction for us was the wildness of the place. There were no tourist facilities apart from the Ferry Croft Tea Room. A walk around the island would stretch your legs for about eight miles, with a good chance that you would meet no one other than the crofting families who live on the island. It is not really on the beaten tourist path but we fell in love with the place and spent the remainder of our holiday there.

We hired a rowing boat from the ferry man. He didn't charge us much because it had 'a wee leak'. It was slightly more than 'wee', because we never went anywhere in that boat without several inches of water slushing around our feet, no matter how hard we baled, but it was great fun. We experienced the wonderful thrill of catching our first mackerel. It was not quite as terrifying as when, about a week earlier, Simon caught a gurnard, a grey gurnard, in Loch Lomond. Actually we were never too sure what it was that Simon had caught because the fish got away, leaped off the line, but we all saw it for one frozen moment in time, when a fish that seemed to be all head, a spiky, open-mouthed head, broke through and cleared the water by several feet. It seemed to hang in the air, glaring at us, before twisting and somehow coming free from the line, then it disappeared into the considerable depths of the Loch. However, our experience of catching mackerel had its own drama.

If you are pulling fish into a boat that has several inches of water slushing about the bottom, the fish begin to swim around your feet. Also rolling about in the bottom of our boat was a short, fat, wooden pole for use as a roller when dragging the boat up or down a beach. Our daughter, Anne, attempted to use this stout piece of wood as a fisherman's 'priest', that is as a club with which to administer 'the last rites' to the fish. We had to beg her to stop because apart from the splash she was making she hit the boat so hard we feared she might drive a hole in the bottom.

There was a bay called Little Horse Shoe Bay which had a row of three cottages. The beach in front of the cottages was littered with generations of crofters' debris: boat hulks, two old tractors half submerged, a huge concrete barge or lighter, the remains of a boat house. Some people would think it looked a mess, but to children it was paradise, an adventure playground arranged especially for them. Mark, our youngest son, who has visited the island recently, says that Horse Shoe Bay has been 'tidied up' and sadly all the relics removed. But it is still a wonderful bay with a great rolling hill behind the cottages, and a half-submerged peninsula which at high tide left a lump of rock protruding from the water, looking for all the world like a submarine about to surface. Naturally we called it 'Submarine Island'. There was another miniature island in the bay which was a haven for oyster-catchers, so Oyster-Catcher Island it was.

At nights, which were sometimes almost as light as day, with, as they say, 'a moon you can read your paper by', there were wonderful luminescent glow-worms. One night, one year, walking home from a wee 'ceilidh' with the Beatons, a Kerrera crofting family, Mark attempted to pick up a glow-worm, only to discover that it was emanating its strobing light from the middle of a cowpat.

Mrs Beaton, who had a cousin on Seil Island who actually owned the cottages in the bay, made arrangements for us to rent two of the three cottages for the following summer.

The next summer we trailed our own boat, the Drascombe Dabber, to Scotland, and had another wonderful holiday. The cottage was extremely basic. The water supply came into a little lean-to at the back and consisted of a tap connected to a pipe which ran up the hillside and drew its supply from a stream. All of this was wonderfully romantic until the day we discovered a dead sheep lying across the stream.

We sailed and fished and tramped over the hills in the pouring rain, and at night we gathered round an open fire in the living room and read to each other. The book we read together was

Arthur Ransome's *Peter Duck*. Our method was to read two pages each and then pass the book to the person sitting next to you. Part of the fun involved imitating whatever voice the previous reader chose for a particular character. We laughed until we cried, and it was all very warm and loving and close, and perhaps one of the best times that I can remember of the children growing up.

I had another contact with Scotland that year, because the London editor of a BBC radio series called *Pilgrim's Way* was taken ill, and I was asked if I would step into the breach. I made three programmes in the series and one of them was about George Macleod, Lord Macleod of Fuinary, the founder of the Iona Community, who in the thirties led the rebuilding of the old Abbey of Iona. I went to the BBC Religious Department in Edinburgh to see if there were any archive recordings of, or about, Macleod that might help the programme I wanted to make. I asked one of the producers what kind of man Macleod was. Did he sing songs, tell stories or, like Lord Soper, did he play a tin whistle? The Edinburgh producer looked shocked.

'You're no going tae ask Lord Macleod if he plays a tin whistle, are ye? Lord Macleod is a very serious man. He has no small talk. The moment he opens his front door he's likely to ask what you think of the situation in Afghanistan.'

That response filled me with some apprehension. I was going to spend a few days with the Macleods and it did not sound as if my stay was going to be a lot of fun.

In fact the Edinburgh producer's image of George Macleod was, to say the least, incomplete. He had seen only one aspect of the man, the public image of Macleod, the Moderator of the Church of Scotland, the elder statesman, the visionary preacher. He did not know him as a friend, or see him as a husband and father. In the days I spent with George Macleod and his wife we did a lot of laughing and he was a very good story-teller.

George Macleod was loved and respected by thousands of ordinary men and women, many of whom had regained their dignity and self-respect through him. Many people had caught hold of the vision that he had inspired in his mission work in Glasgow and Iona. Now you don't do all that if you have 'no small talk'. On the other hand, he was also, undoubtedly, a Scottish aristocrat. A baronet in his own right (made a life peer in 1967), educated at Winchester and Oriel College, Oxford, a First World War Army captain, with a bold moustache, an upright, 'look you in the eye' posture, his looks, voice and natural authority declared his pedigree. Altogether, he was a fascinating and delightful man.

The Macleods took me to their Princes Street club for lunch. It is called the 'New Club', despite the fact that it is one of the oldest clubs in Scotland. Wonderfully situated, in what I believe to be the most elegant street in Britain, it has a very fine view of Edinburgh Castle. At lunch we were waited on by a steward in a kilt, complete with velvet jacket and period lace jabot and lace cuffs. Perhaps because his clothes were so very beautiful the steward was somewhat aggressively macho in his manner.

George said, 'He's a funny chap, that steward. He put a notice in the cloakroom the other day which said, "Would the peer who took an umbrella that did not belong to him, kindly return it." I said, "Look here, Steward, how do you know it was a peer who took that umbrella?" And he said, "Sir, this club was founded for peers and gentlemen – and no *gentleman* would have taken it."'

After the programme had been broadcast George's daughter wrote a very generous letter in which she said that of all the programmes, articles and 'profiles' that she had ever seen or heard about her father, *Pilgrim's Way* had been the only one that had revealed him as the man she knew.

Sydney Carter, the poet and song-writer, was also one of my subjects for *Pilgrim's Way*. I did not want the programme to sound as if it was recorded in a BBC studio so we met in a friend's house in London. Joan Rand (later to become Joan Martin) a friend of our family for years, had, at that time, a lovely miniature Regency house not far from Baker Street. She very kindly gave me the use of it during the day. I wanted Sydney to feel 'at home', so that we would be able to make our recordings in ordinary surroundings, doing ordinary things like making coffee, climbing stairs, opening doors and so on, 'Radio Vérité', I suppose you could call it. I made all three of my *Pilgrim* programmes like this, using the ubiquitous BBC portable tape-recorder, the Uher, which, handled well, could produce an excellent and professional quality of recording. As I had spent almost every day of my life in Bristol lugging one of these machines about, there was nothing that I did not know about its idiosyncrasies.

The *Pilgrim's Way* person who was to make a radical change in my life was Donald Swann. The programme about him was made mainly at his home in Battersea, in his studio/study where he worked at his compositions and performances on a beautiful Broadwood baby grand. We got on rather well, we had similar ideas and I think we made each other laugh, which proved to be rather important to us both in the not too distant future.

All three *Pilgrims* were very well received and the BBC Programme Review Board commented that it was particularly satisfying that these programmes reached more deeply into their subjects than had been expected, in that they were not only entertaining and informative but at times 'moving and profound'. Perhaps it was on the strength of these programmes that I was asked to make a Radio 3 programme with Donald Swann about the interpretation of a poem that he had set to music.

Not long after arriving in Manchester, the head of religious broadcasting in London asked if I would take over the editorship of a Radio 2 series called *Pause for Thought*. The producer at that time was David Winter who passed over the programme, saying that he was honestly quite relieved to hand it on to me. It was definitely time, he said, to let someone else have a go.

Pause for Thought is not an easy programme to produce. The problem was, and is, that the vehicle for this particular religious strand is a light entertainment music programme. When David handed over the reins to me the Radio 2 morning sequence was being presented with airy and inconsequential good humour by Terry Wogan, and the religious 'slot' came between Frank Sinatra, Doris Day and the racing tips from Newmarket. Not an easy task for any religious broadcaster. David Winter had very sensibly decided that as it was a light entertainment music programme, he should endeavour to get broadcasters who were involved in that field. The difficulty is that there are simply not enough Christian singers or entertainers who are able to write original scripts. Whilst most are able and willing to express their faith, this kind of 'witnessing' soon becomes predictable and, I am afraid, repetitive.

At Radio Bristol I had tried a number of experiments in religious broadcasting, one of which was to present ideas and stories through imaginary characters. If the character is amusing, then blending into a light entertainment programme might be easier. At the same time if the blending is so smooth that you hardly notice it is happening, then all your efforts might be wasted; swallowed up, as it were.

It is said that the large majority of Radio 2 listeners stay with the station all the time. The channel is like a friend in the house, a pleasant, undemanding, occasionally amusing friend. Less kindly, some people have referred to Radio 2 music as 'wallpaper music', meaning that pleasant as wallpaper is to have around you, you don't spend a great deal of time looking at it. On the other hand, you do look at the pictures hanging on the wall. The 'pictures' are things like news and information, the weather forecast, and of course, guests in the programme. In the area I lived in in Manchester, the local library had a picture-borrowing scheme, whereby you could change your picture, usually a print of some famous work, every week. So, I thought, *Pause for Thought* should be an interesting picture on the wall, but one that changes every week.

I believe that the ideal *Pause for Thought* should 'entertain' at two levels. First, it should entertain on the surface, at a superficial level, that is to say the presentation should be amusing, clever, interesting, or simply a 'good listen'. The script should also entertain at a deeper and more important level, in its content. So that whilst during the actual broadcast you are 'held' by the presentation, during the piece of music that follows you should still be 'held' by the thought that was at the heart of the broadcast. As a producer all you need is to get people who can do that. Which is easier said than done. There are not many people who have the scripting skills to entertain at two levels, because, ideally, you need theological knowledge combined with an understanding of entertainment and story-telling.

There was a character called Margaret, played by the actress

Cass Allen, who also wrote her own scripts. Her character took texts from her kitchen calendar and mused on what they meant and how they applied to her. They were very good scripts and the character was popular. What I wanted was to find other forms of light entertainment scripts that would entertain at my two levels and complement 'Margaret'.

One of the characters that I had invented in Bristol was an old cowboy called Stubblechin Jones. For my first set of *Pause for Thought* scripts I decided to use this character to tell New Testament parables set in an imaginary place called Fishpool City. The stories were called, *Stubblechin Jones and the Tales of Preacher Claybody*. His signature tune was 'Hand me down that can of beans' from *Paint Your Waggon*. The stories had quite an impact. They were lively, funny, and presented by an amusing character – that was level one – and the content was pure New Testament; that was level two. Eventually *Stubblechin* came to the attention of the *Pick of the Week* team, and at the end of 1972 he appeared in the *Pick of the Year* programme which means that that particular broadcast has now been immortalised somewhere in the bowels of the BBC's archives.

One day a BBC producer rang me up and asked how he could get hold of Stubblechin Jones because he would like to have him as a guest on his music magazine. I told him that Stubblechin did not exist, that he was an imaginary character.

'Who is the performer then? Who plays the part?'

'I do.'

The stunned silence was followed by deep scepticism. The only way I could convince him was by producing Stubblechin Jones there and then on the phone.

And then he said, 'Well, the invitation still stands.'

The end result was that not only did Stubblechin appear as a guest telling stories but in time he was persuaded to sing. At first Stubblechin sang standards like 'Mine eyes have seen the Glory', and then I began to write some original songs and eventually the producer presented a *Stubblechin Jones Special*, an entire thirty-minute programme of the songs and stories of Stubblechin Jones.

Apart from editing the *Pause for Thought* programmes I was also producing other regular programmes such as *Sunday Half Hour* (Radio 2), *Choral Evensong* (Radio 3), *The People's Service* (Radio 2) and the outside broadcast from a church, *Sunday Service* (Radio 4).

In 1973 we moved to London, when I became the editor of several 'strands' of religious broadcasting. For a short while we lived in Guildford, and it was from Guildford that we went up to Scotland with the Drascombe Dabber again.

It was another time of exploring the island with our children, finding the secret lily pond and swimming in a bay with seals in the offing. That year we discovered an old ruined building on a hillside that led down to what looked like a miniature harbour, but in fact it was a disused tidal fish trap. When the tide was up a net had been stretched across the 'harbour' entrance so that when the tide ebbed the fish were trapped. The ruined building, we learned, was known to the islanders as the Uaini, pronounced 'ooni'. It means 'the green place'. We got very excited about an idea to restore the building and June and I even got as far as having tea with the Laird in her lovely house in Oban, but it was not to be.

That year the Darch family, Pam and Dave and their children, friends from Brighton days, came up to Scotland and camped on the mainland near Kerrera and joined us during the day. One night we rowed them back to the mainland in our Dabber. We had hoisted an oil lamp to the masthead and sang sea shanties as we rowed. The following day one of the islanders told us they had heard our singing and had looked out and seen our masthead light in the dark. We were a little concerned that we had disturbed the peace of the island, but when we apologised we were told, in that wonderfully precise and sibilant accent of the islanders of the West Coast, 'Och, there iss no need to apologise, you and the children were making such a happy sound. We were enjoying it. Sure you would have to be very miserable not to smile at children singing.'

We moved from Guildford after only a few months to live in Palmers Green in North London. We had the use of a Methodist minister's manse; oddly enough it was the manse that Derrick Greeves had lived in before he moved to Chelsea. It was very conveniently situated near a gate into Broomfield Park, a lovely park with an aviary, a garden of fragrances for the blind and two small, formal lakes in front of a house that used to be the home of Sir Thomas Lipton. This was to be our home for the next three or four years.

I don't suppose there was any direct influence, but we were living more or less just around the corner from where the poet Stevie Smith had lived, and it was here that I first began my attempts at blank verse. Actually I didn't 'attempt' to write them, they thrust themselves on to the blank pages in front of me, forced themselves into my pen. They didn't give me a great deal of choice really.

One of the characters that I introduced into *Pause for Thought* at that time was a Scouse, a Liverpudlian called Ginger Kelly. He was what the Irish and the Scottish Highlanders would call 'a wee bitty fey', which fitted in very well with the fey humour of Terry Wogan with his imaginary 'Vestal Virgins' dancing on the roof of the BBC. Ginger Kelly's 'feyness' involved a weekly telephone conversation with the Almighty. God's telephone number, by the way, is Jeremiah 333. (If you look it up in the Bible, Jeremiah, chapter 33, verse 3, you will find it says, 'Call on me, and I will answer you.')

Ginger Kelly was immensely popular for a number of years. CTVC (The Churches Television Centre) made a number of cassettes called 'Voices in my Mind' which featured Ginger.

Ginger's telephone conversations with God gradually revealed an entire community of people who lived in the streets around Ginger Kelly's home. He talked about the difficulties of bringing up children, the ups and downs of married life and about his relationship with the next-door neighbour, Billy Thompson, which was a kind of 'love-hate' relationship.

I had deliberately chosen the name Billy Thompson after the father of my old friend and colleague, in Manchester, John Thompson. Billy Thompson was the head of a large Catholic family, rich in nuns and priests, and he had been ill for a considerable length of time. For a long time he hovered uncertainly at death's door. Every now and then he would take a turn for the worse and his considerable family would fly to his bedside from a variety of places around the country, but time after time, from his bed, with the family gathered round, he would open one eye and make an apologetic joke about not having gone yet. Whenever my fictitious 'Billy' appeared in a Ginger Kelly script, neighbours from the local Catholic church would pop in and say, 'Eh, Billy! Ginger Kelly's after you!'

Years after the 'Ginger' series had finished there were a number of requests from listeners for his return. I did attempt to bring him back but, possibly without the sympathetic 'feyness' of Terry Wogan, his return was short-lived.

For special weeks, such as Holy Week, *Pause for Thought* might take the form of short dramas. One year John Farrell (who, thinking of 'feyness', could tell a fey Irish tale like nobody else I knew) wrote a series of passion 'cameos', conversations which took place in the Roman officers' mess, Jerusalem, when Pontius Pilate was Governor.

David Kossoff, of course, was telling his superb *Bible Stories* and his Rabbi stories. And Stuart Jackman, who wrote the controversial play *The Davidson Affair*, in which the Passion story takes place in modern times and is reported as news by radio and television reporters and the press, was also a regular contributor to *Pause for Thought*. One of his outstanding series was called *Conversations with my Conscience*, in which he talked himself in or out of various situations, arguing with his conscience, a very plain spoken character who seemed to be speaking from inside Stuart. This was achieved by a very subtle change of acoustics every time 'Conscience' spoke. Another regular on the team was Bernard Jackson. Every week we would meet to discuss which person, famous or otherwise, would make a good contribution to *Pause for Thought* through an interview or conversation.

One weekend, I had been away, preaching at Kingswood School in Bath. I had hoped to get home fairly early in order to write some scripts for a *Pause for Thought* studio booked for Monday morning. But as it turned out I was very late leaving and did not get back to Palmers Green much before midnight. I was very tired and yet I

knew that I dare not go to bed before I had written the four scripts
that would be expected in the studio on Monday morning. I began
to panic. I realised that I had left it too late. To write a series of
'Ginger' scripts required a good deal of craftsmanship; I couldn't
just dash them off. The same applied to any kind of script. What
on earth was I going to do?

The most difficult stage in writing, no matter what form of
writing, whether it is radio scripts, plays or novels, is beginning,
actually starting to write. The longer you put it off the more
difficult it becomes. Knowing this, I did what I frequently do
when desperate. I picked up my pen and began to write, anything,
the first thing that came into my head, hoping that by some magic in
the actual movement of the pen across the page, something would
emerge. The curious thing is that it usually does.

On this occasion I began to write about how I felt about
myself at that particular moment. Short, terse bursts of anger and
self-disgust. Not complete sentences but sharp little explosions of
words scratched across the page. Something like this . . .

Oh God. I'm tired.
Why am I such a fool?
Why do I always leave everything
To the last minute!

Not just work,
I procrastinate about life!
Dying, I'll protest
that I haven't had time
to get started!

Why? Idleness? Laziness? Fear?

Fear of failure?
After all, if you don't do anything,
You can't do it badly, or wrong.

You can't be judged. Can you?

> Dear God, who am I trying to fool?
> Forgive me for so much waste;
> Waste of talent,
> Waste of time,
> Waste of life.
>
> Lord, in your mercy
> Let me not live to be useless.

When I looked at my jagged scrawls across the page I saw that there was something there, something strong, something arresting in the way the words seemed to have fallen on to the blank sheet. Apart from quoting John Wesley in the last line, there was something fresh about it. If you are a script editor, over a period of time you see hundreds of scripts, and you develop an eye, a feeling for scripts. Just looking at a page sometimes – it's rare – but sometimes you can feel the hairs prickling the back of your neck, you feel goose pimples and you know that you are on to something. Looking at this page of scrawl I felt that something had been released. All I had to do was recognise whatever it was and use it.

You know when you have lost something, put it down some-where, but no matter how hard you look you simply cannot see it? The best thing to do in those circumstances is to retrace your steps very carefully, and suddenly you find what you have been looking for.

So I asked myself, 'What have I done? What was I trying to write?' I was trying to tell myself, honestly, with no frills, just exactly what I was feeling at that moment. And the undecorated, bald outburst of truth about myself was quite arresting. Now, supposing I try to write an undecorated, no-frills statement of what I feel is the truth about my relationship with my wife. Dare I put that on paper?

Could I write in a similar, open, honest way of how I feel about my children? My job? My faith? Suddenly it was four in the morn-ing and I had a set of scripts, nothing like any that I had ever written before. I was a little worried that they might be too explicit, too personal; but it was far too late now to do anything else, so I would just have to go ahead with them.

At the BBC I chose a piece of music, the Adagietta from Rodrigo's *Guitar Concerto*. The scripts seemed to fit the music like a glove, as if they had been written to complement each other, giving time to listen to the words and to listen to the music.

The day after the first of these scripts had been broadcast, I arrived at my office at the BBC to find that an unusually large amount of mail was waiting for me. It was all in response to the broadcast. The following day there was more mail and there was a telephone call from programme enquiries saying that they had rather a lot of mail about the *Pause for Thought* broadcasts and did I want it sent to my office. During the week Terry Wogan's office rang up to say the same thing.

At first there was a feeling of success. Gosh! I must have hit the nail on the head. What a wonderful response! But the euphoria began to evaporate rapidly as I started to read the letters. One after another, people poured out their anxieties, their problems, their pain. 'Your broadcast,' they said, 'could have been written for me.' 'You have put into words what I have felt for years but could never express.' 'I feel that you would understand . . . that you would be sympathetic . . . that you could help.'

There were letters from people who were ill, or who were dying, from people whose marriages were breaking up, who had lost their jobs, or who were seriously distressed about their children. My first concern was how could I answer these people? What did I know about terminal illnesses, or redundancies, or the wide variety of problems that all these people were writing about? Nevertheless, I felt that I should attempt to answer the letters even if I could not possibly give advice to everyone. Sometimes I could suggest a line of action that people might take, or sometimes I could make suggestions about people in their own area they might turn to for help, but frequently the only thing I could do was say, 'I'll pray for you.'

Some months later it was suggested that I should repeat these 'meditational' broadcasts. Although I was persuaded to do so, I didn't seriously think that they would have the same response as the first time. I was wrong. For a second time the letters came flooding in. And it became clear to me that when you are broadcasting to millions of people, every day some of those people learn that they have a terminal illness, every day some people hear bad news about their work, their health or their families. Because of the large amount of correspondence it was decided that we should attempt to have a meditational broadcast once a week, every week.

My sense of inadequacy about being able to respond to people's needs and concerns was eased a great deal as I began to realise that in most cases the real therapy had already occurred in the listener's initial letter. In actually putting a problem on to paper you isolate it, reduce it, make it clearer to yourself and therefore because you have its measure you are able to understand it and deal with it or, at the least, fear it less.

Often people say things like, 'I have so many problems, I don't know where to begin.'

But if we try to write out a list of our concerns it becomes clear that we do not have a multitude of problems, but only one or two, from which everything else stems. Perhaps we have only one grievous problem, which so colours all our thinking that it seems, by association, that everything is a problem.

Time and again I have been convinced that the Holy Spirit has spoken to people through these broadcasts. Listeners have written from opposite ends of the country, from totally different situations and concerns saying, of the same script, 'I felt that your broadcast spoke directly to my need.'

And I have felt bound to reply saying something like this: 'If you feel that you have been guided or helped, in any way, through this programme, please be assured that it is not me, but the Holy Spirit who is speaking to you through the broadcast.'

If, all those years ago, I questioned what on earth I was doing in the ministry, or what on earth an actor with a gift for dialects had to offer God, or the Church, I now know that it has less to do with the gifts of those who are called, and more to do with God's love reaching people in spite of the inadequacies of the messengers.

Not long after these broadcasts began, Alec Gilmore, who was then the commissioning editor of Lutterworth Press, and himself a regular broadcaster of religious programmes, wrote to me to ask if Lutterworth could publish a collection of my meditational scripts as a book. The first short anthology, *Lord of the Morning*, was published in 1977.

8   Swann with Topping

In the summer of 1975 we took the Drascombe Dabber down
to Keyhaven and sailed across to the Isle of Wight. In Shalfleet,
alongside the quay, we saw a small but beautiful little cruiser, a
Finesse, mahogany on oak, brass fittings, brass portholes. In short,
it was love at first sight. Both June and I were enchanted by it. We
met the owners, John Hyatt and Barbara his wife, who were fellow
members of the Hurst Castle Sailing Club. They invited us on
board, and by the time we left we had made an offer to buy their
boat. By the end of the summer we had bought it. As a family we
decided that it had to be called the *Wildcat*, which is the name of
the yacht in Arthur Ransome's book, *Peter Duck*, the book that we
had read together on Kerrera.

We started our 1976 holiday by sailing to the Isle of Wight,
around to the east side of the island, to Bembridge Harbour. We
intended to collect Anne from Portsmouth but when the day came
it was far too windy, so Anne took the ferry to Ryde and we met her
there. We then sailed from Bembridge, after some difficulty getting
out of the harbour because of a rather powerful form of seaweed
that had begun to take over and could clog a boat's propeller in
no time. We sailed into Newtown river which is almost opposite
the Beaulieu river on the mainland.

As you enter the Newtown river you have the choice of continuing up to Shalfleet or taking the inlet that goes to Newport. As
we only wanted to stop the night and then continue west toward
Christchurch Bay and Poole, we took the Newtown turning and
moored alongside several other bigger yachts also spending the night
there. We had dropped our anchor in order to bring us in line with

the other anchored yachts and our stern swung round to lie about fifty or sixty feet from a tidebreak, a wall of rocks placed there, no doubt to protect the shoreline from erosion.

By the early hours of the morning the wind had become very strong; out in the Solent it was probably blowing a Force 8 gale. I woke up suddenly and looked out of my porthole. We did not seem to have moved. I lay my head down and almost immediately heard an ominous rumble. I sat bolt upright and looked out again. We were slowly moving away from the other anchored yachts. Then I realised what the rumble was: we were dragging our anchor!

I leapt out of my bunk, shouting to the others, 'We're dragging our anchor!' We had to do something quickly because we were moving, slowly but surely, towards the tidebreak and the rocks. Out in the cockpit I could see that we were also dragging sideways towards quite a big yacht, the *Cenarea*, lying alongside us. Considering how little space we had on our boat it was amazing how quickly everyone was out and about and doing something useful. Simon was getting out the spare anchor, June was standing by to fend off the *Cenarea*, which we came alongside very swiftly. We did not crash into her, just gently knocked twice, like someone coming to call. We immediately caught hold of her with lines to stop our sternwards drift towards the rocks.

At this moment the owner of the *Cenarea* emerged to see what was going on. He took in the scene very quickly and pointed out, quite calmly, that his anchor would not hold both yachts for long. Miraculously, the *Wildcat*'s engine started first time. Anne was at the helm, and Mark, who was officially designated 'Engineer', was at the engine controls, gears and acceleration. I warned our crew that we were about to let go of the *Cenarea* and therefore would need full throttle forwards. We let slip the lines we had hitched on to the *Cenarea*. I went forward to take up the anchor chain as we slowly moved forward. Suddenly we were free of the *Cenarea* and moving forward slowly into the teeth of a very strong wind.

We moved into the channel of the river and headed for the junction with the Shalfleet lake. There was no way that we would even consider poking our nose out into the Solent. What we wanted to do was re-anchor safely, or pick up an empty mooring buoy. This was far easier said than done. It was very dark, there were no lights of any kind, the wind was strong and the water rough. June went up into the pulpit at the bows with a torch and I took over the helm from Anne, who went to add an extra pair of sharp eyes to the pulpit look-out. We turned into the Shalfleet river, trying to keep well away from the lines of moored yachts, which we could not actually see.

It had been the combination of wind and high tide, and the fact that we had not paid out enough chain that had lifted our anchor. Although we were in line with the other yachts, their anchors must have been considerably further out on much longer chains than ours. In our progress towards Shalfleet that night we actually sailed over a landing jetty. The jetty was submerged beneath the high tide. It was only when we passed, very close, to the wrong side of the post that marked the end of the jetty that we realised where our course had taken us but, somehow, we touched nothing.

At the helm I was almost totally blind. From the bow June was shouting directions, 'Go left! Left! Left! Go right! Steady as you are!' Eventually we came to another junction in the river and here we decided on a second attempt at anchoring. If we could anchor with our stern towards the spit of land that formed the junction, even if we dragged anchor again, here we could only drag on to mud. Nevertheless, we let out the maximum amount of chain and this time we were firmly anchored.

How we managed to tear along that river in the dark and not actually hit anything I will never know, but somehow we escaped without a scratch. However, it was a very frightening way of learning about the height of the rise and fall of a tide and the compensating amount of chain that must be paid out to keep you attached to the ground.

It was not possible now to go straight back to our bunks; too much adrenalin had been flowing. We all needed to wind down. So with dawn's first light beginning to reveal the obstacle course that we had just sailed through, we put the kettle on and dug into a hearty and early breakfast. You will not be surprised to hear that June and I enrolled in a Royal Yachting Association Yachtmaster theory class that September, a class that we followed through both theory and practical training at sea for the next two years, completing the Coastal Skipper's course and the Yachtmaster Offshore course.

The rest of that holiday was spent, happily, in glorious sunshine in Poole Harbour, around Brownsea Island and in Studland Bay. We had an inflatable dinghy which enabled us to scull to sandy beaches and to flop in and out of the water for swimming.

Over the next few years both June and I became immersed in sailing. All our spare time was spent sailing in tall ships, or Ocean Youth Club ketches, or in our own and other people's boats. June went a great deal further than me, acquiring every conceivable qualification certificate in sailing, from motor boat handling and dinghy sailing, and marine radio operating, to becoming an Offshore Yachtmaster, an RYA Senior Sailing Instructor and, as if that were not enough, she has recently taken up sailboard sailing.

During this time I continued to produce *Pause for Thought* and the meditations became a regular part of the output for a number of years. To my surprise my first book, *Lord of the Morning*, sold extremely well for a religious book, and soon had to be reprinted. It was published in America by the Fortress Press and was translated into Chinese in Hong Kong.

Life in the Religious Department of the BBC in London offered me a great variety of opportunities. I wrote a nativity play with songs, in some ways a companion play to *On the Hill*. The nativity play was called *A Particular Star* and it was produced on Radio 4 by Angela Tilby. The play is set on Merseyside or, more particularly, on a Mersey ferry boat. Joseph and Mary are a homeless couple, the Three Shepherds are local shipyard workers, and the Wise Men are a Polish refugee, a school teacher, and a Catholic priest.

In those days almost all Daily Services came from All Souls, Langham Place, and were conducted week by week by the department's staff on a rota. I think the first time the Daily Service did not come from London was when the BBC singers were in Manchester, which happened to be when I was the RBA North and I conducted the service from a BBC studio concert hall in Manchester. As all Daily Services were live broadcasts, you can imagine my alarm when I realised that the studio clock had stopped. This meant doing sums on a stopwatch in order to finish, as we did in those days, neatly, in time for the Greenwich time signal. I can tell you, that was nerve-racking, to put it mildly!

Radio 4's *Thought for the Day* was being presented as a recorded programme because of a broadcast made by the Reverend Dr Colin Morris. At the time he made the broadcast a Bill was being presented in the House of Commons which was about the repatriation of immigrants. I think the Bill was going to require immigrants to be at least second generation in the UK if they were to be allowed to stay. Dr Morris spoke very strongly and very amusingly against it. He pointed out that a considerable number of Life peers would probably not qualify for permanent residence under this Bill, and possibly quite a few sitting Members of Parliament. He said that the Bill was not only sub-Christian but sub-human. He listed a number of parliamentarians with rather foreign sounding names and wondered if they would be able to prove that their grandfathers were British. When he finished he handed back, leaning rather heavily on the presenter's name, which was Jack De Manio.

There was an uproar from the Commons with letters flying to the Director General of the BBC. Now I would have thought that the one freedom one could expect as an automatic right for any presenter of *Thought for the Day* was freedom of thought and freedom of speech, providing it was within the bounds of propriety and the law. As far as I can see Dr Morris offended neither, and surely he was entitled to express his opinion. One might have expected the BBC to have replied on those lines. But to the amazement of many, the BBC issued an apology saying that the broadcast was 'an error of judgment' on the part of the Religious Department producer. And Dr Morris was not heard on the radio for some time, at least a year, I think. Rather amusing to think that in later years Dr Morris not only became Head of Religious Broadcasting in the BBC, but also became a very senior member of BBC management as head of the BBC in Northern Ireland.

Michael Mayne was the Head of Religious Radio when I moved

down to London in 1973. Two years later, in 1975, although I was the editor of *Pause for Thought* Michael asked if I would also look after *Thought for the Day* on Radio 4. I was very keen to get it back to being a live broadcast and not a recording, and so was Michael. I went to see the producer of the *Today* programme to discuss the possibilities. He reiterated the old argument that there was no control over a live *Thought*. More particularly *he* had no control over the *Thought* slot. I could appreciate his argument. I would not be a hundred per cent happy if I was the editor of a radio news magazine in which there was a slot that was just taken out of my hands by another department and I had no say about what went into that particular part of the programme.

I suggested that the *Thought* producer should not be an 'outsider' but part of the team and that the contributor and subject could be changed if he, the editor, thought that a particular topic should be addressed. He said that sounded attractive but in the end once you give somebody a live microphone they could say anything they wanted to. I pointed out that he had to trust every *other* live broadcaster who appeared on his programme and they ranged from politicians to criminals and from people being interviewed in the studio to those broadcasting from a radio car. Was he saying that the only person he could not trust was a parson? And wasn't this insistence on the religious broadcast being pre-recorded so that it could be vetted as 'safe', a form of discrimination that was not compatible with the concept of freedom of speech usually associated with the BBC? In order to allay further fears I offered to be in the studio myself every morning to check the script of every *Thought* contributor.

In the end it was agreed that I would liaise with him about my contributors and that I would be in the studio to go over the script or put any suggestions to the contributor that might help his piece relate to the rest of the programme.

Thought for the Day was live again. It ran into controversy almost immediately, mainly because I invited controversial people to present the *Thought*. Radical politicians from different parties, priests whose faith demanded political involvement, mixed with good story-tellers and preachers and theologians. Oddly, it was frequently the messenger rather than the message that was attacked. For instance, there was more 'thunder' from 'upstairs' and management 'sabre rattling' when I invited Mary Whitehouse to contribute her *Thought* (on the Child Pornography Bill,) than ever occurred with any other contributor throughout the time I was the producer of *Thought for the Day*.

At the same time I was still looking for ideas for the *Pause for Thought* programmes. By chance one day I met Donald Swann in a corridor in Broadcasting House. As he walked towards me an idea sprang into my mind and, after our initial greetings, I said, 'Donald, if I wrote the lyrics, do you think we could write a song a week for thirteen weeks?' Donald blinked for a bit and then said, 'Well, I suppose we could try.'

It was in 1976. A pattern began to develop: over the weekend I would write a lyric and on Monday I would take it to Donald's house in Battersea. A day or so later, or sometimes the same day, we would be rehearsing and recording the completed song. The songs were recorded at first in a small studio, without an audience. This was perfectly acceptable for songs that did not require an audible response, but with humorous songs not having an audience was rather strange. It was like telling jokes to people who were not allowed to laugh. However, the songs seemed to work. They certainly attracted attention, and quite a warm response from the listeners. Again, *Pick of the Week* tuned in and gave us a second airing.

Pick of the Week of course is a Radio 4 programme, which meant that devoted Radio 4 listeners heard our Radio 2 contributions. Not surprisingly, when I was in the *Today* studio with my *Thought for the Day* contributor, Brian Redhead or John Timpson, having heard the *Pick of the Week* programme, pulled my leg about being a Radio 2 'singing' star. I think it was Brian Redhead who said, 'Those songs that you do with Donald Swann, they're more Radio 4 than 2, don't you think?' The upshot was that we decided to try a few of the songs on the *Today* programme because some of them were very immediate and topical. Well, you can't get music much more contemporary than a song written yesterday afternoon.

Between 1977 and 1978 we wrote about thirty new songs. The

response on Radio 4 was absolutely marvellous. However, we were convinced that if we were to continue writing songs for the radio the recordings had to be made in the presence of a studio audience. In fact both of us had songs tucked up our sleeves that required audience participation. Accordingly, in early 1979, we booked a fairly large studio in Broadcasting House, S1, and arranged for chairs to be brought in for forty or fifty people. People were informally invited to attend the recording session, BBC colleagues and their families, other broadcasters, actors and musicians, friends who would be appreciative, hopefully.

It was the informality of our invitation that was our undoing. We did not send tickets, simply an invitation. 'Do come, if you can, and bring a friend.' And they did. They brought their sisters and their brothers and their fathers and their mothers, their uncles and their aunts . . . and their second cousins too! A few hasty telephone calls and new arrangements were made. We were lucky that the BBC Concert Hall in Broadcasting House was not being used so we moved there. Instead of forty or fifty, the audience was nearer a hundred and forty or fifty.

We did not immediately realise what this meant in terms of performance. Instead of forty or so people sitting on the same level as the performers in a studio with acoustic pegboards on the walls, the audience were now sitting in plush theatre seats in steeply rising stalls, and Donald and I were on a wide sweeping orchestral stage. The setting transformed the performance. It was not a studio performance, it was a theatre performance. The environment demanded that you pull out a few stops. I had written some linking material so that even in the studio setting there would be some flow and continuity to the session, a few stories, some light relief between the songs, but this audience more than drew us out of our shells.

Our audience consisting, as they did, mainly of actors, writers, broadcasters and their families and friends, had come along willing to play the part of a good audience. They were, of course, excellent, and our performance had to rise to theirs. The warmth of their response released something in us. Like the rubbing of Aladdin's lamp, some genie was set free, a genie who cast a spell over performers and audience, a genie who had a vast barrel of stories and voices and jokes into which he could dip, and whose timing was impeccable. Telling a story under this spell the audience anticipated the coming of the joke; I can see in my mind's eye Gerald Priestland and Sydney Carter chuckling in expectation, encouraging with half laughs and then letting rip with the big one on the punchline. All this went without a single prompt or cue because audience and performers were one. The recording had an uproarious Hoffnungian quality to it. The result was that when the extracts were broadcast in the *Today* programme they sounded like extracts from a West End show.

One Monday, shortly after this recording, Donald and I were working on a lyric in Donald's house in Battersea when the telephone rang. Donald answered it, and after a conversation in which Donald seemed to be agreeing with someone rather a lot, he hung up the telephone and said, 'That was an invitation to bring our show to the Opera House in Jersey next April. He sounded a rather nice chap so I agreed.'

'But Donald,' I said, 'we haven't got a show.'

'That's true,' said Donald, 'but we do have until April to write it.'

It is not always easy to write and plan when the telephone or the doorbell keeps ringing. We never seemed to be able to achieve an uninterrupted hour, so we decided to move away from the bells for a short time; anywhere out of reach would do.

In October 1979, rather out of season for boating, but a quiet time to be on the Norfolk Broads, Donald and I hired a little wooden old-fashioned Broads cruiser called *Water Gypsy*. The idea was to find the seclusion that we felt was needed to work on our show. I arranged with a local Methodist church, the one at Thurne, to have access to their church hall and the use of their piano. Donald was not able to get to Norfolk for the first day so we agreed that I should pick up the boat in Wroxham and take it to Norwich. The river is very close to the station in Norwich so it would be quite convenient for me to moor alongside the quay at the yacht station on the River Wensum and simply cross the road to Thorpe Station to meet the London train.

Actually it is quite a long way from Wroxham to Norwich by boat, so I wasted no time in setting off. I planned to sail under the Vauxhall Bridge above Great Yarmouth Harbour on the last of the ebb tide so that the incoming flood would take me across Breydon Water and up the River Yare.

This might sound a bit daft, but what follows can best be imagined if you can visualise what I was wearing. Because most of my sailing at that time was coastal, my sailing clothes were more appropriate to being at sea than on the Broads. I was wearing a polo-necked sweater, a navy double-breasted seaman's reefer jacket, Navy trousers tucked into seaboots and seaman's white seaboot stockings rolled over the top of the boots. On my head I had a black peaked cap with an embroidered Royal Yachting Association badge. The gold wire of the crown in the badge had gone green with the mildew caused by exposure to seawater and air. In a word I looked a modern version of a bearded Ancient Mariner, and somewhat over the top for the Norfolk Broads.

I was using a pair of binoculars to pick out the position of the channel markers ahead when, through the mist, I caught sight of a building which appeared to be at the end of a promontory. I consulted the chart (note the technical term!) and saw that it could possibly be a public house, rather isolated, probably there to serve the holiday boating trade. I looked at my watch and thought, 'Good. I should get there before closing time if I get a move on.' So I opened up the *Water Gypsy*'s little throttle as far as I dared and made for what was now emerging as the pub jetty.

Having executed a reasonably successful single-handed, 'coming-alongside', I tied up, strode along the path to the pub door and lifted the latch. I don't know quite what I expected but somehow the pub being completely empty took me by surprise. Well, it wasn't completely empty. Behind the bar was a barman. I made a second false assumption in expecting to hear the light tune of a Norfolk dialect from this barman, but when I said, 'Hello. Could I have a pint of Guinness, please?' his reply was in broad, unmistakable, Glaswegian. 'Ay, I'm sorry but there's nae Guinness.'

I managed to conceal my surprise by keeping both of my eyebrows firmly in place. 'Ah, I see. Do you have any stout?'

He did not hesitate or look under his counter but answered, immediately, 'No. There nae stout either.'

I laughed an embarrassed little laugh. 'Ha, ha. Don't tell me I've come to the original "pub with no beer"?'

This time he did glance swiftly under his counter. 'We've two cans of pale ale, an tha's all.'

He could see that I was now not just puzzled but bewildered. He attempted to explain. 'See, we close at two o'clock.'

That did not exactly answer all my questions, so I asked, 'Do you always run out of beer at two o'clock?'

He threw back his head and laughed. 'Och no! I mean that today we close for the rest of the year!'

Suddenly the penny dropped. Nevertheless, I was still amazed that he had managed to run down his stock to the last two cans of pale ale. I bought one of the cans, which he opened and poured into a glass for me. I paid for it and then went to a table in a corner, by a window, so that I could look out on the river. In those days I used to smoke small cigars, so I sat down and lit up.

I don't know if everybody at some stage in their life experiences a sense of not being welcome, but on this occasion I became aware of a distinctly hostile, frosty attitude emanating from a woman who appeared from the nether regions of the pub and began to pick up chairs and put them upside-down on the tables around me. She then began to sweep the floor around my feet. I was aware of her sneaking ill-concealed hostile glances at me. Every time I knocked cigar ash into my ashtray, in a flash she emptied it into a bucket and flicked at the ashtray with a duster produced from her apron. I don't know if her behaviour was part of a deliberate plan to force an exchange of words, but after she had done the ashtray emptying twice, I was beginning to feel a bit oppressed, so I said, 'If you leave the bucket by the table, I will put my ash into it, directly.' This was the opening she had clearly been working for. She said, with an accent that was as Lancashire as Gracie Fields, 'Excuse me, luv, but are you a German?'

I began to think that I had wandered on to the set of a Pinter play, or perhaps it was Franz Kafka in translation.

'A German? Whatever gave you that idea?'

She sniffed. 'Your English is too good for an Englishman.'

I was baffled, so I just said, 'Well, I *am* English, and always have been.'

She was clearly unmoved and unconvinced. She delivered her knock-out punch. 'The moment you walked through that door I said to m'self, "U-boat commander"!'

The mind boggled. The thought of a German U-boat commander surfacing from two inches of Breydon Water in the late nineteen-seventies, walking into a Norfolk pub and asking for a glass of Guinness in a too perfect English accent, almost defeated me, but not quite. I remembered that for my mother all history was in the present. She had no sense of time or distance. To my mother London was 'far away', just as Hong Kong was 'far away'. Four centuries after the Dissolution of the Monasteries she could walk into an Anglican cathedral and say, 'This is one of ours, isn't it, Frank?' Clearly, my Norfolk Gracie Fields had the same 'mind set' as my mother. I knew that I could reiterate my denial about being a German U-boat commander, but I also knew that it was unlikely to be believed. I did reiterate. She sniffed and swept off, leaving me the bucket.

When I came to leave, I walked over to the door and lifted the latch. The Gracie Fields lady was standing behind the bar with the Scotsman. I turned to say thank you and goodbye. They were both staring at me.

I could not resist it. I clicked my heels and bowed, '*Auf Wiedersehen, Fräulein.*'

As I turned back to the door I caught sight of Gracie elbowing the Scotsman and saying, 'I told yer! Din't I? I told yer!'

On our return from the wilds of Norfolk we continued to work on the show. We tried out some of our work with Sydney Carter in a concert at St James in Piccadilly. We also continued to write songs for broadcasts. I was aware that people would make comparisons with Michael Flanders. We were both bass baritones, bearded and English but we had little else in common. I worried, without need, about Michael's widow, Claudia. Would she resent someone playing her husband's part? I was to discover that Claudia was an exceedingly generous woman. She came to see our show a number of times and every time she was full of encouragement and advice. She said, quite rightly, that I laughed too much, that the humour was stronger when it came from a straight face. Michael Flanders, a superb performer, with a genius for humorous verse, was very sparing with his smiles on stage. I knew that I did not have his gifts, nor did I wish to attempt to imitate him. I do have a gift for regional and national accents and dialects, and somehow the timing of a story always seems to come out right. I knew that the only thing I could do was use what gifts I had to the best of my ability.

The first few months of 1980 sped by and suddenly it was April. We had an informal dress rehearsal with a few friends in Donald's house in Battersea. Then we flew to Jersey. At first there was some concern about the sale of tickets, but then one evening the doctor, a local GP whom we were staying with, a relation of Marian McDonald, my secretary at the BBC, came home bearing good news. 'It's going to be all right,' he said. 'It's going to be a sell-out.' Naturally we wanted to know why he felt so sure about this, and he told us, 'The Governor is going. Anything that he attends officially is always attended by everyone who considers himself to be prominent in Jersey society.' If you know that living on this small island there are over eleven hundred known millionaires, you will also realise that there are quite a few people who consider themselves to be 'prominent'.

I wish I could do justice to the encouragement and practical support that Marian McDonald gave throughout the whole of this time. She was and is a true friend.

We had a delightful surprise on opening night. June turned up in our dressing room at the Opera House in Jersey, just before we went on. People who sing the virtues of their partners run the risk of being suspected of either sentimentality or self-indulgence, but I am prepared to take that risk because the memory of June coming to the theatre has brought a rush of other incidents to mind, typified by this particular memory. So often it has been my lot to be the one on the platform, behind the microphone or in front of a camera, but there is no such thing as a 'one-man show'. Throughout my career, in all the wild projects and enterprises,

I have always known her enthusiasm and encouragement, her comfort when things have not worked out. Her unshakable faith in our shared adventure is so much a part of me that I could easily adopt the royal 'we' in telling my story. I have been supported by her love in thousands of ways, and her turning up at the theatre was a practical and typical example of her love.

The airline tickets to Jersey, for Donald and me, were paid for by the backers of the Opera House Show. However, they did not throw in tickets for our wives. On the other hand June had decided that she was going to be there. She arranged for a theatre ticket to be reserved for her. She travelled the cheapest way, which included an overnight ferry, sleeping on a bench surrounded by the merry sounds of late-night revellers and the resounding noise of bottles breaking at frequent intervals. Her description of the journey horrified me. For the return journey I managed to get her a seat on an aeroplane, but it was typical of her that she made such a wonderful effort to be there. It was a lovely and loving gesture, and so good to know that there would be at least one vociferous supporter in the stalls.

The performance at the Opera House was a great success with both audience and critics. We had decided to call the show quite simply, *Swann with Topping*. A Jersey clergyman had designed a very clever poster which incorporated a swan in the 'S' of Swann and an inverted top hat formed the first letter of Topping. The design was so simple and effective that we asked for permission to use it in our publicity material when we opened in the London Fringe Theatre.

There are few, if any, experiences to compare with performing before a packed and excited theatre; roars of laughter that echo in your mind for years, and gasps of silence so intense that you can hear people breathing. Later, at the Edinburgh Festival Fringe, I found that the size of the audience was not as important to the performance as the relationship created between actor and audience, the magic that you mutually consent to share. It is a very potent medicine to pour into anyone's veins. I was then and I am now, hooked. I chose the word 'magic', deliberately, because in many ways it is still a mystery to me. I know that Ralph Richardson said that acting was just a 'trick', but I am not convinced about that. If it was only a trick then presumably anyone could learn to do it, just follow the formula and Hey Presto! Magic! There is, I think, more to it than that. 'Magic' was a key word for us in writing and rehearsing. Donald would frequently say, 'We must create magic.'

Walking into an empty theatre on a wet afternoon, I have sometimes found it hard to imagine that the same spell will be cast, that the same relationship, the same unspoken contract between audience and actors will be agreed, the 'willing suspension of disbelief' when for an hour or two we are no longer in Woking, or Liverpool, or London, but in North Africa in 1943, or medieval Italy, or wherever the play takes us. An hour before the audience arrives, walking across a dark and lifeless stage and into the dressing room corridor, you wonder if it will happen again. Then through the dressing-room speakers you hear the audience beginning to take their seats. There is a knock on your door and a disembodied voice calls out, 'Beginners please!' The excited hubbub of voices suddenly dies as the houselights dim. The curtain or a stage light rises, an actor speaks . . . and there it is, the spell is cast.

Later still, if direction, writing and actors are gifted, we find we have not simply been taken to a place, but into the heart and mind and life of a make-believe character. So deeply involved are we, that when this person smiles, we smile, when they weep, we weep, and when we leave the theatre, we take arguments, feelings and experience with us. This is not just a trick, or sleight of hand, it is genuinely deep magic.

The news of our success spread and very shortly after our return from Jersey negotiations were opened for us to take the show into the London Fringe. There was still a great deal of work to be done, tightening up the script, writing new songs and improving those we had already performed.

I was still fulfilling my normal BBC workload. There was very little free time in this year. My second book, *Lord of the Evening*, had been published the previous year and this year the third book in the series came out, called *Lord of my Days*. These three books proved to be so popular that the following year all three were published together in a special hardback edition.

When a new book is issued a good deal of work is put into its launching. Publishers try to arrange 'events' that will help to publicise the book. Radio and television interviews, national or local, guest appearances wherever they can be arranged, bookshop signings, literary luncheons or suppers. David Kossoff once told me it was possible that more of his books were sold at the conclusion of his evening entertainments than were sold over bookshop counters. For this reason publishers are always pleased to have an author who is involved in any form of public life, or is at least willing to 'go on the road' with a new book.

On July 17th, 1980 Donald and I opened at the Upstream Theatre Club in Short Street, Waterloo, opposite the Young Vic and just down the road from the Old Vic. Although this was an extremely pressurised period, it was also a very exciting and happy time. Upstream Theatre is a church hall conversion, a visionary enterprise of the parish church of St James. The full title of the theatre is 'Upstream with St James'. One of my favourite songs from our show was written with Upstream in mind. It is called 'The Salmon and the Trout'; both are fish that go upstream, against the flow, in order to reach their spawning grounds. Donald sang the dreamy tenor 'Trout' part:

> I hear you calling, how like a dream,
> Pools of enchantment, far up the stream.

And I played, or sang, the 'Salmon' part, a bold, north-country, 'self-made' fish:

> Jump! Jump! Jump!
> Oh, I can hear the trump, trump, trump
> that's calling from the deep, deep, deep
> That's calling me to where the Salmon leap!

We sang it as an Edwardian parlour duet, and as the last song in the show, ending on a very high *and* an extremely low note, it was always received with warmth and a great deal of laughter.

Battersea, where we spent so many hours working on the show, also inspired a song which embraced all the glamour of Battersea Park, the dogs' home and the power station.

Upstream Theatre Club was supported by a very faithful body of subscription members, and the advance publicity quickly resulted in 'sell-out' houses so far ahead that we were, in fact, sold out for our entire run at that little theatre.

I am not sure whether or not any other new show opened in London on our opening night, or whether it was entirely due to our excellent publicity manager, but for whatever reason, one by one, nearly all the theatre critics of the national press turned up, certainly most of the national broadsheet newspapers. I can remember the excitement backstage as people from the front of house sent messages saying, 'John Barber of the *Daily Telegraph* is here!', closely followed by breathless and hysterical whispers hissing, 'Good heavens! *The Times* and *The Financial Times* are here!' The reviews were extremely good. John Barber wrote, 'As fresh as the first crocus ... Songs serious about funny things, songs funny about serious things. I enjoyed myself hugely.'

On the morning after the first night, unknown to us, the impresario, Harold Fielding, telephoned John Barber to confirm that he really meant what he said, that he was not being generous to Donald for old times' sake. On the second night Harold Fielding came to see the show for himself. The following morning, at Donald's house in Battersea, the telephone rang. There was not much conversation. Donald said things like, 'Really?' and 'Well, that's marvellous!' Not much else. When he hung up there was a seraphic smile on his face. He turned to me and said, 'We've done it.' As I had no idea what he was talking about I said, 'Done what?' Donald laughed his famous laugh and said, 'That was Harold Fielding, the impresario. He wants to transfer us to the West End.'

A few days later found us in Fielding House, in Bruton Street off Berkeley Square discussing the possibilities with Harold Fielding. It was like a dream, like something out of one of those glamorous Anna Neagle and Michael Wilding films, *Maytime in Mayfair* or *Spring in Park Lane*. Even the language was strange to me. When

Harold started to talk about the design of the 'electric sign', it took me some time to realise that he was talking about our names and the title of the show being put up in lights outside the theatre.

Of course we still had a contract to complete with the Upstream Theatre and you cannot simply move straight into the West End. A theatre has to be found, the right theatre. In our case it turned out to be the Ambassadors, next door to *The Mousetrap* at the St Martin's in West Street, off Cambridge Circus, Shaftesbury Avenue. A public relations agency was employed to publicise the show. This involved photocalls in strange places in order to sell a story to a newspaper. Generally speaking, an article or a feature in a national newspaper is far more valuable than hundreds of classified advertisements. The articles and the linked subjects are sometimes stretched in order to make a credible link. For instance we had written a song that mentioned Battersea Dogs' Home. A photocall was therefore arranged at Battersea Dogs' Home that resulted in a photograph of me holding some poor unfortunate dog and an article in the *Daily Express* under the headline, 'THE TAIL OF TWO WAGS'. This was followed by a jokey article about Donald and I planning to raise the 'Woof' at the Ambassadors.

Our daughters, Natasha and Anne, were photographed buying seafood from a street stall at the end of West Street on the grounds that we had written a song about fish. It was all a bit daft, exciting, and a great deal of fun.

There were a great number of radio interviews and several television appearances. Perhaps the biggest 'coup' pulled off by our public relations agency was being interviewed by Sue Lawley on the BBC television evening news sequence. A lot of these appearances depend, as it were, on the luck of the draw, or rather what's in the news. Somebody might be interested in your slot as an amusing filler, so the item would be used if it wasn't pushed off the running order by stronger news stories.

Here all my experience in local radio of having to adapt to any programme and to think on one's feet came into its own. Some interviewers knew exactly where they were going, others more or less handed the spot over to us. We needed to be armed with items from the show that we could adapt to whatever current news story was the talking point of the day. This experience has proved useful ever since.

In the last few weeks I have been appearing on breakfast television reviewing the papers. That is a very immediate thing to have to do. It is so early in the morning that you haven't had time to read through all the papers. You learn to skim at speed through the summaries, picking up whatever catches your eye. On the air there is no script, you either think on your feet or you are not likely to be asked very often. It is possibly this acquired ability to provide instant comment that has resulted, on several occasions, in being called on in emergencies to do live *Pause for Thoughts* or *Thoughts for the Day*.

For instance, at the time of that terrible day when Lord Mountbatten was murdered, all three of the radio religious slots, *Pause for Thought*, *Thought for the Day* and *Prayer for the Day* were pre-recorded and none of them were appropriate. I was called that day to present 'live' alternatives to the recorded programmes. A similar thing occurred when the Gulf War began. That evening I went into the BBC and listened to the news as it came in from the Middle East throughout the night, making 'live' comment whenever it was requested. During the run of *Swann with Topping*, I was called to appear on many kinds of programmes as an instant expert on all things moral, ethical or religious. On one particular programme, discussing the reform of insurance policies I was asked what I thought about the 'Act of God' clause. My reply seemed to throw the 'insurance experts' in the studio into some confusion. I said, 'Well, apart from being rather weary of people blaming God for anything and everything they can't explain, I think the "Act of God" clause is grossly unfair to atheists.'

This was greeted by the silent raising of eyebrows. So I continued, 'It also presupposes that all insurance salesmen are God-fearing people and therefore will have passed some form of theological examination before being employed as insurance salesmen.'

'Good God,' said one of the experts.

'Now *there*,' I said, 'I couldn't agree more.'

I've been for a walk down to the sea to clear my head and get a little fresh air into my mind. I find looking out at that vast horizon and feeling the prevailing south-westerly in my face somehow lifts my spirits and helps me to get things into proportion. Collecting thoughts and ideas together in this attempt to tell my story, it has become clear to me how many different 'personas' or images an individual presents to the world. And that any single image is not the whole person.

To tell the story of 'the Writer', or 'the Broadcaster' or 'the Actor' or 'the Preacher', is to place a particular activity of one's life into a frame. Each frame is different, and each picture is mounted on a different background. But the frame limits the picture, and anyway the picture is only two dimensional.

To my wife and children I am not 'the Broadcaster', or 'the Writer', although I am both of those things. It would be perfectly possible to write three or four stories about the same person, looking at him separately from several different points of view. Seen as 'the Father' or 'the Husband', 'the Son' or 'the Friend', all would be quite different and yet all of them could be absolutely true.

Even if you were to mix the portraits together, make a montage of them, it would still be a fractured and incomplete picture. There are so many things missing. I don't mean the things you cannot tell because they might hurt someone; or the things you cannot bear to tell because the pain in the memory is too intense and close, and probably always will be. I mean, simply, that the context in which everything happens is always complex. Nothing happens in isolation. Wars and earthquakes happen around us as we struggle to make a living. Families endure traumatic experiences and children grow up. For my montage to begin to make a complete three-dimensional picture it would need to have national and international events woven into it. It would need conversations, beliefs, betrayals, intimate relationships with individual members of my family, family meals and birthday parties, triumphs and grief, and the ache of love growing in and around the people I have been given to love; all this would need to be threaded through each image that I have presented. The problem is not that such a task cannot be attempted but that no one has the right to reveal that kind of intimacy about the people they love. I think I understand now why people write epic novels. It is the only way to get close to telling the truth.

Becoming a West End 'Star' has a strange effect on your positioning in the theatrical league tables, for a time at least, although Noël Coward's dictum is, 'once a star always a star'. Rightly or wrongly you are now accepted as a 'First Division' player. This gives you an entrée into all kinds of fields. As you can see from the stories I have told, you are now entitled to be a 'special guest' on a variety of radio and television programmes. You now receive invitations, almost daily, to attend 'celebrity' gatherings, usually for charity. You are also invited to submit items of your personal property to be auctioned for charity, to open exhibitions and garden fêtes and to give prizes at school speech days. You are only too glad to do most of this, especially if it means utilising your good fortune for the good of the less fortunate; it eases your conscience a little and frequently turns out to be a very pleasant experience.

Moving into this league also means that you are prey to those charlatans who have devised myriad ways of using your name to make a fast buck. Over the years I have made a variety of commercial recordings, that is records, singles, LPs and cassettes that are offered to the general public for sale, from the long playing record and cassette of *Swann with Topping*, to religious cassettes, like 'Voices in my Mind', consisting of meditations and sketches using the radio characters from *Pause for Thought*, to a seriously and worryingly sentimental single that moved, briefly, into the charts, and an LP of a concert by the London Emanuel Choir which I introduced. Whilst making these recordings I met some very good, honest people who paid their dues, bills and royalties in the most above-board manner possible. But I have to say that I have also met more charlatans and been left with more nasty tastes in my mouth in connection with the recording industry than in any other line of business of which I have had experience. My advice to any would-be recording artist is

(a) Don't do anything until you have a contract.

(b) Get it checked by two different legal experts.

(c) Take up skydiving instead, it's safer.

We recorded the LP of *Swann with Topping* at the Abbey Road Studios, famous as the Beatles' recording studio, and performed the entire show before an invited audience. We did it in one take, which the studio people found remarkable but if you are performing in the theatre every day of the week you don't find this difficult.

In the audience at the Abbey Road Studios was a television producer from Yorkshire Television called Terry Heneberry. After the recording he talked to us about a possible television series. It was the first of many talks that ended up in a series called *Sunday Best*. It was a thirty-five-minute Sunday evening religious slot. The idea was to construct a programme that took a particular theme, such as 'Love' or 'Faith' or 'Forgiveness', and then explore it through music, sketches, interviews or whatever lent itself best to the subject.

There was a resident team involved in presenting the programme. I was the anchor man who also had a 'performing' spot. Donald was at the piano, either to sing solo or with me. Marian Davies was our roving reporter who provided the programme with filmed inserts, though sometimes I would also go out and about to film. In the studio every week, providing a weekly 'Thought', was an Irish priest, Monsignor Michael Buckley. In our first programme we had Tom O'Connor doing a stand-up comic spot on the theme of religion and comedy. Our guest singing star and harpist was Mary O'Hara. Week by week there was a wide variety of actors, sports personalities and singers, including Sir Harry Secombe, Vince Hill, Julian Pettifer, Johnny Morris and Rabbi Lionel Blue. It was a good programme. Some traditionalists would have preferred a programme devoted entirely to hymn-singing, but it was liked by the general public and received good audience ratings from the ITV audience researchers.

In December 1980 we recorded a half-hour programme at the BBC Paris Theatre in Lower Regent Street to be broadcast on Radio 4 on Christmas Day. We also recorded another thirty-minute television programme with Mavis Nicholson called *Afternoon Plus* for her Christmas show.

A slightly more surprising programme to find ourselves not merely appearing in, but, as they say, 'topping the bill', was an ITV variety programme called *Starburst*. Variety is real 'star spangled' glamour, from the studio sets to the chauffeur-driven limousine service offered to its stars. It could make one slightly schizophrenic if one took it seriously. For a few days you have the 'star' treatment, being looked after as if you were Royalty, the posh dressing room, the personal 'dresser' from wardrobe who looks after every item of your clothing, the make-up artists who pat your brow if you begin to perspire, the call-boy who will bring tea to your dressing room, and then you are actually taken home in the chauffeur-driven limo.

The following day you are back to normal, back to queuing at the supermarket checkout and wondering why it is that whenever you buy a copy of the *Guardian* it is always the last one and, 'Sorry, guv,' it is the one that was on the bottom of the pile when it was thrown off the truck. Once more you are wrestling with that other immutable law of the universe which says that it shall in all circumstances be impossible to eat bread and honey without getting the honey on every conceivable surface, fingers, knife, table, cup handle, your new lambswool sweater and your three-year-old granddaughter. The return to earth from the glamour of your all-too-brief period of 'stardom' is so sudden and so inescapably real that all you can do is laugh, at yourself.

In 1985, our son Mark acquired a beautiful old wooden boat called *Colleen*. It had two masts with tan sails. One day, when June and I were sailing the *Colleen* across the Solent, June's woolly hat blew into the sea. We almost recovered it. We went about quite rapidly, came alongside and reached out for it, but it submerged just beyond our reach, weighed down, I think, by whatever stiffener had been used to give it a little peak, like a cap.

We were rather sad about its watery demise mainly because of the sentimental attachment June had about how she came to get the hat. Early in 1981 we were involved in delivering a caravan to a mountain village near Naples. There had been a terrible earthquake in the Naples region and an appeal had been made for people to supply temporary homes, in the form of caravans, to those who had been made homeless by the earthquake. As many of the homeless were in mountain villages and as it was winter, they were struggling to survive in sub-zero temperatures.

All kinds of charitable organisations had rallied to the call and a group of local churches had raised the money to buy the caravan that we were to deliver. That, of course, had been one of the needs, drivers to deliver the caravans from all over Europe to Southern Italy. There happened to be a gap in our theatre and television activities so June and I were able to volunteer as driver-deliverers. It was to be a wonderful adventure with events we would never forget and the making of friendships that would be lifelong.

Because of wintry conditions we had to drive around the Alps rather than through them. We drove down through Lyons to Aix-en-Provence and then along the Riviera through Cannes, Nice, Monte Carlo and on through all the long coastal tunnels, such as the Ventimiglia, cut into the mountains, where the Maritime Alps sweep down to the very edge of the sea. Then into Italy and over the viaducts and flyovers which at Genoa seem to be so high in the air, with acres of tomato-producing greenhouses on the mountain slopes beneath us, glinting in the winter sun. Then we started the long run south, with the Apennine Mountains, the 'spine' of Italy, keeping company to the east of us all the way to Rome and further south to Naples.

At Naples we had been advised to take the Tangenziale, a great ring road, which has an exit at a place called Averna where there is an 'English holiday club'. The English club has an area of several acres of landscaped chalets or bungalows, built especially for the tourist trade, but now, out of season, it provided a convenient place to house the people who were delivering caravans to the victims of the earthquake. We almost made it. Unaware that we were being followed, we had no idea that we had been selected as a target by a minor branch of the local Mafia.

The robbers must have made their move at the Tangenziale toll booth, because no sooner had we begun to drive away from the booth and on to the motorway than we realised something was wrong. It was a puncture in the right-hand tyre of the caravan. Once we had established that this was the problem, the next question was, how could we get off the motorway in order to do something about it? There appeared to be nowhere to go, the motorway had no hard shoulder, so we trundled along the Tangenziale, very slowly, desperately looking ahead in the hope of seeing an exit or some way of getting off the motorway. Suddenly June said, 'Look! There's a lay-by, up ahead!'

Patiently we coaxed the lame caravan up to the lay-by and pulled off the motorway. (Which was of course exactly what the robbers wanted us to do, but we were not thinking about robbers, we were just wondering how we could get a puncture mended.)

We had hired a large Ford Transit van to act as the towing vehicle. In this van there was a wooden dividing screen behind the driver and passenger's seats. Sitting in the front seats the screen was about shoulder height, which made it possible for us to drop things over the screen, handbags etc., so that they were out of sight from anyone casually observing the front seats. June was carrying a small knapsack in which we kept our passports, our travel documents and our money. Oh yes, and, amongst other things, our English-Italian phrase book.

As we drew to a halt, June, who had been travelling with the knapsack at her feet (in fact for most of the journey she had never let the bag out of her sight) for safety, dropped it behind the wooden screen before we jumped down to go and look at the punctured wheel. As we were crouched down, examining the tyre, we heard lots of car horns being sounded. That is not exactly unusual in Italy, but this time there were so many horns hooting and honking that we looked up. To our amazement we saw a man running across six lanes of Tangenziale motorway holding above his head a bag, our bag – the knapsack that contained all the important documents for our trip, passports and money! When he reached the far side of the motorway, he jumped into a waiting car and drove off in the opposite direction from us.

With a terrible sinking feeling, we realised that there was nothing we could do. We were completely helpless. June recognised the getaway car. It was a blue car that we had seen and passed, earlier, apparently 'broken down' on the motorway. We learned later from the police that it was not unusual for thieves to mark out travellers, particularly foreigners, and to follow them for miles, making a note of who carried the important money, (usually 'Momma'), who paid when the travellers got out at service stations or went to a restaurant; what kind of bag was used for money and important documents, and where it was put when they left the car.

Standing at the side of the Tangenziale, we were shaken and amazed that someone could risk his life in a wild dash across a motorway for such a comparatively small amount of money. However, within a few hours we were to gain some idea of what real poverty can mean. We had to inform the police and get help for our punctured tyre (there was no spare caravan wheel). Two young men pulled on to the lay-by and we asked them if they would telephone John Campbell at the British Consulate. We now had no money either to telephone or to pay the toll to get off the Tangenziale. After the young men had gone, we realised that we were not totally convinced that they had fully understood our predicament, nor that they would, in fact, do anything, even if they had understood. We decided to unhitch the caravan and leave it in the lay-by. We also thought that any idea of splitting up, such as one of us staying to 'look after' the caravan, would be extremely foolish. So we unhitched and, together, set off down the Tangenziale.

We were looking for the nearest exit so that we could leave the motorway and find a police station. Not long after we had left the caravan we saw an exit and took it. Suddenly we found ourselves in an extremely alien and threatening environment. It was as if we had slipped back a century into some Dickensian part of London, like 'The Cut' at Waterloo, where 'thieves' kitchens' existed on every corner, and street urchins slept under waggons and carts, or sometimes huddled together for warmth under a pile of old sacking. Of course it wasn't a time-slip, we had merely wandered into one of the poorest quarters of Naples. The houses were very close together, so close that it seemed dark. Washing lines were strung from one side of the street to another. We both had an uncomfortable sensation of being watched; peered at from windows, and squinted at from doors and dark alleyways. We may have been suffering from an attack of paranoia, but, as the saying goes, 'Just because you are paranoid, it doesn't mean they are *not* after you.' We also had a feeling that the blue car might belong to an area such as this, and we did not really want to meet the thieves here, not in their part of the jungle.

We never learned the name of the district we had wandered into, but, at that time, we were mutually agreed that the best course of action was to get out, quickly. We turned around and retreated the way we had come. I still don't know how we managed it, but somehow we found ourselves back on the motorway without having gone through a toll gate. People may say this is impossible; all I know is that we did it. We did not travel far along the Tangenziale before we saw a 'Carabinieri' car parked at the side of the motorway. (The 'Carabinieri' are a local police with a status that is different from the National Police, though I have never understood the difference.) We drew up alongside their vehicle. They got out as we did and without the aid of our phrase book, we attempted to explain our predicament to them. There was much arm-waving but not much comprehension. A young Italian drew up in his car and offered to help. He spoke very good English. However, another problem presented itself.

The evening 'rush-hour' was building up and motorists began to 'Rubber-neck'. Suddenly there was a series of familiar noises, 'Crash, tinkle, tinkle. Crash, tinkle, tinkle', as motorists ran into each other whilst watching the gesticulations of Carabinieri and distressed travellers on the roadside. In complete contrast to the measured solemnity of the British policeman, the Carabinieri abandoned us and rushed on to the motorway, slapping the cars like farmers herding cattle and shouting, '*Avanti! Avanti!*' The drivers returned the compliment by shouting something like, '*Mamma mia!*' at the Carabinieri and making that strange, loose-wristed hand shaking gesture, the full significance of which can only be known to the born Neapolitan. The young man, who had stopped to help, advised us to drive on and report to the *other* police. We pulled on to the motorway, which was clear ahead of us, but behind us lay a motorway that was stationary apart from umpteen people bouncing bumpers free and exchanging insurance details and intriguing gestures with the apoplectic Carabinieri.

As we drove on towards Averna, June hit on the excellent idea of drawing a series of matchstick-men cartoons which would tell the story of our Tangenziale adventure. Her cartoons were very explicit and graphic, and worked like a charm. The man at the toll gate took one look, gave us a sympathetic face and gesture, and then waved us through without arguing about payment.

At the English club at Averna we met Sheila Damiani who helped us to telephone John Campbell at the Consulate. (He had *not* heard from the young men whom we had asked to help.) John immediately took charge. He collected us and took us to his house in the Consulate building. His wife, Shirley (who had recently been robbed herself, by a group of young men on scooters), insisted that we stay with them rather than at the club in Averna.

The house of Her Majesty's Consul General for Naples and Sicily was rather splendid. Typical of many large Italian city houses, there was a very tall double door which opened into a courtyard and with the gate shut behind you, the noise and heat of the street disappeared and another more gracious world was revealed. Having been on the road for several days it was marvellous to have a civilised hot shower before dinner, and to come out of the bathroom and discover, waiting on the dressing table, a tall aperitif clinking with ice, and glittering in sparkling crystal. As post Highway-Robbery therapy I can recommend it. After dinner John and I went off to remove the wheel from the caravan, to get the tyre mended. We took the wheel to someone who assured John that it would be ready by the morning, and it was.

The following morning June and I collected the mended tyre and set off for the caravan. We were driving along the Tangenziale on the opposite side of the motorway to where we had left the caravan, intending to turn around at the toll booths. Looking across as we drew level with the caravan we noticed that its door was open. I knew it had been locked the previous night when John and I were removing the wheel. As we passed we could also see that the number plate had been removed.

'June,' I said, 'someone is trying to steal the caravan!'

I put my foot down and raced for the toll booths. Somehow I took the wrong approach and went through a booth which put us onto the road for Salerno. Desperately trying to work out how I could get back on the road into Naples I suddenly spotted ahead a stretch of road that had no central crash barrier. As luck would have it there seemed to be no other vehicle near us at that moment.

'I'm going to make a u-turn and get back on the opposite carriageway!'

I checked the mirrors. We were still a long way from other vehicles, so I made the turn and went racing back to the toll booth, hoping and praying that we could reach the caravan before the thieves took it. The only thing in our favour was the fact that they would need a spare caravan wheel, and because this particular caravan was a rather old model they would need a very particular size. Within minutes I had drawn up yet again at the toll booths, this time facing the right way.

The man in the toll booth was looking at our ticket, scratching his head and saying, 'Not possible. This ticket is not possible.'

I could see his problem. He was looking at a ticket stamped as being issued only minutes earlier for the opposite direction. I tried to explain to him that I was desperate, that I had made a u-turn on the motorway because at this very minute someone was stealing my caravan.

'Not possible,' he kept repeating. 'I must speak to Supervisor.'

He began to leave his booth but stopped when I started to shout, 'Mafioso! Cosa Nostra! They are stealing my caravan! Call the police! Carabinieri!'

I turned to June. 'If he doesn't let me through in a minute I'm just going to drive on. If they send the police after me I'll just lead them to the caravan, if it's still there. I can't wait here much longer.'

I don't know if the toll collector understood anything I said, or whether he simply recognised the note of desperation in my voice, or whether someone shouting 'Cosa Nostra' worried him; whatever it was, he suddenly made a decision. He handed me a new ticket and waved his arms. '*Avanti! Avanti!*'

Before he opened his mouth for the second '*Avanti!*', I had gone.

A minute later I screeched up beside the caravan. As I did so, a truck a little way in front of us on the lay-by pulled away so fast that its tyres skidded and left a small cloud of blue smoke.

'That's them! They were going to hitch it to the lorry!'

We had arrived in the nick of time. A few minutes later and they would have put some makeshift wheel on the caravan and it would have disappeared from the face of the earth.

We checked the caravan for damage. The door had been forced but it was not difficult to make it shut again. Cupboard doors were open inside but there had been nothing worth stealing. It was also possible to tie the number plate back into position. We put the repaired wheel on the caravan and set off for our rendezvous with two other British caravans that were to be delivered to the same village, high in the mountains. The village was called San Gregorio Magna.

The road to San Gregorio Magna was rough and tortuous. The congestion in the streets of mountain villages often seemed insoluble, but we managed. We frequently worried, as we struggled around precipitous mountain bends, about what on earth we would do if we met something coming the other way, but by some miracle all our encounters with other vehicles occurred near some form of passing place. At one resting place our guide pointed to a village up ahead of us that seemed to be hanging off the edge of the mountain.

'Is that San Gregorio Magna?'

'No. San Gregorio,' he sniffed, 'is higher.'

We reached the village at about four o'clock in the afternoon. This high on the mountain there was snow and a bitterly cold wind. We could see the effects of the earthquake. People had made makeshift shelters out of bits and pieces, cardboard boxes and sheets of polythene. I saw an old lady coming out of one of these 'shelters' and I felt ashamed that we had not filled up the caravan with as many useful items as we could have laid our hands on. Suddenly all the problems we had faced in the last twenty-four hours seemed minor, trivial.

We were met by the Protestant pastor of the village who led us to where the caravan was to be parked and introduced us to the married couple who were going to move into it with their family. Young soldiers manhandled the caravan into the exact position required. These young men were marvellously cheerful, in spite of the fact that their tented encampment was sited on the top of a very cold and exposed hill.

The village grocer (it seemed incongruous, somehow, that his shop was a 'Spar' grocery store) whose name was Giuseppe Policastro, had lived in America, and therefore spoke fluent Brooklyn: 'Hey! What can I tell yer? Call me Joe, huh?' He offered to take us in his tiny Fiat to look at the buildings in the old part of the village that had been most affected by the earthquake. We were perhaps a little nervous because there were earthquake tremors of varying degrees every day. We squeezed into his car, which had recently been occupied by a pig, and found ourselves bumping down a street in which buildings had collapsed.

There was a war-torn, bombed and shelled look to many of the buildings, especially those which had walls broken away to reveal intimate interiors, just how the houses of near-by Salerno must have looked during the Allied landings in 1943. They looked like open dolls' houses, with linen hanging off a bed and flapping in the breeze, a kitchen table with plates and a carafe of wine, and a mantelpiece with photographs still standing next to a candlestick.

Suddenly the little Fiat screeched to a halt, and Joe slung it into reverse and started zig-zagging violently back the way we had come.

'What's the matter?'

'De rubble! Dat rubble across the street!'

'Yes. What about it?'

'It wasn't der half hour ago. Dat's what!'

In Joe's shop a small group of us gathered round and prayed. To our embarrassment, the woman to whom we had presented the caravan had brought us a gift, a two gallon polythene container of home-made red wine. We made brief and polite protest but clearly it would have been hurtful not to have accepted it.

Joe then decided to introduce us to his fellow shopkeepers in the Piazza Amendola. In one shop, a clothier's, which stocked working clothes, overalls, lumberjack shirts, thick sweaters, socks and work boots, June tried on a knitted hat, a warm woollen hat with a kind of peak, like a cap. Many of the local farmers wore them. Joe Policastro insisted on buying it for June. It was to survive many sailing trips before finally coming to rest, off the south coast of England, at the bottom of the sea.

That night, a Saturday night, we dined at the Consulate with two young men, Geoff and Roger, from England. They had flown over in order to teach the local people how to construct the prefabricated buildings that had been donated to the earthquake villages. It was essential that the local people became involved in the work tomorrow, Sunday, because Geoff and Roger had to fly back to England on Monday. However John Campbell was meeting resistance to this idea simply because very devout Catholics in Southern Italy believe in keeping Sundays 'holy'. In the end I believe John himself rolled up his sleeves and was chiefly instrumental in laying the concrete bases for the buildings in San Gregorio Magna. I cannot begin to describe the amount of relief work that the Campbells were involved in with the local communities at this time. Suffice it to say that they were up to their necks in work and that British 'stock' in Naples was never higher.

On Sunday I had to do a live broadcast from Naples into the Radio 4 Sunday morning magazine programme, *Sunday*. Some of the newspapers in England had picked up a story that charitable gifts, intended for Italian earthquake victims, were being stolen. A consignment of blankets had gone missing, a caravan, things like that. There had been sensational headlines about the Mafia ripping off their own people. These stories had become so widespread that there had been a dramatic fall-off in charitable giving to the victims of this disaster, in which many people had died, been injured or become homeless.

In my broadcast I described what I had seen in the mountain villages, the cardboard shelters, the elderly and the children suffering in the extremely cold winter nights. And then I referred to the stories of so-called 'Mafia' rip-offs. I tried to remind people that wherever there was a tragic catastrophe there would be unscrupulous people who would scavenge, shoplift, steal and generally attempt to take advantage of the chaos. But that did not mean that we should give up our attempts to help the victims of the disaster.

'It's true, there are thefts, and there always will be. That does not alter the fact that I saw an old lady crawling out of a makeshift cardboard shelter, in the middle of winter, on the top of a snow-covered mountain. What am I to say to her? "I'm sorry, I have brought you nothing, because someone is stealing blankets."

'More than ninety per cent of all the charitable gifts sent to Italy *have* got through, but there are still people in desperate need, people who are cold and homeless, ordinary people from hard-working farming communities, who, unless we help them, have nothing with which to survive what looks like being a long and hard winter. They do not deserve to be abandoned because of the actions of a few sad and criminally disturbed people, or the ravings of a sensationalist press.'

Years later John Campbell told me he believed that the broadcast from the Consulate that morning had turned the tide in regard to charitable giving. I have no idea if my broadcast really had anything to do with this. At any rate, according to John, there was a sudden and marked improvement in funds received immediately after the broadcast. It certainly would be nice to think that it had had some positive effect.

After the broadcast that morning I preached at the English church in Naples, which was attended by British ex-patriots and American staff and their families from the Naples Nato base. Down at sea level the weather was warm and gentle, like a mild English summer's day, and after the service we had lunch sitting out on the Campbells' roof, looking out across the Bay of Naples. Very romantic.

The following day, after some shopping for the return journey,

Shirley Campbell led us out of the town and put us on the road to Rome. We were a bit like tourists going home. June paddled in the sea and just south of Formia we bought a brightly painted milk jug from a local potter.

Having become permanently paranoid about being robbed or losing our money, travel documents and passports, we split what money we had between us and carried the passports and documents in a cardboard folder. (You need quite a lot of documents if you have been 'exporting' something like a caravan.) We took it with us whenever we got out of the vehicle. Even doing this we nearly came unstuck again! In France, near Aix-en-Provence, I left the safe and secure folder with our new temporary passports and documents on the counter of a shop. The shop was empty and closing even as we left it. I remembered the folder just after the shop lady had departed for home. However, the shop was attached to a restaurant and the restaurateur was also the owner of the shop, so he opened up and returned the folder to us – phew!

In Central France and further north it was snowing heavily. Some mornings we woke to very heavy frost and ice on the roads. The drive from Naples to England took us four days. We had left England on 26th January and returned on 5th February, eleven days in all, and we had driven a total of 3,222 miles. Apart from three nights in Naples we had driven almost continually and slept either in the caravan or in the back of the transit. It had been a wonderful mixture of hard driving, highway robbery, earthquake villages, mountains, Consular comforts, a long distance broadcast and a friendship that is still enjoyed a decade later. All in all, a wonderful adventure.

9 Treading the Boards Again

Moving house is said to be an extremely traumatic experience; to be rated amongst the Top Ten Life-Shortening Events, such as losing your job, or getting divorced. Since the day of our marriage we have moved house so many times it requires a concentrated effort to remember all the places. When we moved to Milford-on-Sea it was our seventeenth move. I don't know if we have now become inured to the house-moving trauma, but we certainly seem to be able to take it in our stride. For those who are fascinated by chronological lists, perhaps I should include a table of 'Houses we have lived in' at the back of the book.

Among the many houses we have enjoyed, there was one magical year when we lived in the swirling mists and against the dramatic backcloth of the mountains of the Lleyn Peninsula in North Wales. It was such a wonderful year, like a fairy tale. Even now I have to ask myself did it really happen or was it just a dream? But there are the photographs, winter, spring, summer, harvest; sheep, cattle, horses and haymaking. Somehow, like the children in C. S. Lewis's *The Lion, The Witch and The Wardrobe*, we had stepped out of our own time and place and found ourselves in a country where mystery and magic was the norm, a land whose language and mountains embraced legend and myth as naturally as breathing; and the house in which we lived had a magical name of its own, *Ty'n Y Gors*, or, in English, *The House on the Marsh*.

Ty'n Y Gors could be described as a small hill farm, twenty-eight acres of rough grazing, divided into twenty-one fields of eccentric shapes. Worked as a farm, it would be difficult to achieve anything above subsistence farming, though it would offer scope to the very dedicated as a self-sufficiency smallholding. However, it was not its farming potential that attracted us, it was the setting.

The entrance gate to *Ty'n Y Gors* is marked by two large white stones. About a hundred yards through the gate there is a cattle grid. Every time I crossed this grid I had the feeling of crossing a divide, a bridge between the mainland and the island of *Ty'n Y Gors*. Once across this 'bridge' I had breached a magic circle, entered a ring within which I was secure, protected from the real world. The illusion of being on an island is encouraged by the fact that most of the fields are divided by drainage ditches which, for most of the year, run like streams down to dew ponds and the little river that borders the fields beyond the house.

Standing at the 'bridge' you look towards mountains whose peaks frequently rise clear of low and swiftly moving cloud. It is as if the mountains are alive and the movement of the clouds, and shafts of sunlight falling across their faces, reveal their moods, sometimes severe, sometimes benign, but always powerful. It is no wonder to me that Moses climbed a mountain to receive the Ten Commandments. Who else could inhabit such mysterious places; who else could live amongst ancient and unchanging crags shrouded in mist but spirits, or gods; who could if they wished, send down wild-eyed giants to prophesy.

The farmhouse stands on level ground at the foot of the Yr Eifl mountains. Beyond the house is a line of tall trees, ash mainly, and then there is a field bordered by a small river, the River Erch, hardly more than a deep stream at this point, but a trout stream nonetheless, which winds its way down to the sea at Abererch and Pwllheli. The river marks the boundary between *Ty'n Y Gors* and the mountains. On the other side of the stream the fields slope up towards a plantation of trees inhabited by foxes, which we sometimes glimpsed and whose night barking could send shivers down the spine. Above the trees the land climbed more steeply to the peaks.

Standing on the 'bridge', with your back to the house, you look towards the 'wild place', six acres of *Ty'n Y Gors* that lie across the road from the gate, uncultivated fields of bushes, trees and ponds, once the home of a lonely donkey called Benjamin (whose story,

I'm glad to say, had a happy ending). The last two, furthest-away acres are fenced off. It is 'wetland', a field of fascinating but treacherous sphagnum moss.

Local legend has it that a cow strayed on to this moss and sank, completely disappeared. I could believe it. Mark and Simon, our sons, terrified us by jumping up and down on the sphagnum and making the surface shift and heave over a considerable area. It was like poking a pie crust floating on a huge tray of stew. The sphagnum acres halt, and *Ty'n Y Gors* farm ends in the shadow of a dense forest of pine trees.

From the 'bridge', walking towards the farm buildings, you are protected from northerly winds by a gorse-covered bank which is a blaze of yellow blossom for month after month from summer to autumn. Butterflies live here, brown, red and delicate blue. Everywhere you look there are saplings. Before we arrived, in 'The Year of the Tree', over six hundred young trees had been planted, along the lane, on the bank, in a triangular corner, in strips in between fields, amongst the older trees, alongside the ditches, in every possible gap or wasted space. I was never able to identify all the varieties, even though I bought two books about trees and spent hours examining leaves, bark and pine needle formations.

One part of the farm takes a sizeable turn to the south and ends in a wonderful meadow that sweeps down to the tree-lined little river where cattle stand to drink. I loved this field, a secret field, hidden from the world in a fold of land. For one whole wonderful year we were the guardians of *Ty'n Y Gors*, its streams, pools and fields; surrounded by forests and mountains, high up on a plateau, four hundred feet above sea level on a peninsula which thrusts itself into the Irish Sea. From the slopes of Yr Eifl we could see the bays and rocky inlets on both sides of the peninsula. It was, and is, an enchanted place which welcomed us with the best summer in living memory.

Whilst we were there we experienced the tremors of a Welsh earthquake, so violent that they were felt as far away as Broadcasting House in London. Later we discovered, through a visiting team of Cambridge scientists, that *Ty'n Y Gors* was practically the epicentre of that earthquake. Mark, who was upstairs in his room when the earthquake occurred, heard a terrifying rumble; he could not at first imagine what had caused the noise, or made the house shake. The first thing that came to his mind was the thought that the cattle had somehow got into the house and were stampeding through the living room. Amazingly, no damage was caused to any of our buildings.

Living at *Ty'n Y Gors* introduced us on a personal level to sheep, calves and vets, hens, ducks and a lively, anxious-to-please, sheepdog who answered to the name of Fred. It also introduced us to a warm and sturdy people who relieved the hard life of hill farming with humour, stories, eisteddfods and singing that surprised you with its skill and beauty.

Ty'n Y Gors was not merely a hill farm, but another world, a dream come true, and I miss it, yet I am glad to have been part of it even if for so short a time. But how did it happen? How did we get there? Well . . .

After *Sunday Best*, Yorkshire Television asked me to present a new series for Sunday evenings, called *Topping on Sunday*. Like *Sunday Best* it was to be networked nationally. *Topping on Sunday* ran for several happy years. Each programme had a theme, such as *forgiveness*, and all the songs, stories and quotes would be closely related to the theme. The centrepiece of each programme was an interview with someone who had a particular interest in the subject. Lord Denning for instance discussed the place of forgiveness in the law. Delia Smith and Rabbi Lionel Blue talked about the religious significance of various items of food. June and I spent many pre-show evenings at the Queen's Hotel in Leeds discussing the following day's recordings with our guests. They were wonderful evenings, exchanging stories with people like Thora Hird Chay Blyth, Chad Varah, Lord Soper, Bob Champion, Lady Sue Ryder, Moira Anderson and so many people who had wonderful stories to tell. At the beginning of the series, June and I, and the family were living in Kent. For a year or two we commuted to Yorkshire. The programme required me to be in Leeds for two days a week, and I also met the producer in London to talk about the script, which I wrote week by week. June came with me to Leeds and looked after the guests on the programme. Like filming, there is often a great deal of waiting around in television studios, and for contributors waiting to make their contribution this can be very tedious. Most people came up the night before the recording and stayed at the Queens Hotel. We would have dinner with them at the hotel so that by the following day we were reasonably well acquainted with each other.

But let's get back to *Ty'n Y Gors*. Rudyard Kipling, who knew Cecil Rhodes very well, tells of how one day, in South Africa, Rhodes, apropos of nothing in particular, had suddenly said, 'What's your dream?'

It's a very good question. Everyone should have a dream, even if it's an impossible dream. To fall short of your dream might mean falling a great deal further on than would have been possible had you never dreamed. *Ty'n Y Gors* was a dream which came true for us, for at least one, blissful year.

Naturally, June and I have individual dreams of our own, but we also have a shared dream. We've talked about it sitting by firesides on long winter nights, walking down country lanes and trundling around the country in our various jalopies. It changes shape a little from time to time but not much. Both of us enjoy entertaining people; by that I mean looking after them. Both of us would like to have the means and a home large enough to invite a small number of guests to house parties, with no object other than to enjoy each other's company and conversation, to eat good food, to walk in the country, to laugh and sing and to send people on their way refreshed; to be able to offer different forms of retreat from stress and pressure, ways of slowing down, taking stock or just relaxing, retreats with a difference for some secular, for some religious, all therapeutic.

We began to look at houses in Kent during the *Topping on Sunday* run, but every place we looked at that had possibilities always turned out to be far too expensive. We decided to search further afield, perhaps in areas where houses might be a little cheaper. We looked in East Anglia, and then began to look at what we called the Celtic Fringes. Our daughter Anne suggested looking at the *Sunday Times* property pages. I thought this might be too expensive, but in fact we discovered that not everything in the *Sunday Times* property columns was out of the question.

We saw a particular property advertised in North Wales which looked as if it might have possibilities. We had now begun to think that if we lived a little nearer to Leeds the property would be less expensive and it would make our commuting easier. We decided to take a trip to the Principality.

The first place advertised in the *Sunday Times* that we went to see, was a wonderful house near Port Madoc. The house was called *Cefn Coch*. It was a large stone house with a fascia of local, blue-grey dressed quarry stone which gave the house a very elegant appearance. We got very excited about this house, and almost bought it. *Cefn Coch* stood in about three and a half acres of land and had quite a number of outbuildings, including a coach house. It was beautifully situated on a hill facing towards the sea.

We thought it had great possibilities and made an offer which was accepted, providing we could sell our house in Kent and raise the money for *Cefn Coch* before anyone else did. Apparently there was someone who wanted to buy *Cefn Coch* but simply could not get a buyer for his own property. The couple selling *Cefn Coch* were very anxious to sell, in fact they had already left, so it was simply a case of the house going to the first person who could raise the money. Our house in Kent, in the village of Upnor, next to a yacht club and with a study that overlooked the only green-banked and tree-lined tidal reach of the River Medway would not be difficult to sell. In fact we were convinced it would sell quickly so we began to explore the possibilities for *Cefn Coch*; the whole family were involved in planning what we might do with it.

In our excited imagining the coach house was converted into rooms for retreatants; the outhouses into quiet rooms and a little chapel. The house itself had two stairways, one in the servants' quarters, a 'back stairs', and one serving the principal rooms. The main sitting room looked out on to a patio above a garden, which was terraced into the hillside.

There was an enormous kitchen, or perhaps more properly it was called the servants' hall. There was a butler's pantry discreetly situated between the sitting room and the dining room. There was also a disused but beautiful wood-panelled lavatory which I could imagine owed it workings to the system favoured by medieval castles. I think it worked by gravity down a pipe that led to goodness knows where! We could not decide on a new use for this closet. The children made various suggestions such as turning it into a confessional box or perhaps an internal wishing well with a bucket suspended halfway down the shaft to catch the coins, a novel kind of offertory box of somewhat doubtful theological value. I expect we would have converted it into a cloakroom of some sort.

One part of the house that offered a great deal of space for development into possible extra retreatant rooms was the enormous attic. However, it was also a part of the house that filled us with a certain amount of sadness. To use a crude expression, it 'gave us the creeps'. It was an area that one did not want to linger in because somehow there seemed to be a contagious and almost overpowering feeling of depression about that part of the house, in complete contrast to the sunlit living rooms.

The attic was reached by the back stairs. In a corner of this cavernous space there was a very crude room formed out of thin partitions. It was constructed like a stage set with wood-framed panels that did not reach the roof. It was perhaps quite literally a 'box' room, only the box did not have a lid. Some attempt to make it more homely was evident in the wallpaper that lined the inside of the box, but it was still a dark and cheerless hole, more like a cell than someone's room. All around the house were servants' bell wires, most of which went to the enormous kitchen, but one of them came up here into this desolate makeshift chamber. We felt very sad for the poor little skivvy who had obviously had to live up here. It was sad to think of some girl clambering up to this eerie place, clutching her candle, freezing in winter and airlessly hot in summer.

So committed were we, and so sure that we would be the purchasers, that we arranged to stay a night in the house, camping style, with sleeping bags and Gaz stove. The nearest neighbour was a marvellously welcoming family who lived about two miles further up the hill. This neighbour now farmed the land around *Ceyn Coch*. The farmer's wife invited us to call at her house for tea when we came to stay the night. As it turned out, the day we were to stay she had an appointment elsewhere, but she wrote to us saying that she would leave some food in her kitchen and that we were to let ourselves in and help ourselves.

It was a strange feeling to walk into the kitchen of an isolated farmhouse and sit down to tea, seeing no one except the two sheepdogs in the yard, who had greeted us as if we were old friends, despite the fact that we had only met once before. It was a very generous tea, and the kindness typical of the people we were to meet in the North Wales farming communities.

Sadly we never saw that lady again. Somehow, the other party raised the purchase money the day before we sold our property. So now we had sold our house but had nowhere to go. However, perhaps it was just as well. After it had all fallen through June confessed that she had not been entirely happy with the Feng-shui – the spirit of the house itself – maybe that little girl in the attic had been trying to tell us something.

We decided to make a concentrated search in roughly the same area. Surely there must be other houses available that were similar to *Cefn Coch*. June was working in Kent in one of the several posts she held as warden of a sailing centre or senior teacher at an outdoor pursuit centre. At this particular time she was the warden of the Cliff Sailing Centre, on the Thames side of the Hoo Peninsula, so she was not free to go roaming around North Wales, but her twin brother, John Berry, was free and he agreed to come with me to house-hunt in Wales.

At that time we were enjoying the folly of owning an elderly but wonderful old Daimler, sleek and elegant in dark British 'racing green', which is quite my favourite colour for a car. John and I threw a tent into the boot and swooshed up to Wales.

It was October, and the holiday season was well and truly over. Nevertheless we found a camping site that was still functioning, near Port Madoc, and we flung up our tent amongst the hardy few that appear to be devoted to Welsh hill walking all year round. I suppose I ought to count myself amongst the winter adventurers.

It was in October that Donald Swann and I went boating on the Broads to write songs; it was in the depth of winter that we tackled a snow-clad mountain in Southern Italy, with a caravan; and here I was once more, in a tent, out of season, hardly a dozen miles as the crow flies from Mount Snowdon.

Mentioning Donald Swann and thinking about mountains brings to mind a slightly curious experience that Donald and I shared, up a mountain. We were performing at the Isle of Man Music Festival. Donald had telephoned Richard Adams, the author of *Watership Down*, who happens to live on the island. Donald did not, at that time, know Richard Adams, but he was never inhibited about telephoning people. He told me that he had once telephoned a famous cartoonist, whose work he had long admired, in order to tell him that he had long admired his work. He might have been a bit long-winded doing this, because whilst Donald was waxing eloquent about the humorist's skill and talent, the famous cartoonist suddenly cut across him saying, 'I'm terribly sorry, Mr Swann, but my wife has collapsed in the kitchen and I was about to telephone the doctor when you rang.' Whether or not this was true we shall never know, but as a conversation stopper it must be hard to beat. On this occasion there was a more positive outcome; Richard Adams invited us to lunch.

We hired a car, which Donald drove because he had brought his driving licence with him and I hadn't. Someone at our hotel had suggested, 'a more interesting route than just following the main road. It's a very minor road, but it will give you a wonderful view of Snaefell.'

It began to rain not long after we had set out. The further away we moved from the principal roads and signs of human habitation, the darker the skies became. A few miles on and the wind increased noticeably; then we heard the first crash of thunder. We were too committed to turn back, and in any case, roads as narrow as these make it rather difficult to turn. The rain was now very heavy and streams of water were running mud brown from the fields and down the sides of the road. Pools, to be forded carefully, had formed in dips in the road. Trees rocked and swayed in the wind, their glistening leaves flashing in unison with the lightning. It was as if we had stumbled into some wild act of worship, in which every green and growing thing in the earth was paying homage to the God of the Tempest. Not only were we visiting Richard Adams, we were entering his kingdom, the forest world of *Shardik*. Then I noticed that we seemed to be very low on fuel.

'Donald, did you start off with a full tank?'

Donald peered at the petrol gauge. 'The garage didn't say anything about petrol, so I never gave it a thought. I just assumed there was plenty. It does look rather low, doesn't it?'

We crept, as economically as possible, around the mountain and then, thankfully, began to descend towards a village in which we could see a petrol station and some clear signs of life on its forecourt. But even as we drew into the petrol station we realised that we had not left Richard Adams' enchanted world. Standing in the doorway of the office was a witch, complete with black pointed hat and black scarecrow-like garments. Only as we drew level with the witch did we recognise that black plastic bags over your shoulders and a black plastic bag folded to make a conical hat does make a rather convincing witch.

Nor did Richard Adams' house release us from his primordial grip on our imaginations. We passed the entrance to his house unaware of its presence. Only on returning very slowly down the lane did we see that his house name-plate was lying flat on the ground.

'There it is!' I shouted. 'Knockharry!' (Or was it Knobkerry? I can't remember.)

Entering his drive there was further illusion. From the drive the house gave the impression of being a very modest bungalow. It was only when the driveway swung us to the side of the house that we realised that we had only been looking at the top of the house. The rest of it clung to the side of a very steep hill. I seem to remember that part of it was supported by stout legs.

Inside the house, Richard's study seemed to be suspended in space because it overlooked the steep drop to where a lake was being excavated, far below the house. A suitably magic setting for a creator of magical stories.

Meanwhile, let us return to the Welsh mountains, and the tent

in a field near Port Madoc, where my brother-in-law and I were
evaluating the small stack of estate agents' 'House for Sale' details
that we had collected on our way through the town. We spent the
evening sifting and translating the information we had acquired.
By now I had become expert at such interpretation. I could speak
fluent Agentspeak. Here are a few examples of how to translate
Estate Agentspeak.

> Cottage with immense character – Derelict.
> Considerable potential for imaginative purchaser – Needs a
>   bathroom.
> In need of some repair – Riddled with damp and wood rot.
> In need of modernisation – Has outside lavatory.
> In need of decoration – Not quite derelict.
> Tremendous Old World Charm – either, a) Watch your step
>   going up the stairs
> or, b) Derelict.

Most house-hunters are familiar with phrases such as 'Surprisingly spacious interior', which means, 'The outside may look like
a Norwegian troll's hovel, but an interior wall has been removed
giving you room to swing a very small cat (should you require room
for such an activity).'

'Convenient parking space' means there is a rusting Hillman
Minx and half a Cortina in the front garden. 'Greatly improved
by present owner' means 'There isn't a level shelf in the house
and the built-in wardrobe is covering a huge crack in the bedroom
wall.' 'Featured fireplace' is a nice one. It means, 'There are
some incongruous lumps of stone set around an imitation coal,
"flicker"-effect, two-bar electric fire.'

House agents' hyperbole can provide an amusing half hour in
a tent in a field on a rainy night in North Wales, but it tends to
pall as the rain seeks out the leaks in the canvas. By morning we
had made a shortlist and a plan of action for the day.

I had noticed a place advertised in the *Sunday Times* that seemed
too good to be true, asking a very reasonable price; in fact it was
about the same price as *Cefn Coch*. The property included a

farmhouse, outbuildings and twenty-eight acres. With all the cynicism of the seasoned house-hunter I thought that at such a price, and with all that land, there must be *something* wrong. However, I telephoned the owner and arranged to see the house in the afternoon, after we had seen all the other properties.

One by one we worked our way through the list. We explored narrow lanes, negotiated hairpin bends and bumped along ill-repaired farm tracks. In hill-top houses and in cottages hidden in folds of the land we were polite, in the reserved and non-committed manner of the house-hunter. Eyes everywhere, we nodded as we listened to stories of 'home-improvements' and exchanged glances as we spotted the damp patch or the ominously bulging ceiling. Some of the houses were in good repair and beautifully decorated, but there was a 500-foot television relay aerial ('They do pay an annual rent') towering over the house, or there was no approach road, except along the pot-holed farm track. 'We have got planning permission to build a road, but . . .' One house that had a lot of possibilities as a retreat house was somewhat marred by a neighbouring and highly visible farmyard which housed a motley assortment of old buses, trucks and a furniture removal van. I felt sorry for the embarrassed young agent who was showing us around the house.

Certainly one of the best places we saw was a rambling old manse or vicarage near Criccieth. But the estate agent told us that it was being sold by the church to the highest bidder and then proceeded to tell us what offers they had received so far. I was not quite sure of the ethics of being told what somebody else had bid, and as I had neither the time, the resources or the inclination to get involved in an ecclesiastical gazumping game we crossed it off our list.

We made the acquaintance of a number of animals in strange places. Cats and dogs one might expect, even the occasional goat, but not a pony in a kitchen or a llama in the front garden. Llamas at close quarters are surprisingly tall, with doe-like eyes set in a camel-shaped face. This llama took a particular interest in John's ears, I don't know if it was attracted by his after-shave or what, but despite being assured that it was harmless we were no more

convinced than we had been by similar declarations made on behalf
of teeth-bared Alsatians.

Gradually we ticked off each house and cottage until the only
place left to see was the hill farm with twenty-eight acres. By now
we were weary and a little depressed and as this property was
further to the west than any of the others, and particularly as I
thought we would be on a wild-goose chase, we were almost of a
mind to scratch the appointment. However, we had set the course
for the day and felt that we ought to complete it.

We searched the Ordnance Survey and discovered that we would
need to take the road that runs close to the sea on the north of the
Lleyn Peninsula. We cut across country, joining the road at Clynnog
Fawr. With the sea on our right and Bwlch Mawr towering to the
left we drove along the coast road.

At Trevor the road turns due south, leaving the sea and passing
through a mountain gap. The left side of the pass is guarded by
a mountain called Gurn Ddu, and to the right, or west, there
is a dramatic sweeping saddle-back mountain which falls steeply
into the sea. It was my first sight of Yr Eifl. It was so impressive
that I remember exclaiming to John, 'Wow! Look at that! It's
breathtaking!'

As we drove through the village of Llanaelhaearn, which the
English in time learn to pronounce, we passed a public house
called 'The Rivals', clearly an anglicisation of Yr Eifl. John
consulted the directions we had been given. 'Look out for a
forest on the left and two white stones on the right about half
a mile from Llanaelhaearn.'

'There they are! The stones!'

We turned in through the gateway and stopped. The afternoon
sun was shining on a plateau of fields and lighting up the mountains
on the horizon. About half a mile ahead we could see a white farmhouse with a spiral of blue smoke drifting from its chimney. Sheep
and cattle cast long shadows in the fields, and in the distance, near
the house a dog barked. Neither of us spoke. There was a feeling of
space and freshness, peace perhaps. Slowly we rumbled across the
cattle grid and quite suddenly I knew, without entering the house,
that this was it, the place we would make our home, *Ty'n Y Gors*.

Ty'n Y Gors was owned by Sheila and Terry Potter, an English couple who had worked hard to improve both the house and the land. The principal improvement to the land had been in field drainage and re-sowing. This improvement was quite dramatically evident. From the top of Yr Eifl you can see right down the peninsula, miles of bays and inlets. From this peak you have an aerial view of the land below, a patchwork of fields, lanes, forests, streams and isolated farmhouses. Most of the land is either forest or rough grazing, thinly grassed scrub. From the mountain *Ty'n Y Gors* is very visible because of its greenness. The field drainage, re-sowing and the planting of so many trees has transformed the land.

Sheila Potter welcomed us and showed us around the farm-house, or perhaps I should say 'houses'. From a distance only the white house is visible; closer you begin to see that there is more than one building. The original farmhouse was a typical Welsh Longhouse, a single-storey building for the most part except that at one end there is a 'crog-loft', that is a storage room, in this case built above a pony trap house. I discovered later that the word 'crog' meant 'hanging', so the crog-loft was where the farmer would hang items he intended to keep out of the reach of cats, rats and mice. Against the crog-loft end of the Longhouse stood a brick 'pump-house' which housed an electric motor that operated the pump which drew water from the well.

At the other end of the Longhouse, and attached to it, is a two-storey Victorian house, and at the end of that building is a big conservatory, and at the end of the conservatory is a timber pergola covered in Russian ivy. Both the Victorian building and its Welsh Longhouse companion have additional rooms at the back, some on different levels, including a small breakfast room that enabled you to consider the mood of Yr Eifl whilst you marmaladed your toast. It had wood-burning stoves, stable doors, an inglenook and an interior doorway into the crog-loft that was halfway up a wall.

I loved the house, with its eccentric rooms, particularly the wonderfully long sitting room with the enormous fireplace, but most of all I loved its setting. Sheila Potter produced a large-scale map of the farm and we walked a little way around the fields. It was too late in the day to walk the boundaries, but I was convinced that this was the place we had been looking for.

Sheila was naturally a little worried that I was making a decision without June having seen the place, but I assured her that I knew June would love *Ty'n Y Gors* and that I would bring her to see it at the first opportunity; meanwhile would she please consider the place sold. This time there would be no delay as the sale of our house in Kent was all but complete. On October 3rd, 1983 we stood in our own little farmyard and watched 'Daves Removals' reverse slowly down the half-mile drive that led to *Ty'n Y Gors* farmhouse.

An image that lives with me from the day we moved into *Ty'n Y Gors*, is the look of hurt astonishment on the face of the man who laid the carpet in the long room. He was having a tea break, sitting on the floor, on a section of carpet successfully laid, when a colleague drew his attention to a problem that lay ahead, that of having to cut the carpet around a boulder protruding from one of the walls. He carefully laid his sandwich in its greaseproof wrapping on his copy of the *Daily Mirror* and stood up.

At that precise moment, a prowling cat passing the open door seized his opportunity – the carpet-layer's lunch! In addition to the carpet-layer's look of astonishment I have a cartoon-like image of the cat, with a ham sandwich gripped firmly in its teeth, streaking out of the door and into the farmyard. The carpet-layer stood open-mouthed, for several seconds, before hissing with all the inflection, syncopation and rolling of 'r's' peculiar to the Welshman of the North. 'Thie-fing li-ttle bug-gerrr!'

I believe this particular epithet, the final word at any rate, has a different meaning when translated into the Welsh; at least it does not have the same force as the English. The most courteous and respectable farmers, Sunday collar, no tie, chapel-goers steeped in Bible-rich language, seem to use the word as a triumphant demonstration of their command of English. Such men, who rarely speak English, when taking Sunday tea at *Ty'n Y Gors*, even in the presence of the ladies of Llanaelhaearn, would lower a delicate china cup clutched between gnarled fingers and solemnly announce, 'Mr Topping Bach, I'll tell you this, I love horr-ses, but *mares* – is bug-gerrs!' Heads would nod in agreement with the profundity, but not an eyelid batted at the use of the explosive word.

It was an idyllic year. June took to farming like the proverbial duck takes to water. Gradually we bought calves and sheep and hens and ducks. And from time to time we trekked across the Pennines to Yorkshire Television.

Simon, our elder son, prior to going to Cambridge to read Theology, was working in Liverpool assisting the Methodist chaplain to the university. Simon brought a party of students to *Ty'n Y Gors* for a retreat weekend. A Methodist minister and his family brought their caravan for a holiday on the farm. John and Shirley Campbell, our friends from Naples, and their son, Piers, came to stay. Friends from Kent and Marian McDonald, my BBC colleague, found their way to Yr Eifl, and so did my mother and my Aunt Winnie and Uncle Arthur. My mother, Winnie and Arthur were with us in spring, when we let out the calves who had wintered in the cowshed. Our daughter Anne and her fiancé, Robert Pardoe, were with us at the time. (Robert's parents, Sheila and Bob, also came to stay.) When the calves were released they gambolled like lambs, running and leaping. We needed to move the calves from one field to another, and the antics we performed as we tried to drive the calves to where we wanted them reduced Uncle Arthur to tears of laughter.

Anne was married from *Ty'n Y Gors*, in the chapel of her old school, Kingswood, in Bath, where she had been Head of School. Mark was at King's College, London University, in the final year of his degree. He spent the summer with us and helped with the harvest.

I have been very fortunate in my long association with the Religious Department of the BBC, not only in the matter of the privilege of being allowed to broadcast for so many years, but in the large number of friends that I have gained in the broadcasting world: producers and producers' assistants, studio managers, fellow writers and broadcasters, and also listeners who generously write to say that they include me amongst their old friends. From time to time I make forays, religious and secular, into Radio 4, from the *Daily Service* to *Down your Way*, but most of all I have been associated with Radio 2. For instance, 1993 will be my twentieth year of presenting *Pause for Thought* on Radio 2. During the year in Wales I became rather worryingly unwell, but I was able to continue broadcasting through the BBC studios in Bangor.

Over the years I used to have a recurring problem with my back. During this particular year in Wales it gradually became chronic. In the past there had been a certain amount of spasmodic pain but now the pain was becoming more or less permanent. I began to find physical movement, particularly walking, painful and difficult. I went to the brand-new hospital near Bangor where it was possible to have a very comprehensive X-ray whilst lying on a highly manoeuvrable X-ray bed. Some spinal fluid had been replaced with a dye that made it easier to read the X-ray. One is required to stay overnight in the hospital, propped up to prevent the dye from getting into your head and giving you a nasty headache.

Shortly afterwards, my doctor told me that the X-ray had revealed a small tumour on my spine. This growth was likely to be interfering with the messages that are sent through the nerve system of the spine and causing the pain and difficulty of movement.

Being informed that you have a tumour, does, as they say, 'concentrate the mind'. Inevitably, you begin to think about the future as realistically as possible. The basic question is, 'If it turns out that the amount of time I have left is short, what do I do with that time?' Curiously enough I was not nearly as afraid as I thought I ought to be. If I looked at my life, June, the children, the theatre, radio, songs with Swann, the West End, books, my own television series, I could hardly complain, 'I was robbed!'

By this time six of my books had been published, and there were two just about to be published, one with Lutterworth and the other with Collins. Sarah Baird Smith, who was the Religious Books editor for Collins, came with her family to visit us at *Ty'n Y Gors*. I cannot remember if she knew about the problem of the tumour hanging over me or not, but she commissioned me to write another book, and left the subject entirely to me. In many ways that commission was a life-saver. I threw myself into writing the book which, of all the books I have written, gave me the most satisfaction. It is called *An Impossible God* and it is a study of the Passion of Christ as seen through the eyes of people who witnessed the events. I asked myself, 'How would those who saw these things happen have understood them?' It was an attempt to put myself in the shoes of those who were intimately involved and those who were simply bystanders. For instance, I asked myself, 'Supposing I was a servant in the house of Caiaphas on the night Jesus was arrested, what would I think was going on? How would I describe what I thought was happening to my friends?' 'If I was Simon of Cyrene, or a soldier, or a disciple, or Mary, the mother of Christ, given the particular cultural and historical environment, how would I interpret what was happening?'

This was the first time I experienced what Kipling described as his 'Daemon', the feeling that all I had to do was put my pen on the page and watch it write. A great deal of mystic nonsense is talked about this experience. I believe it simply means that you are writing at precisely the time you are *ready* to write that particular book. When all your research, all your reflecting (what I call 'mulling') and the structure has been shaping itself in your head and when, at the same time, your enthusiasm for telling the tale has reached its peak, when all these things coincide, then the book 'writes itself'. Having written the book under these agreeable conditions, it still has to be rewritten, edited, wrestled with and, generally, handed over to the publisher with the usual sense of deep despair and utter regret that you ever embarked on the project.

Nevertheless, having said all that, I still have to admit that there is a kind of alchemy that happens in the writing of a book, in the writing of anything really, a song, a poem, a play, a radio script. There is a sense of something having been created, words and images conjured from a well-fertilised imagination, and that process, no matter how cynically you analyse it, can never really be deprived of an element of wonder and mystery, even for the magician who has waved his inky wand and invented his own magic spell.

June typed the book from my longhand. She found it difficult to keep up. I was writing faster than she could type, mainly because, unusually for typists, she got caught up in reading the text instead of just typing it.

As my pen scratched its way across the pages, eventually the answers to the questions about what I would do with my time if there was not much left became clear to me. In many ways these simple, but hopefully not simplistic, answers would apply to me whether or not I had a short or long time to live. The questions were, 'Where should I spend the time? Doing what and with whom?', and the answers were, 'I want to be near those I love, doing what I do best for as long as I can'.

All our children had begun to carve out independent lives for themselves in England, and *Ty'n Y Gors* was a two-hour drive from the nearest motorway. June's family, her father, her twin brother, her sister and their families all lived in the South of England. What I felt I did best was write and broadcast, but was *Ty'n Y Gors* the best place to do it? I remember once driving the comedian Ted Ray to his home in North London when we had lived in Palmers Green, and in conversation about working in the theatre and broadcasting Ted said, 'A lot of people have a little success and then move out into the country, but they make rods for their own backs. If you are a factory worker and you want to work regularly, you should live near the factory.'

At this time I was also acting as the National Chaplain of Toc H. I feel rather guilty whenever I think of the kindness they showed me, because in the circumstances I was not able to give them full value, but Toc H continues to count me one of their own, and I am grateful. I am particularly grateful to Jo and Eddie Godfrey who were very warm and generous in their friendship. The headquarters of Toc H is in Buckinghamshire, and a house was provided for the chaplain in Princes Risborough. June and I decided that we should move back to England. We could sell the farm, and live in Princes Risborough whilst we looked for a place of our own.

We left *Ty'n Y Gors* almost exactly a year to the day that we had arrived. There are few places I have left with such regret. The dream of a wonderful retreat centre and house party home had not exactly been achieved, but, who knows, perhaps it was, as the Communion service says, '. . . a foretaste of the heavenly banquet.'

I will not echo my grandfather, from whom we received 'threepence' for patiently listening to a detailed medical bulletin that covered everything from a sore throat to an aching knee joint. Suffice it to say that, after visiting several hospitals from Bangor in Gwynedd to the Radcliffe in Oxford and a short stay at Stoke Mandeville, ultimately, I emerged from *Ty'n Y Gors*, Wales, and the tumour, to find myself living in a cottage by the sea in Hampshire with a clean bill of health and as fit as the proverbial fiddle.

Despite having moved house so many times, the New Forest and its Hampshire coastline has been one of our unchanging points of reference, largely because June's mother and father retired here, but also because we have maintained a number of interests in the area, such as membership of a sailing club and keeping our boats here. Even the family beach hut has featured as a constant in the lives of several generations, with great grandparents at one end, and great grandchildren at the other. Wildcat Cottage is close to several branches of June's family, within easy reach of our own children, and a fast train to London places us near, if not exactly outside the gates of the 'factory'.

In the summer of 1985, June launched her own seasonal sailing school, and as our name seems to have a kind of nautical ring to it we christened the school, 'Topping Sailing'. At almost the same time we also launched a very small travelling theatre company. It consists of June and me, and occasionally Mark. The company bears a name which we fondly believe is appropriate for wandering players, 'Emmaus'.

Not long after we had moved here, in the winter of 1985, I was asked by the Snap People's Theatre Company if I would consider being involved in the adaptation of a book, by John Steinbeck, to be presented as a one-man play, and also to be the 'one man' and perform the play in a variety of venues from studio theatres to public libraries. It was a project that opened up some new and exciting avenues.

In 1943, the novelist John Steinbeck became an accredited war correspondent for the *New York Herald Tribune*. The writing style of the dispatches he sent from Europe revealed more of the novelist's art than that of the war correspondent. Steinbeck was less interested in reporting military statistics and strategy than he was in understanding the heart and mind of the ordinary soldier trying to come to terms with the war and his part in it. He also revealed his own developing thoughts, from his initial desire to 'get where the action is', to his eventual rage at the mindless waste of war.

Steinbeck's dispatches were collected together after the war and published as a book entitled *Once There Was a War*. The collected essays are alive with humour and shrewd, sensitive observations of how people lived through the violence of the bombing raids over London; of how desperate hospital doctors coped with the massive influx of maimed and wounded; of how American city slickers and bucolic country boys found themselves in an army in North Africa preparing for the landings on the beaches of Salerno and Anzio, and how they survived or died. He had an acute ear for the rich dialogue emerging from people from the complex multi-culture of the United States thrown together by war.

Reading his book, I became more and more aware that any attempt to lift, single-handedly, from his pages, Irish, Jewish and Italian Americans, farmers and cattle men, the kids from Brooklyn and the kids from Harlem, and parade them in the flesh in a theatre was, to say the least, going to be as challenging as any project I had ever previously contemplated. The difficulty was not accents and dialects. There were more basic questions to be answered. Did I have the staying power, the physical and emotional strength and stamina, the technical skill and, above all, the charisma, the personal alchemy that enables a lone actor to bewitch an audience, nightly, for at least an hour and a half? There was only one way to find out.

The director was Chris Barton, a man of great enthusiasm and infinite patience. Together we assembled the material, the dialogue, the speeches that would recreate the Second World War as seen through the eyes of John Steinbeck, and the drama of being anyone living in Europe in 1943. We rehearsed in the gymnasium of a school in Bishops Stortford. Gradually a 'set' was assembled.

Act One: Steinbeck's quarters, somewhere in England. A room furnished with the simple 'utility' furniture of wartime Britain: a bed, a table, a typewriter, a phone, a lamp standard with a terrible hand-painted lampshade.

Act Two: North Africa and inland from the beaches at Salerno. Boxes and packing cases, but the thing that really sets this scene, draped at an angle behind the ration boxes, a huge khaki-green camouflage net, the kind of net that might camouflage a tank.

Add to these, a collection of sound effects, the rumble of aircraft, an air-raid siren, incidental and interval music of Vera Lynn, the Andrew Sisters, and Glen Miller's Orchestra pumping out his big-band versions of 'American Patrol', 'Little Brown Jug', 'Chattanooga Choo Choo' and 'Tuxedo Junction'. Now add one actor in American press corps uniform, set before an audience, mix the whole concoction, gently at first, and then stir, increasing speed as required.

All the props and all the scenery had to be packed away after every performance in a rather small hatchback car, driven by an indefatigable stage manager called John Cann, an excellent name for someone capable of overcoming every conceivable problem to be found in village halls, schools, churches and occasionally, joy of joys, a real live country theatre, called 'The Barn', or 'The Stables' or the 'Little Theatre'.

During the rehearsal weeks I stayed with an old chum from college days in Bristol, Roy Crew and his family. The Crews lived in Winchmore Hill in North London and Roy was the minister of the Methodist church known locally as the Church in the Orchard. It was very convenient for nipping up the M11 to Bishops Stortford, and it was good to renew an old friendship. Roy had also been the Methodist minister in Sidcup in Kent when our daughter Anne was a student at the Rose Bruford College of

Drama in Sidcup, so, one way or another, we had kept in touch since we were students together.

One-man theatre, in the kind of halls we played in in East Anglia, is very intimate, and the actor is very close to his audience. Fortunately I had experienced this before at the Upstream Theatre in Waterloo. In East Anglia, we rarely had an actual stage; a 'space' is what we were generally given. So much depended on the audience seeing what the actor was seeing, knowing the limitations that he knew, entirely from his belief in the existence of his boundaries or in what he could see in his mind's eye. Chris Barton was absolutely insistent that when I looked at something that existed only in my mind, I had to know its precise position, exactly where it was to the inch, and to know its shape, size and texture.

Later, when Emmaus Productions was under way and we were presenting a passion play, there is a particular moment when one of the characters turns to face the risen Christ. Several times people have told me afterwards that for one terrifying moment, even though there had only been one actor on the stage for over an hour, so caught up were they in 'seeing what I was seeing' that they actually expected to see Christ at the same moment I 'saw' him. For which, thank you, Chris Barton.

When we first took the Steinbeck play out in February 1986, it was called by the same title as the book, *Once There Was a War*. When we took the production to the Edinburgh Festival Fringe it was called, *Steinbeck: Dispatches*. Getting Steinbeck's name into the title was a good idea. The original book has long been out of print in this country but, of course, Steinbeck's name and reputation is assured.

There was a school teachers' overtime ban in force when we began our tour. Would it be cynical to suppose that there may have been one or two school bookings arranged by desperate head teachers who saw the visit of a one-man play as a means of 'occupying' the children for a few hours without the need for too many supervisory teachers? Whatever the reason, performing in an understaffed comprehensive school gymnasium on a Friday afternoon will test the actor's concentration, reactions, stamina and personal charisma in a way that few other audiences or environments will.

One night we played at a youth centre and the acting 'space' turned out to be a kind of bear pit, with some of the audience leaning on a railing and looking down at the performer. I don't know how the evening was paid for, but clearly many of the young people did not know there was to be a play performed, and from our cupboard, allocated to us as a 'dressing room', we could hear whining and perhaps understandable complaints about not being able to play snooker or table tennis.

I think this would probably rate as the fastest performance of the Steinbeck play I ever achieved. I was galvanised not only by the sight of cigarette ends being thrown into the 'pit' as I made my first entrance, but also by the quickly acquired knowledge that the concentration span of this particular audience began to disintegrate if a silence lasted for much more than three seconds. In a curious way there was a kind of poetic 'rightness' about this particular venue. It was as if I was playing under wartime conditions, albeit in the trenches of the Second World War. It is a tribute to Steinbeck and Chris Barton's production, and possibly to the innate politeness of the young people, that no one left, and that in the final scene you could, as they say, 'have heard a pin drop'. Perhaps the most satisfying critical assessment of that night's performance came from a member of the audience, now chalking his snooker cue, who spoke to me as I left. 'That was good, that was, mate. You're okay – for a Yank.'

In absolute contrast, the next day could find us playing in a wonderful drama studio, to a mixed audience of sixth formers and locally invited old-age pensioners, whose intelligent involvement, laughter and applause would have been envied in Drury Lane.

Repertory theatre 'studio' audiences were wonderfully committed and enthusiastic. I remember playing at one theatre (actually in the theatre, as opposed to the 'studio'), where the Steinbeck was being presented as the principal performance of the evening, when I was introduced to a lady who was the secretary of the English section of the John Steinbeck Society. Such people know all the works of their heroes intimately, so we were especially encouraged when she gave the production and the performance her personal seal of approval.

Emmaus Productions began with an adaptation of the book that I had written during our year at *Ty'n Y Gors*. A drama group in Canterbury, called Group 81, founded by Maurice Copus in 1981 with the sole purpose of producing plays suitable for performance in cathedrals and churches, had invited me to be one of their patrons, the others being the Right Reverend Richard Third (the Bishop of Dover) and the playwright Christopher Fry. Group 81 were now performing parts of *An Impossible God* as a play.

Prior to *An Impossible God* I had written a book called *God Bless You, Spoonbill*. This was a kind of pastoral theology in which a young minister exchanges letters with an old minister, called Walter Spoonbill, over a period of three years. During that time they discuss a great number of pastoral situations as they arise in the life and work of the young minister. In Belfast, a Methodist minister called Harold Good was teaching Pastoral Theology to theological students and ordinands, and he had included my book on his students' reading list. After *An Impossible God* was published in 1986, Harold Good invited me to come to his church in Belfast and take part in a series of Holy Week interdenominational Services of Reconciliation.

All denominations were invited to take part, Protestant and Catholic. Despite ominous and threatening telephone calls to both Harold Good and to the headmistress of the Catholic convent school that had agreed to take part and provide a choir, the services went ahead with packed churches, revealing once again that both Catholic and Protestant Church people not only want peace and reconciliation but are prepared to make a public stand on the issue. For me it was the beginning of my involvement with and commitment to the reconciliation movement between the Churches in Northern Ireland. I have been invited now on a number of occasions to share in a variety of reconciliation events and in the process I have made some very good friends, both Catholic and Protestant.

As it was Holy Week, I chose to read a different character from *An Impossible God* every day of the week. Reading the speeches aloud, and perhaps especially in the heightened atmosphere of a packed Belfast church, the dramatic potential of the speeches became very evident.

Back in Hampshire I had been invited to present a kind of *Evening with Frank Topping* at a church in the West Country. The man who had invited us said that as we would have to make a rather long journey to visit his church he would try to arrange *Evenings* with one or two other churches in order to make the journey worthwhile. So June and I discussed how *An Impossible God* might be adapted as a one-man play, as a possible production to take to the churches in the West Country.

Key characters were chosen, their speeches edited and committed to memory and then we began to build a production. We decided to put some of the techniques of the Steinbeck performance to use in this play. Props, furniture and stage lights must be kept to a minimum. The furniture should consist of pieces that we would find available in any church that we were likely to visit. A wooden table, desk size, a chair for the table and a separate chair, probably one of the rather imposing chairs that are usually to be found in the sanctuary of any church. If the big chair can also be placed on a different level, well and good. We also required a step, or a box, anything that would enable me to stand up about a foot higher. That is the furniture dealt with. The 'costume' consisted mainly of some lengths of cloth which because of different colours and ways of draping, helped to suggest different characters.

Each character has a distinct voice. When one speech is finished the lights slowly fade on that character and dramatic 'mood' music fills the brief darkness that follows. When the lights come up again they do so on another part of the stage where a different character, draped in a different colour and shape of cloth, speaks with a totally different voice. The play flows on at a very swift pace and by the interval people who know there is only one actor feel that they have seen perhaps a dozen quite different characters. The formula is simple but it works. The result is both powerful and effective.

Just as, whatever activity I am involved in I always, somehow, manage to continue to broadcast on BBC Radio 2's *Pause for Thought*, so, with the encouragement of Anthea Morton-Saner, I also manage to bring out a new book at regular intervals. Anthea is a director of the literary agents, Curtis Brown, in Regent Street, and has looked after my literary and other contractual interests for many years. She not only negotiates my book contracts, but she also persuades people to translate the books into different languages, including exotic ones such as Chinese and Afrikaans. In addition, she also looks after my television contracts, both as a scriptwriter and as a performer. I stumbled into writing books and I was fortunate to be introduced by another writer, Stuart Jackman, to Curtis Brown. I have since learned that authors say that it is slightly more difficult to get a good agent than it is to find a publisher. I seem to have been blessed, without trying, on both accounts and can therefore only be grateful for my good fortune.

When Emmaus Productions took to the road in the spring of 1986, we extracted a leaf from David Kossoff's book, so to speak, and took with us enough books to set up a bookstall at every venue. I am delighted to say that this idea is always welcomed by the people we visit and book-signing is a regular feature of an Emmaus visit.

The period of my being unwell in Wales, and all those hospitals (to whom I will always be grateful), put me out of mainstream circulation for a while. There is a belief that is current and popular in the media world which implies that if you have been out of circulation for more than six months, the likelihood is that you are dead. As I had passed the six-month 'deadline' I knew that to many I was undoubtedly no longer in the land of the living. I therefore had to reveal that I was still alive and kicking. In order to put my name back on the map we decided to perform at the Edinburgh Festival Fringe, where I would do not just *one* full-length one-man show but *three*.

The 'two or three churches' in the West Country ended up as over one hundred and sixty performances all over the United Kingdom, the bulk of which had been performed before we arrived at the Edinburgh Fringe. Mark, our younger son, became my 'roadie' for many of the one-man shows, whilst June got on with 'Topping Sailing'. Mark and I occupied ourselves during the long hours of cross-country driving by singing along with various tapes picked up at service stations. The result is that we now know by heart an entire collection of Andy Williams' 'Golden Hits' and two LPs of Glenn Miller numbers. Yes, that's right, we sing saxophone and trombone fluently.

That summer, in 1986, Emmaus Productions took *An Impossible God* into the frontier world of Fringe performance. At Edinburgh we had two different venues. One was St John's, the church at the end of Princes Street where we alternated every lunchtime with a different show, either *An Impossible God* or *Out of my Mind* which is a light-hearted entertainment of sketches, stories and songs. In the evening we were at a beautiful Georgian Methodist church in Nicholson Square, where the play was either *Steinbeck: Dispatches* or *An Impossible God*. The collection of plays was advertised as 'One Man, Three Plays'. It was a pretty wild adventure which involved a daily removal of lights from one venue to another. In Nicholson Square it meant June, and any family assistance she could get, lugging the lights up and down the stairs to the balcony, and of course re-setting the stage and the lights and operating lights and sound for every performance.

We stayed with an old Kingswood School friend of our children, Andrew Wright, known as 'Augie', who had a flat within walking distance of Princes Street. What we had not envisaged was the number of other people who were also sleeping at the flat, on the floor, in the living room, in the corridor, in fact wherever there was a space. Nevertheless Andrew kept his word to us and the bedroom he allocated to us was kept sacrosanct, until that is all the Toppings arrived and slept – at the side of our bed, in the corner, at the end of the bed. It was great fun and by anyone's standards we were a success. We achieved what we set out to do. Financially we broke even, which apparently is unusual; most Edinburgh Fringe shows lose money, and frequently lose a lot. Basically people don't go there to make money, mostly they go for the fun.

We received three good reviews in *The Scotsman*, one for each performance, and BBC Radio 4 in Scotland devoted a forty-five-minute programme to *An Impossible God*. There were interviews on the local radios, BBC and Independent (one programme was devoted to performers of one-man shows, so it would have been difficult to have left me out of that one). There was also an invitation to appear on BBC Radio 2's special nightly Festival programme, Brian Matthews' *Around Midnight*. We could not have hoped for more. The Festival is a very exciting thing to be involved in, and there is a special camaraderie amongst performers, helped enormously by the existence of a performers' club where performers could get a chance to hear bits of each other's work. Truly exciting, but also truly exhausting!

At the North End Buoy, a small yacht, a Westerly Centaur, has just changed course and is making for the channel beyond Hurst Castle. I hope she keeps clear of a local phenomenon marked on the charts as 'The Trap', which is a nasty patch of turbulence over a hole in the sea bed. A number of boats have come to grief at that point. They drop in the 'hole' and, depending on the depth of tide, hit or miss the shallow edge of the under-sea hole as they emerge from the turbulence. It's a place best left well alone. There is a steady south-westerly blowing today, Force 3 or 4 perhaps.

June and Simon are coming down to the beach hut shortly for a brew-up, so I'd better clear my papers a bit and make sure there are three clean cups. I've just discovered that I'm low on water. I'll trot along to the stand-pipe and fill up the container.

Clean cups, kettle on and here they are. The Westerly Centaur is well clear of 'The Trap', I'm glad to say.

'Let's have a look through your binoculars, Dad.'

'I've brought some fresh milk, darling, just in case you're low.'

'Great, hang on, the kettle's boiling.'

'What are you smiling about?'

'Well, I've just thought of a title for our next show.

'Really?'

'Yes, it's something you accuse me of doing, from time to time.'

'I'm intrigued, what is it?'

'*Laughing in my Sleep.*'